A HISTORY OF BRITAIN BEFORE 1066

VOLUME 2

The Anglo-Saxon Invasion
410 A.D.-802 A.D.

A HISTORY OF BRITAIN BEFORE 1066

VOLUME 2

The Anglo-Saxon Invasion 410 A.D.-802 A.D.

Charles Oman

LEONAUR

A HISTORY OF BRITAIN BEFORE 1066
VOLUME 2
The Anglo-Saxon Invasion
410 A.D.-802 A.D.
by Charles Oman

FIRST EDITION

Leonaur is an imprint of Oakpast Ltd

Copyright in this form © 2021 Oakpast Ltd

ISBN: 978-1-78282-964-5 (hardcover)
ISBN: 978-1-78282-965-2 (softcover)

http://www.leonaur.com

Publisher's Notes

The views expressed in this book are not necessarily
those of the publisher.

Contents

CHAPTER 1

The Anglo-Saxon Invasion (410–616 *A.D.*)

From the landing of Julius Caesar down to the year 410 the history of Britain can be traced with a fair amount of continuity, though it is full of dark corners. But for more than a hundred and fifty years after the obscure revolution that followed the Edict of Honorius which bade the British communities "defend themselves," there is a sheer break in the sequence of the narrative. We know what was the condition of the island in 410, and we know what was its condition in the end of the sixth century. But of the stages of the transformation, by which the Roman provincial Britain of Honorius became the Anglo-Saxon Britain of Aethelbert and Aethelfrith, we have little certain knowledge. There is a complete solution of continuity in the tale; six generations pass by in which we have but the scantiest glimpse of what was going on in the island.

There is only one literary document of some length which belongs to this period, the *"Liber Querulus"* of Gildas, and that, as we have already seen, is full of notorious errors concerning the earlier part of this Dark Age, and for the remainder of it gives us little more than denunciations in vague language, borrowed from the Prophets of the Old Testament, which reprove certain British kings contemporary with the author. We shall have to ascertain, in due course, how much of solid fact can be elucidated from these jeremiads. To supplement the hysterical periods of Gildas we have three historical narratives belonging to a much later age.

The first is the *Historia Brittonum* or *Volumen Britanniae* of an anonymous author who wrote, somewhere about the year 685, a compilation which—mixed with other and later material—has come to be known by the name of Nennius, a ninth-century redactor of the little work. The second narrative is that of the Venerable Bede, who wrote, about 730, his excellent and scholarly *Ecclesiastical History*, in which he endeavoured to construct a sketch of the early history of Britain from Gildas, combined with the traditions of his own English ancestor, and some small help from writer of the latest Roman period.

The third source is the *Anglo-Saxon Chronicle*, whose earlier section was compiled by the order of King Alfred in the very end of the ninth century. Its annalistic entries covering the fifth and sixth centuries are largely derived from Bede, but are supplemented by many statements, more or less credible, drawn from independent English tradition, of which the greater part are concerned with Alfred's own forebears, the royal house of the West Saxons.

The most cursory examination of the narratives of the *Historia Brittonum*, and of the *Anglo-Saxon Chronicle,* proves that both abound in doubtful matter—as might indeed be expected when we reflect that they were written so long after the events which they purport to record. In especial, the earlier of the two, the *Historia Brittonum*, contains many chapters which are clearly not history at all, but wild legend, full of dragons, enchanted castles, and fires that fall from heaven. That there remains in them a residuum of acceptable fact, when all the errors have been cleared away, our historians agree. Unfortunately, the precise amount of that residuum is hard to settle.

In addition to the four sources which we have named, a certain amount of scattered information may be gathered from other quarters. Some short but useful glimpses of fact may be found in certain early lives of saints—especially from those of Patrick and Germanus. A note or two may be taken from early councils of the Cambro-British Church. There are some entries which seem trustworthy in Irish chronicles, drawn up at a much later date. There are a handful of fifth and sixth century inscriptions on the west side of Britain. A very few mentions of insular affairs occur in continental historians, such as Prosper and Procopius.

But the total amount of external material for checking or correcting the statements of Gildas, the *Historia Brittonum*, Bede, and the *Anglo-Saxon Chronicle* is lamentably small. The spade, so useful in the Roman period, helps us little here: the Teutonic invader has left us no inscriptions earlier than the year 600: his British enemies hardly any, and those of the shortest. Saxon graves of the pagan period give us a good deal of information concerning the social life and culture of the incoming race, but not definite history: in that respect they can only be used like the barrows of the Britons who lived before Julius Caesar.

We left the Roman province of Britain suffering under the simultaneous assaults of the Pict from the North, the Scot from the West, and the Saxon from the side of the Eastern Sea. These invasions certainly did not grow less fierce and continuous when the provincials were abandoned by the central government of the Roman Empire, and told to shift for themselves. We might have expected that the whole island from sea to sea would have fallen a prey to them within a few years—as Spain fell to the Visigoths in this same period, or Northern Gaul to the Franks a little later.

But no such complete catastrophe occurred: the British provincials defended themselves with unexpected resolution, and even a century and a half after the time of Honorius they still retained half Britain unsubdued. The Pict and Scot were beaten off, with singularly little loss of territory on the part of the defenders, on the West and North. The Saxons and their kinsmen made many conquests, yet after great successes at the beginning were brought to a stand, and never completely achieved the enterprise that they had begun.

One would naturally have supposed that of all the districts of Britain that most surely doomed to conquest by the barbarians would have been the Northern region, about and beyond Hadrian's Wall, which had never been properly occupied by the Romans since the time of Commodus, and which had been reclaimed for the empire in name alone by the elder Theodosius. Here the Pict and Scot were near neighbours on the North and West, while the East coast was exposed to the raids of the Saxon. Yet in this borderland of the Britons, through which Pictish invasions must have swept on innumerable occasions, in order to reach the more desirable plunder beyond the wall, and to which the keels of the pirates from beyond the North Sea came early and often, the resistance offered to the external enemy was fierce and successful.

The Picts won nothing more than a small strip of land to the south of the Firth of Forth, (they may even have been holding it since the third century), from the neighbourhood of Stirling to that of Edinburgh, the "Manau" or "Manau Gododin" of the British poems and chronicles. The other Pictish settlement in the Lowlands, that in Galloway, where lay the "Niduarian Picts," was, as we have already seen reason to believe, the prize of an earlier invasion from Ireland, before the Roman power had been broken in Britain, and not a land subdued in the time of chaos that followed the year 410. The Scots seem to have devoted their chief energies to the seizure of regions farther North and South—the isles and peninsulas of Argyleshire on the one side and Wales on the other.

The Teutons won something more than the Picts or Scots, as their settlements on the East coast from Lothian to the Humber seem to have begun early, and always to have been increasing. But at first, they were mere scattered patches on the shore, and it was long before they were united into that Northumbrian kingdom which began to threaten the independence of all the Northern Britons only in the end of the sixth century. At the earliest return of historical twilight, we find them still weak and divided, while the Britons were holding their own, and had even got possession of lands beyond the wall of Antoninus. The strong rock of Alclyde, "the fort of the Britons" (Dumbarton), on the northern shore of the Firth of Clyde, was reckoned not merely as their outpost but as their capital.

The successful resistance of the people of the land between the two walls to their invaders may be ascribed to either—or both—of two causes. It is clear that they had never been absorbed into the area of Roman civilisation like their kinsmen farther South, and military vigour went hand in hand with comparative barbarism. But it is also possible that they may have rallied at the first around the wrecks of the old trained garrison of Hadrian's Wall. Indeed, their first leaders may have been the captains of the auxiliary *cohorts*, which were not withdrawn when the last legion sailed South, to aid the much-vexed Honorius or the usurper Constantine III.

We have one glimpse of the state of the Lowlands somewhere about the year 450 *A.D.* St. Patrick wrote in the later years of his long life (see Bury's *Life of St. Patrick*, where the date 459 *A.D.* is suggested), his "Epistle to the Christians subject to Coroticus," from which most suggestive deductions may be drawn. This chief appears as ruling the land that lies opposite Ulster in the most vigorous style. The saint speaks of him as a Christian Briton whose power depended on the bands of his soldiers (*milites*), a word that seems to imply trained troops and not merely tribal levies, when used by one who was a Roman citizen by birth. He also possessed a fleet, and had used it to carry out a raid—retaliatory no doubt—against the Scots on the other side of the North Channel.

In this expedition his men had surprised, and carried off as slaves, some of Patrick's newly-baptised converts, "with the sign of the cross still fragrant on their foreheads". It was a case, no doubt, of the "stork among the crane"; all Scots were pirates, and fair game in the eyes of the soldiers of Coroticus. But the most striking point in the denunciation of Coroticus, for preying on his Christian brethren, is that we are told that part of his expeditionary force had consisted of heathen barbarians, both Picts and Scots. The former may have been some of those Picts of Galloway, who had been partially converted by St. Ninian some fifty years before; some of them had relapsed into heathenism, or had never deserted it.

But to find Coroticus possessed of a Scottish contingent is more surprising. Had he hired them from the settlement on the Argyle coast, or were they simply broken men, like those numerous Danes of five centuries after who readily took service with a Christian employer? At any rate Coroticus was sufficiently energetic, and (we must suppose) sufficiently wealthy to maintain barbarian auxiliaries, and it was they, and not his own native soldiery, who had slain some and enslaved others of Patrick's disciples. The saint wrote his epistle not to the chief himself, to whom he had already made application in vain, but to the whole Christian community subject to him, including his soldiers, though these last he declares to be:

No fellow-citizens of mine or of the pious Romans, but fellow-citizens of devils, on account of their evil deeds, men who ally themselves with Scots and apostate Picts.

All of Coroticus's subjects who retain a spark of Christian feeling are bidden to bring pressure to bear upon the "tyrant"—Patrick calls him neither king nor general—in order that he may release his captives. They are asked to see that the letter gets to his hands, and then, unless he repents, to boycott him and his soldiers, to deny them the participation of hearth and board, to take no gift from them, and to refuse obedience to their orders until the prisoners are set free. Whether any of the Christians of North Britain tried this somewhat perilous experiment on the tyrant we know not. The darkness descends again for nearly a century on the land between the two walls.

******

A wild Irish legend (see *Tripartite Life of St. Patrick*, ed. Whitley Stokes) tells that Coirthech, King of Alclyde, refused to listen to the saint's pleading, that Patrick cursed him, and that he was therefore turned into a fox by miracle in the presence of his retainers, and never was seen again.

******

But it would seem that Coroticus succeeded in maintaining his power till his death, and passed on his authority to his descendants. For in the genealogies attached to Nennius in the Harleian Manuscript he appears, under the name of Ceretic Guletig, as the ancestor of the sixth century kings of Strathclyde, Rhydderch Hen, Elfin, Clinog, Eugenius, and the rest, down to that Beli King of Alclyde, whose death is recorded under the year 722 *A.D.* (Whereas the later set of genealogies in the Hengwrt MS., which gives the *Bonhed Gwyr y Gogledd*, or "families of the men of the North," wrongly takes back this family to Maxim Guletig, *i.e.*, the Emperor Magnus Maximus.) The family would seem to have had many branches, who followed each other on the throne of Alclyde in a very irregular line of succession.

Probably several princes of the house were often reigning at once, under the *suzerainty* of one of their kinsmen, and the hegemony often passed from one to another cousin. One of the line, Rhydderch Hen, son of Tudwal, is recorded in Nennius as taking a prominent part in the struggle with Hussa, the son of Ida, the first great Anglian king of Bernicia, about the year 580. He was no doubt the same as the Rodarcus, son of Totail, King of Alclyde, who is found in Adamnan's *Life of Columba* sending to Iona to beg the saint to prophesy in his behalf.

The house of Coroticus were not the only family of hard fighters that was produced in the land between Hadrian's Wall and the Firths of Forth and Clyde. It must be remembered that from this same region came that Cunedda, the son of Aeternus and grandson of Paternus, whom we have noted in a previous chapter as descending from the North, in the latest years of the fourth century, to deliver Wales from the invading Scots, who had crossed from Ireland to the lands about the Menai Straits and the foot of Snowdon.

If the date given by the *Historia Brittonum* and the sequence of the later Welsh genealogies be approximately correct, Cunedda had come down with his eight sons and his army, from "Manau Gododin" on the Forth about 390, long before the final departure of the legions under the usurper Constantine III. We cannot tell whether he left Manau because he was driven out by incoming Picts, abandoning a region which could no longer be held, or whether he went as the vassal and ally of Rome, to face in behalf of all the Britons that wing of the barbarian invasion which seemed at the moment the most dangerous. But at any rate "he expelled the Scots with much slaughter from those regions (North Wales), and they never returned again to inhabit them".

The other, or South Welsh holding of the Scots, about Gower and Kidwelly, was finally reconquered by the house of Cunedda, and reincorporated with West Britain, though a strain of Goidelic blood no doubt survived there, and some princely families of South Wales, even long after, traced themselves back to Irish ancestors on one side of their genealogy. (See Zimmer's *Nennius Vindicatus*, and E. B. Nicholson's *Dynasty of Cunedda.*)

But while it is clear that Northern and Western Britain beat off the Pict and Scot, after a long struggle and many vicissitudes of fortune, the history of Southern and Eastern Britain is very different. This, as we have already seen, was the most thickly settled and highly organised part of the island, a region where Romanisation had been complete and thorough. Though often harried on the coast-line by the Saxons before 410, it was still a wealthy and civilised land when we lose sight of it in that fatal year. A century later the eastern side of it, from the extreme north to Southampton Water, was occupied by a number of petty Teutonic kingdoms, while the western side of it was still held by the Britons, who were engaged in an obstinate defence of the South-West and the Midlands against the invaders.

When and how did the kingdoms of the Saxons, Jutes and English come into existence? Gildas gives us almost dateless rhetoric: the *Historia Brittonum* an elaborate legend full of marvels, miracles and folklore tales. Bede and the *Anglo-Saxon Chronicle* supply us with a rationalised version of the hysterical paragraphs of Gildas, supplemented with ancestral memories of the invader's, written down centuries after the epoch to which they are supposed to belong. Most modern writers follow in the footsteps of Bede and the *Chronicle*; and the legend of Vortigern and Hengist, fixed down to the years following 447 or 449 A.D., appears in every history of England. That there is every reason to suspect its details we must now proceed to demonstrate.

When in 410 Honorius bade the Britons "defend themselves" the message must have been delivered to the magistrates of the tribal cantons into which the province was divided, and to the commanders of those *cohorts* and *numeri* which still survived out of the old garrison. "Vicar" and *praesides* there were none, since these governors had been expelled shortly before, when the Britons threw off their allegiance to the usurper Constantine. Perhaps the most obvious course for the islanders to take would have been to proclaim another local emperor: but it is clear that they did not do so. We must therefore suppose that they organised some sort of a provincial league, as did their neighbours on the opposite coast of Gaul, the Armoricans, about the same time.

Since self-protection against the Saxon, Pict and Scot was their most obvious need, they must surely have appointed some military magistrate to take charge of their defence, and there are indications that such a person existed some generations later, and had taken up the title as well as the duties of the *Dux Britanniarum* of the later empire. Probably a vague *suzerainty* on the part of Honorius was still recognised in theory, for till a much later date the Britons regarded themselves as *"cives,"* citizens of the empire, and the term is still used for them in the work of Gildas, written more than a hundred years after this period, though he at the same time blames them for "casting off rather than cherishing the name, manners and law of Romans."

What was the inner organisation of the British communities in the earlier period of their independence we can only guess: presumably in the larger towns, like Londinium, Camulodunum, Eburacum or Lindum, regular municipal government continued for some time to exist. In the remoter districts where towns were few, and the canton rather than the city was the unit of civil life, something like the old pre-Roman tribal chieftainships were soon re-established. For there were plenty of old and wealthy British noble houses, some wholly Romanised, as the names of their members show, other's less so, round whom it would be natural for the peasantry to rally, in a time of unfortunate war and perpetual invasion.

Such nobles would in many cases have held office, civil or military, before the breakup of the empire: the not unfrequent Britons like Magnentius, Gerontius, Gratian Municeps, and others, who occur in the pages of Ammianus and Zosimus, must have been persons of this sort. Starting from the condition of magistrates or local magnates, they and their descendants became in the course of a generation or two real tribal chiefs. To Gildas they had become *reguli, tyranni*, even *reges*. The process must have been assisted by the fact that in the West of Britain a clear and definite kingship was being set up by Cunedda and his sons, who, after expelling the Scottish invaders of Wales, had established real military monarchies on a small scale therein.

Similar phenomena were not unknown elsewhere in the Roman Empire. Not to speak of Syagrius and Aegidius in Gaul, who only just failed to build up a native kingdom on the Seine in the end of the fifth century, there was a prince named Masuria in Africa, who in the sixth century declared himself *"Rex Romanorum et Maurorum"* and held out for some time with that strange title in the recesses of Atlas. We have already noted the parallel case of Coroticus, in the extreme north of Britain, though that chief evidently had not assumed any royal style, and was presumably no more than a military magistrate. If guessing is permitted, we may think of Britain in the early fifth century as a loose confederacy of communities, in which the municipal element was progressively growing weaker and the monarchical element stronger.

It is a curious fact that while the few notices of Britain which come to us from the continent in the first half of this period seem to make the Saxons the chief enemy of the island, Gildas speaks more of the Picts and Scots during the early fifth century, and only begins to enlarge on the ravages of the Teutonic invaders after some time has elapsed. Something may perhaps be allowed for the local standpoint of the informants: the so-called Prosper, writing in Gaul, thought most of the face of Britain which looked toward his own land. Gildas, a West Briton whose outlook embraced only his own half of the island, had received a tradition which told more of the invaders on that side than of those who wasted the Eastern regions.

Be this as it may, the Gaul tells us, under the years 409-10, of the strength of Britain being brought low and the Saxons being engaged in devastating Gaul also, and then in 441 assures us "the Britons after having been long vexed with various disasters and ill chances down to this moment, are now reduced to subjection by the Saxons". This can, at the most, only have been true of some parts of the Southern and Eastern coast, but even in respect to this limited part of the island, his statement is absolutely contradicted by Gildas, who makes the first permanent conquests of the Teutonic invaders to date from some years after the third consulship of Aetius (446 *A.D.*) and then to fall far short of that complete success of which Prosper speaks.

For the years before this Saxon settlement Gildas speaks only of the Picts and Scots as invaders:

> Races differing from each other in part as to their manners, but alike in their delight in bloodshed, and in their preference for covering their villainous faces with hair, rather than their immodest middles with raiment, (the first recorded hit at the kilt.)

According to him the Britons, after suffering disasters for a long series of years from Pict and Scot, at last turn to the unhappy idea of calling in the Saxons to save them from the Northern enemy. To judge from his narrative this would be the first appearance of the Teutonic invaders—which as we know is absurd, since they had given Carausius occupation nearly two centuries before, and had been among the chief foes of Stilicho in 395.

Clearly Prosper and Gildas contradict each other. It remains to be seen what more can be gathered from less obvious sources. Of these the most useful is the life of St Germanus, Bishop of Auxerre, by Constantius, a biography written in the last quarter of the fifth century, and therefore long before the time of Gildas. Germanus was twice in Britain, and his doings there have fortunately been recorded by his disciple. He first crossed the Channel in 429, along with his friend Lupus, Bishop of Troyes, as a deputation sent by the Gallic Synods to preach against the Pelagianism, or semi-Pelagianism, which was invading the Christian Church of Britain at the moment.

We may omit his miracles, which take up much space, but profit us little for historical inquiries. But when they are extracted, we have some solid political information, Britain seems to be still mainly under municipal, not regal, governance: there is no mention of a king, though we hear of "a man of tribunician rank," and are told that the supporters of Pelagianism included wealthy magnates arrayed in splendid apparel. It is most important to note that the Synod at which Germanus and Lupus refuted the heretics was held at Verulamium, where the Gallic bishops venerated the tomb of St Alban. The heart of South-Eastern Britain, therefore, was still intact, and the walls and shrines of its cities were still standing.

But we also learn that the island was being harassed at the moment by a joint invasion of Picts and Saxons, who were not merely co-operating in a general way, the one from the landside, the other from the sea, but were concentrated in a single host "driven into one camp by their common necessity, they undertake war against the Britons with conjoined forces." The invasion must, of course, have taken place somewhere considerably to the north of the region which Germanus had been visiting, presumably in Yorkshire or the North-Midlands, but the locality of the conflict cannot be identified. It was certainly *not* Maes-Garmon (the field of Germanus) in Flintshire, where Welsh antiquarians have placed it: that is too far to the West, and not on any reasonable line for a Picto-Saxon invasion.

The Britons—no mention is made of a king or even of a single general—terrified by the exceptional strength and violence of the raid, sent for Germanus and Lupus to their camp: the step was not destitute of practical wisdom, since the former had been a great man of war in his youth, and had held the high military post of *Dux* of the Armorican region before he became Bishop of Auxerre. The bishops strengthened the hands of the British Army, and induced many thousands of them, who were still heathen, to be baptised before the day of battle. Germanus then selected a defensive position for them, a narrow plain bounded by mountains, on whose slopes many of the Britons were hidden away in folds of the ground, so as to lie on the flank, or even the rear, of an enemy pushing along the central valley.

When the Picts and Saxons had advanced far up the level ground, making for the troops visible in front of them, Germanus gave the signal for a general attack, by bidding the whole army raise the war-cry "Hallelujah," and display itself. The shout was repeated by the ambushed forces all along the hillsides, and the barbarians saw themselves surrounded, as it were, and threatened on every side. Whereupon, instead of attacking, they wheeled round and fled down in the valley in disorder, casting away their arms, and making no resistance when they were pursued and cut down by the oncoming Britons. Many were drowned at the fords of a river which lay behind their line of flight. The "Hallelujah Victory," a rout without a battle, saved Central Britain for at least some years from a repetition of the Pictish and Saxon invasion.

Clearly, however, the results of this well-concerted affair would only be temporary. We have an account of a second visit of Germanus to Britain in 447, when he came accompanied by Severus, Bishop of Trier, once more set on the task of combating Pelagianism, which had raised its head again in the island. Unfortunately, there are no political or military facts preserved in connection with his second mission, whose narrative deals only with his conflicts with heresy. Yet, if there is any truth at all in Gildas, he must have been in Britain just at the moment of its greatest distress, since in the preceding year (446) fell the third consulship of Aetius, to whom, according to that dreary author, was sent the doleful letter called the "Groans of the Britons":

> The barbarians drive us to the sea—the sea throws us back on the barbarians: we have only the choice between the two methods of death, whether we should be massacred or drowned.

Moreover, six years before falls the date given by the so-called Prosper as that of the "falling of Britain under the domination of the Saxons." There can be little doubt that the state of the island must have been much worse in 447 than at the time of Germanus's first visit in 429. Conceivably he was sent for to act as a saviour from the barbarians once more, as well as a champion of orthodoxy. If so, his second appearance had less happy results than his first. He returned to Gaul, to die there in the next year, and the state of Britain grew progressively worse.

It is curious to find that Gildas makes no mention whatever of Germanus, thus showing once more the shortness of his historical perspective. The *Historia Brittonum*, on the other hand, has only too much about the Gaulish Saint, but its narrative is mainly wild legend. The chief work of Germanus, according to this strange book, was to protest against the wickedness of a certain Vortigern, who seems to be represented as king of the whole island, and as reigning from somewhere about 425 down to at least 455. He was not only a tyrant and murderer, but the friend and patron of the Saxons, to whom he betrayed the Britons, and a notorious evil liver who kept many wives, among whom was his own daughter.

Germanus harried him from place to place, "following him with all the British clergy, and upon a certain rock prayed for his sins during forty days and forty nights". Finally, fire fell from heaven and devoured the wicked king in his castle of Caer-Vortigern on the Teifi, together with all his wives and his retainers, male and female. An almost similar fate fell upon another prince of equally deplorable manners called Benlli, the imprecations of Germanus in the legend having the same power as those of Elijah in the Book of Kings.

In this wild fashion do we get our first glimpse of Vortigern, a personage who appears in every normal history of England as the immediate cause of the Saxon invasion. It may be granted, however, that he is probably to be identified with a certain unnamed king, spoken of by Gildas, who (with all his faults) is a better authority for the sixth century than the *Historia Brittonum*. According to the "*liber querulous*" the Britons having failed to get any help from Rome in 447, after their last appeal in the third consulship of Aetius (or Agitius as Gildas calls him), took to defending themselves, not without some success.

> Kings were elected, not by God's ordinances, but such as showed themselves more fierce than other men: and not long after they used to be slaughtered by those who had anointed them, not after any examination of their true merits, but because others more cruel still were elected. And if any one of them seemed milder than the others, and in some degree more regardful of the truth, the anger and weapons of all men were turned against him, as if he were the undoer of Britain.

The island is in a state of elective despotism, tempered by assassination, when a new invasion of the Picts and Scots is announced.

> Then all the councillors, together with their haughty king, are so blinded that, devising a succour (say rather a destruction) for their country, they introduce into the island those ferocious

Saxons of accursed name, hateful to God and man, bringing—as it were—wolves into the sheepcote, in order that they may drive back the races of the North. . . . The cubs from the lair of the barbarian lioness arrive in three *oyuls* (keels) as they call them, that is three warships, with a favourable wind and with omens and prophecies favourable, for it had been foretold to them, by their own best Seers, that they should hold the land to which they were directing their prows for three hundred years, and for half of that time, a hundred and fifty years, should frequently devastate it.

They land first on the eastern side of the island, by the orders of the unlucky King of Britain, and fix their horrid claws therein, nominally about to fight in defence of our country, but more really for its destruction. Their mother-land, learning of the success of the first band, sends over in more numerous companies these dogs of mercenaries, who come across on their ships to unite with their base-born comrades. From that time the seed of iniquity, the root of bitterness was planted among us, and the poisonous growth, as we deserved for our demerits, sprang up on our soil with rank-growing stalks and leaves. The barbarians introduced among us as our soldiers, and ready (as they falsely boasted) to brave every danger in behalf of their worthy hosts, ask for regular pay. It is given, and for some time stops, as the proverb goes, the dog's maw.

Presently, however, they complain that their monthly wages are not supplied in sufficient quantity, deliberately making out a colourable case against their employers, and say that more profuse maintenance must be given, or they will break their agreement and ravage the whole island. Nor is there long delay: the threat is followed by its execution. For the conflagration that started in the east, the due punishment for our previous sins, was spread from sea to sea, fed by their sacrilegious hands; it blazed across every city and region, nor did it stay its burning course until, after devastating almost the whole surface of the island, its ruddy tongues licked the Western Ocean.

Gildas then describes in moving terms the destruction of a civilised community by reckless and ignorant barbarians.

Every colony (*omnes columnae* should clearly be *omnes coloniae*, for which indeed there is some MS. Authority; Gildas), is levelled to the ground by the stroke of the battering ram, the inhabitants are slaughtered along with the guardians of their churches, priests and people alike, while the sword gleamed on every side, and the flames crackled around. How horrible to behold in the midst of the streets the tops of towers torn from their lofty hinges, the stones of high walls, holy altars, mutilated corpses, all covered with livid clots of coagulated blood, looking as if they had been crushed together in some ghastly winepress! And there was no grave for the dead, unless they were buried under the wretched ruins of their homes, save the bellies of birds and beasts of prey—with reverence, be it spoken, of the blessed souls (if indeed there were many found) which were carried at that time by the holy angels to the height of heaven. Of the miserable remnant some flee to the hills, only to be captured and slain in heaps: some, constrained by famine, come in and surrender themselves to be slaves forever to the enemy, if only their lives might be spared—and this was the best that was granted, others wailing bitterly passed overseas.

A remnant, however, as Gildas tells, continued to resist among woods, mountains, and crags by the sea, till the first rush of the invasion was over, and many of the barbarians had retired to their homes laden with plunder. These desperate patriots rallied under the leadership of Ambrosius Aurelianus:

A modest man, who alone was courteous, faithful, strong and truthful, and alone of the Romans was left alive, in the turmoil of this miserable time. His relatives had won the purple, and had fallen in the civil wars of this age: his descendants still survive in our own day: they have degenerated much from their ancestor's virtue, but still make head and challenge the triumphant barbarian to battle; God has granted them victory according to our prayers.

From the time of Ambrosius onwards, sometimes the citizens, sometimes the enemy, have been successful:

Down to the year of the siege of Mount Badon, which lies near the mouth of the Severn, the year of the last and not the least slaughter of these ruffians, which was the forty-fourth (as I know), with one month elapsed, since it was also the date of my own nativity. But even now our cities are not inhabited as they were of yore, but lie in ruins, deserted and wrecked, our foreign wars having ceased, but not our civil strife.

★★★★★★

Note: The date of the Battle of Mount Badon is one of the most puzzling points in the chronology of the English invasion of Britain. The Latin of Gildas in the above-quoted sentence is very peculiar and obscure. Most commentators take this to mean that the battle was forty-three years and one month before the date at which Gildas wrote. Now internal evidence proves the *Liber Querulus* to have been written about 545-46, since Maglocunus, the tyrant whom he most denounces, is recorded as dying in 547 in the *Annales Cambriae*.

But that same compilation gives the Battle of Mount Badon as taking place in 516, which is only thirty years before. Of course, it is a late work, yet it represents the received traditions of the Welsh. Some students have wished to make out that the date of Maglocunus's death is wrong, and that of Mount Badon correct, running the former on to the year 560, so as to get the forty-four years' interval from 516 correct. But this seems dangerous, because the tyrant is recorded to have died in the "Great Mortality," and the famous plague which swept from Persia over all Europe can be accurately dated from Procopius and other sources to 543-44 in Constantinople and Italy, so that it might naturally ravage Britain in 547.

If this date, therefore, is certain, and Gildas's words are taken in the usual sense, the Battle of Mount Badon and the birth of Gildas ought to have fallen somewhere between 500 and 503, according as the *Liber Querulus* was written two, three or more years before the death of Maglocunus. Mommsen prefers this explanation, fixes the battle in 500, and throws over the date of 516 given in the *Annales Cambriae* as simply wrong.

But we have another curious note to make. Bede, copying Gildas otherwise almost word for word, about the Battle of the Mons Badonicus, says that it took place *quadragesimo circiter et quarto anno adventus eorum (hostium) in Brittaniam*, as if he had a manuscript before him which had contained these words, "*adventus eorum*," in the middle of the clumsy sentence of Gildas. As he seems to place the advent of Hengist somewhere about 447-49 this would make the battle fall in 493. Some foreign commentators (*e.g., La Borderic Rev. Celtique, vi*. 1-13), accept this view.

Yet another suggestion has been made. Mr. E. B. Nicholson, wishing to keep both the dates in the *Annales Cambriae*, 516 for the battle, and 547 for the death of Maglocunus, as correct, makes the forty-four years run from the appearance of Ambrosius Aurelianus counting forward, not from the date of the writing of the *Liber Querulus* counting backward. This ingenious explanation would make the appearance of Ambrosius fall about 472—a date against which there is nothing to say—and leave 516 for the battle and the birth of Gildas; but Gildas would have written his book at the age of about thirty, instead of about forty-four. The *Annales Cambriae* gives Gildas's death under the year 570: if we take Mr. Nicholson's hypothesis he was then fifty-four: if Mommsen's, he was about seventy; if Bede's, he would be about seventy-seven.

If we accept 472 for the date of the appearance of Ambrosius, it must clearly have been not that prince but some other leader who led the Britons to victory forty-four years later, in 516. This allows space for the campaigns and successes of Arthur, if we accept the existence of that much discussed personage, as I am inclined to do.

It may be remarked that if Ambrosius was alive and fighting in 516, and if Gildas wrote the *Liber Querulus* in 545, only thirty years after, it is a little surprising to find the latter describing the princes of his own day as the grandsons rather than the sons of Ambrosius—they have degenerated *avita bonitate* not *paterna bonitate*. But if Ambrosius flourished 472-500 the generations seem to fit in better. Mr. Nicholson's hypothesis, therefore, is well worthy of consideration.

★★★★★★

Gildas then proceeds to denounce five British kings of his own day for their evil life and perpetual turbulence. It is notable that they all dwell on the western side of Britain, one in Damnonia, one in Demetia (South Wales), one in Venedotia (North Wales), the other two, as it seems, respectively on the Severn and on the southern shore of the Bristol Channel. But of these princes more hereafter.

It will be observed that this narrative, though vague and lacking in names and dates—Ambrosius Aurelianus is the only person specifically named in the fifth century, and the year of the Battle of Mount Badon the only epoch fixed—contains little that seems impossible or even unlikely. It thereby differs *toto caelo* from the wild tale of the

Historia Brittonum. There is nothing improbable in the story that the Britons hired barbarian auxiliaries—their Roman predecessors had done so a hundred times. The only error of importance seems to be that the Saxons are represented as new visitors, whereas we have seen reason to believe that their attacks had been continuous ever since the Roman Empire began to grow weak.

It is possible, also, that Gildas gives too much the impression that Britain was under one king only about the year 460, by talking of a single superbus tyrannus, when really Vortigern (or whatever his name may have been) was at most the chief among several contemporary dynasts. But in one respect his narrative seems to fit in with archaeological evidence in a way that the ordinary received tale of the Saxon conquest fails to do. He represents the disaster to civilised Britain as being sudden and fearful, as a conflagration that spread from sea to sea in a short time, and then retired from a great part of the area that it had devastated, leaving irreparable ruin behind.

Much of the island was liberated by Ambrosius, but it was never restored to its old state of wealth and culture. This is precisely what we should guess from the condition of the old Roman cities when they are excavated. In hardly one of them, even in those of the West Midlands, do we find any trace of a continued occupation by civilised Romano-Britons going on for many years after 410. Nearly all, so far as we can see, show signs of having been burnt or deserted at a comparatively early date, and never inhabited again, even though their sites were not permanently occupied by the Teutonic invaders till the sixth or seventh century.

There is no satisfactory evidence for the existence of an independent British Colchester, London or Lincoln, or even of a survival of York, Chester or Wroxeter. The only known exception to this general rule is Calleva (Silchester), where a single post-Roman inscription in Ogham letters has been found, commemorating a certain Ebicatus: it seems to belong to the second half of the fifth century. But there are strong reasons for supposing that Calleva was evacuated by the Britons before that century was over.

It is quite possible to believe that the date 441, given by the so-called Prosper as that of a complete domination of the Saxons in Britain, really represents a moment when the invaders seemed to inundate the whole south and east of the island, though they ultimately lost their hold on great part of it.

The *Historia Brittonum* gives a much longer account of this period, but one that does not at all square with the narrative of Gildas. Since, however, it was compiled not earlier than 685, while Gildas was writing in 545, the later book can have no authority when it conflicts with the earlier. Moreover, Gildas gives a possible series of events, while the *Historia* is replete with wild miracles and obvious folktales. Told shortly, for what it is worth, the version of this strange book runs as follows.

About forty years after the death of the tyrant Magnus Maximus, *i.e.*, about the year 428, Vortigern reigned in Britain, and was distracted between three fears, that of the Picts and Scots, that of the Romans, and that of Ambrosius (apparently a competitor for his throne, but clearly not the Ambrosius who flourished in 472-500).

To him came three ships from Germany, in which were the brothers Hengist and Horsa, exiles, and their war-band. Vortigern gave them the Isle of Thanet to live in, and hired them as allies against the Picts and Scots. About this time St. Germanus came to Britain and wrought many miracles, especially the portentous destruction of the tyrant Benlli by fire from heaven. (Here then we seem to be in 429, the time of Germanus's first visit.)

After a time, the Britons grew weary of paying their Saxon auxiliaries, and began to quarrel with them, but Hengist persuaded the king to retain them as his guard, and even to send for sixteen more ships' crews of his countrymen. With this second party of the strangers arrived the daughter of Hengist, a girl of surpassing beauty, with whom the king fell desperately in love. He was so infatuated with her that, to buy her hand from her father, he gave him the whole region of Kent, though that was at the moment the patrimony of a certain British prince called Guoyrancgon.

At the same time Hengist persuaded his son-in-law to enlist more mercenary bands, headed by his son Ochta and his nephew Ebissa, to whom he allotted for settlement the lands near the Great Wall. They came with forty ships, sailed around the coast of Pictland, devastated the Orkneys, and seized several tracts lying beyond the *Mare Frenessicum* (whatever that may be—possibly the estuary of the Forth) as far as the boundary of the Picts. Hengist meanwhile with his own band occupied great part of Kent.

At this moment the evil life of Vortigern, who had just added polygamy and incest to the list of his offences, drew down on him a second visit from St. Germanus. He was cursed by the saint and all the British clergy, and felt himself so insecure that he fled into the mountains beyond Severn, where he purposed to build himself an impregnable castle. Here follows a wild tale about a mysterious boy, certain wizards, two dragons, and some *ex-post-facto* prophecies about the fate of Britain. The boy, whom the king had at first intended to slay, revealed himself as Ambrosius, the son of a Roman consul, and showed such marvellous knowledge that Vortigern fled, and built, in another spot than that which he had chosen, his refuge-castle of Caer-Vortigern.

Meanwhile, the king being apparently disgraced and discarded, the Britons took as their leader his son Vortimer, a hard-fighting hero, who fell upon Hengist and the Saxons, and after four general actions drove them out of Kent, and even from their original grant in the Isle of Thanet. The battles seem all to be placed in Kent—the first on the Darent (*flumen Dergwentid*), the second:

> At the ford which is called in their tongue Episford, but in ours Rithergabail. (This in the *Saxon Chronicle* appears as Aegelsthrep—Aylesford—and as a victory for Hengist, under the year 455. Rithergabail means "the ford of the horses".) There fell on the one side Horsa and on the other Categirn, the second son of Vortigern and brother of Vortimer. The third conflict was at the Inscribed Stone, which stands on the shore of the Gallic Sea; there the Saxons were forced to flee on board their keels, and were entirely driven out of Britain. (Lapis Tituli is perhaps Stonar, near Deal and Richborough. Evidently there was a large Roman inscribed monument near it.)

But Vortimer died not very long time after his last victory, and when he was gone Hengist and his Saxons came back in force. Vortigern, who seems to return to power on his son's death, was ready to receive them on friendly terms, because of his affection for his Saxon wife. A conference was arranged between 300 deputies on each side, who were to come unarmed; but in the midst of the proceedings the Saxons, who had hidden daggers in their boots, fell upon and massacred the British delegates, all save the king, whom they held to ransom. As the price of his life Vortigern ceded them the regions afterwards known as Essex and Sussex.

Thoroughly discredited among the Britons, Vortigern fled after this last disaster to his own special dominions beyond the Severn. He was pursued thither by St. Germanus, who came to give him once more a spiritual castigation. The king avoided him, slinking from place to place, till he reached his stronghold of Caer-Vortigern on the Teifi, where the saint blockaded him, as it were, praying and fasting for three days outside the castle gate. On the fourth night fire descended from heaven and destroyed the king, his *harem* of wives, the castle and its garrison.

But others say that he was not thus slain, but wandered as an outcast from place to place, banned by everyone, till he died of a broken heart.

His third son, Pascentius, succeeded to the heritage of two regions, Builth and Vortigerniaun, and ruled there under the *suzerainty* of the celebrated Ambrosius, who was afterwards chief among the kings of Britain. And Fernmail, his descendant in the tenth generation, was reigning there when the last recension of the *Historia Brittonum* was made in the year 820, "the fourth year of King Mermin," who reigned from 816 to 844.

Meanwhile Hengist the Saxon died, and his son Ochta came from the northern side of Britain to the kingdom of Kent, and from him descend the kings of the Kentish men. The Saxons "increased in multitude and grew in Britain" till they were checked, not, as we should expect from Gildas, by Ambrosius Aurelianus, whom the *Historia Brittonum* only mentions incidentally, but by Arthur, a new name to us, though it is destined to be so famous in British story. Of him we are told that:

He used to fight against the Saxons in company with the kings of the Britons, but was himself *dux bellorum*.

A title which seems to descend from that old Roman *dux Britanniarum*, of whom mention has already been made. Arthur defeats the Saxons in twelve battles, most of whose names present difficulties of identification, though the tenth of them is that of Caer-Legion, *i.e.*, Chester, and the twelfth, that at Mons Badonis, is clearly the same as the victory of Mons Badonicus, of which Gildas speaks. Of it we are told "there fell in that one day 960 men before the assault of Arthur, and no one felled them save he alone". No cessation of the Saxon attack is mentioned as following the battle of Mount Badon, though Gildas has told us that forty years of comparative peace were won by it. But the *Historia* merely says that:

Routed in all these battles, the enemy sought succours from Germany, and were increased in numbers without intermission, and they brought over kings from Germany, to reign over them in Britain, down to the time when Ida came to be king, who was son of Eobba, and was the first king in Bernicia.

Quite at variance both with Gildas and the *Historia* is the tale told by the *Anglo-Saxon Chronicle*, which represents the conquest of Eastern Britain as having been made, not by one wide-spreading incursion, led by Hengist, but by the separate enterprises of many different war-bands, Saxon, Anglian and Jutish, who worked very slowly forward, and conquered small patches of territory at long intervals of time. According to this narrative, only put together at the end of the ninth century, the course of the invasion was as follows:—

First, in 449 Hengist, a Jutish adventurer, with his brother Horsa, landed in the Isle of Thanet, at the summons of Vortigern, who offered them land in the south-east on condition that they should fight against the Picts. They drove off the northern barbarians, but soon quarrelled with their employer, and were for twenty years and more fighting to win the mastery of the land of Kent; Hengist proclaimed himself king in 455, and after many victories drove the Britons as far back as London in 457. But his subsequent battles were in Kent, and the last mention of him, in 473, does not imply that he had won any more than the single district where his descendants are found reigning a century later.

Secondly, in 477, Aella, the Saxon, and his three sons land on the South coast, establish themselves in Sussex, and in 491 besiege and take Anderida, its chief town. Their efforts do not extend beyond the forest of the Weald, the limit of the later South-Saxon kingdom.

Thirdly, in 495 Cerdic, another Saxon adventurer, and his son Cynric, land somewhere on Southampton Water, and after many battles with the Britons, all apparently in Hampshire, are hailed as kings in 519. A second contemporaneous invasion in the same region is made by one Port, who lands with his sons "at the place which is called Portsmouth," slays many Britons and makes a settlement. The relations of this certainly fictitious person (who is no more than the eponymous hero of Portsmouth) with Cerdic are not explained. But in 530 Cerdic conquers the Isle of Wight, and in 534 he dies. Since nearly twenty years later (552) the West Saxons have not yet occupied Salisbury, which they win in that year, it is clear that Cerdic's kingdom is conceived as covering no more than Hampshire, with, conceivably, parts of Berkshire and Surrey.

Fourthly, we are given a short notice of the establishment of an Anglian kingdom north of the Humber by Ida, who began to reign in 547, lived twelve years longer, and fortified the royal stronghold of Bamborough.

Fifthly, we get a mention of Aella, the first king of the other Northumbrian kingdom of Deira, who is said to have received recognition as king in 560.

No statements are made in the *Chronicle* as to the foundation of the other primitive Teutonic States in England, such as those of the East Saxons, East Angles and Mercians.

The great irruption of the invaders into Central Britain is said only to begin in 571, when, under the West Saxon king Ceawlin, the grandson of Cerdic, a great battle is fought at Bedford, and the four towns of Aylesbury, Lenbury, Bensington and Eynsham, all north of Thames and south of Bedford, are taken. Clearly, then, the *Chronicle* conceives that the Britons were still holding the South-Midlands more than a hundred and twenty years later than the supposed date of the landing of Hengist. The first penetration of the Saxons to the western side of the island follows a few years later, with Ceawlin's victory at Dyrham, in South Gloucestershire (577), after which he took from the Britons three cities, Gloucester, Cirencester and Bath.

It is clear that this ninth century narrative, evidently composed from the ancestral memories of the invader's, with no direct help from Gildas or the *Historia Brittonum*, and much from Bede, contrasts in the strongest way with the version of the Saxon conquest given by the fifth and sixth century writers. Nor can we doubt that when they come into collision, we must trust the earlier rather than the later authority. In a similar way Gildas must give way when he comes into conflict with the *Vita Germanic* which was written sixty years before his time. And the *Historia Brittonum* must be rejected when it conflicts with Gildas, whose testimony is good for the sixth century, in whose very commencement he was born, though it is not to be trusted for the early fifth century, of which he clearly had only a knowledge in outline. Indeed, the *Historia* can only be used with discretion and doubt for any history earlier than the eighth century, in whose end it was first compiled.

Putting the whole of these authorities, whose weight varies so much, into historical perspective, the version of the Saxon invasions, which we are forced to construct, must run somewhat as follows:—

Down to about the year 429, the time of the first visit of St. Germanus, Britain was assailed by Pict, Scot, and Saxon simultaneously, but, though suffering severely, more or less held its own. The heart of the Romanised Eastern and Southern Britain was still intact, but local kingships were beginning to spring up both in the West and the North, and these were Celtic rather than Roman in character: in fact a kind of Celtic revival was in progress, as is shown by the fact that the recorded names of princes are often non-Roman—*e.g.*, Cunedda, Coroticus, and a little later Vortigern. A side-light on this movement may be got from the unique fifth century Ogham inscription at Silchester, which proves that barbarism was making its way towards the eastern side of the island.

As already stated, it gives the name of Ebicatus written in the rude Celtic character common in Ireland, but rare in Britain, which begins to be used about this period. Apparently, the words are in a Goidelic dialect, and Ebicatus may conceivably have been a visitor or immigrant, and not a citizen of Calleva.

Somewhere in the middle of the century, the Pictish invasions, checked for a moment at the "Hallelujah victory" of 429, grew again so dangerous that the Britons hired Saxon or Jutish mercenaries against them. We must conclude, from Gildas's mention of a "*superbus tyrannus*" and *consiliarii* that there was at this moment a federation of kings and cities over which one prince held some sort of *suzerainty* or presidential power. And there is no reason to doubt that this was Vortigern, though his name is not given by Gildas. We must conceive of him as being a king of South Wales, since his descendants were reigning in Builth and Radnorshire when the *Historia Brittonum* was written, and the site of his castle was remembered to have been on the Teifi.

There is no reason for distrusting this pedigree—and Vortigern was not an ancestor so creditable that anyone would wish to claim him, unless there was good reason for so doing. The names of his predecessors in the pedigree, Vitalis (Guitaul), Vitalinus (Guitolin), Bonus, and Paulus, show that they must have been Romanised British nobles. He was clearly not "King of Britain," but one of many kings, who whether by election, or by force of arms, enjoyed a preponderance over the rest.

That Teutonic mercenaries, when they had accomplished the task of fighting for which they had been hired, often turned against the hand that fed them, is a well-known phenomenon of the fourth and fifth centuries, all over the Roman world. I see no reason to doubt that Gildas's story concerning the breach between the British king and his mercenaries may be true. And we may allow that the chief of the Teutons was named Hengist, not so much because the *Historia Brittonum* so, nor even because the English remembered him as founder of the Kentish kingdom, when Bede wrote in the eighth century, or when the *Chronicle* was compiled in the ninth, but because we have a much earlier authority for the fact. This is the anonymous "Geographer of Ravenna" who, describing the world a century before the *Historia*, and writing in a region where British or English legends were equally unlikely to penetrate, says that "the race of the Saxons, coming from Old Saxony, under their prince Anschis settled the island of Britain some time back." (For Mr. Chadwick's idea that Anschis = Oise, see *Origins of the English Nation*, but those who take it as a form of Hengist are more numerous.)

What followed the breach between the Britons and their danger-ous *employés* must have been something much more resembling the tale of Gildas than that of Nennius or the *Anglo-Saxon Chronicle*. That is to say, we can hardly doubt that the Saxons swept with fire and sword all over Eastern Britain, and even as far as the Western Sea, dur-ing the course of a comparatively few years. They sacked all the great cities, probably with details of horror as great as those detailed in the lurid paragraph of Gildas quoted above. They massacred, drove out, or enslaved the whole population, and firmly established themselves all down the length of the shore from Northumberland as far as South-ampton Water. How far to the West these ravages may have extended it is impossible to say; we have the definite statement of Gildas that:

> The conflagration which started in the East, did not stay its course till, after devastating almost the whole island, its ruddy tongues licked the Western Ocean.

This may mean, and probably does mean, nothing more than that the farthest raids of the Saxons touched the Bristol Channel, or the estuaries of Dee and Mersey. The area of permanently conquered ter-ritory cannot have reached nearly so far. But there is no reason to doubt that there came an end, somewhere about the middle of the fifth century, to all the Romano-British states, municipal or monar-chical, along the eastern side of Britain. When Gildas wrote, his list of surviving British kingdoms seems to include nothing that lay east of the basin of the Severn, and of the line drawn from its southern edge to the English Channel across Wiltshire. He seems to have no knowl-edge of the eastern side of the island. Yet he tells us that since the year of his own birth, early in the sixth century, nothing more had been lost to the barbarians, and the Britons had been comparatively free from foreign—if not from domestic—strife. The victory of the Mons Badonicuus and the rally headed by Ambrosius Aurelianus had saved the West but had not recovered the East. London and Camulodunum, Lindum and Eburacum, were lost forever.

We are forced to conclude that, starting before the year 441, which the so-called Prosper gives as the date of the overrunning of Britain by the Saxons, the wave of invasion swept in one (or at the most two) generations up to the central watershed of England, and was then checked by the rally of the Britons. The devastated eastern half, which had once been the most populous and civilised part of Roman Britain, remained with the invaders; the western half had crystallised into a number of native States, which maintained their independence, but had lost in the time of chaos nearly all traces of the Roman culture, which had never bitten deep on the western side of the island, save in a few isolated districts like the Valley of the Lower Severn.

There seems no reason whatever to doubt the historic existence of Ambrosius Aurelianus, whose grandsons "much degenerated from their ancestor's virtue" were still reigning in some part of Britain when Gildas wrote about 545. The genuine tradition concerning great historical figures extends with ease over a period so short as sixty years, which must be about the interval between the exploits of Ambrosius and the date of Gildas's book. The other great British hero whose name falls into this period has caused much searching of heart to historians. Is it possible to believe in Arthur, *"dux bellorum"* and victor of Mount Badon, as he is described in the *Historia Brittonum?*

Arthur is not mentioned by name in Gildas, nor in Bede, nor in the *Anglo-Saxon Chronicle*. The chapter dealing with his twelve battles in the Historia was not written till 685 at the earliest—a date nearly two centuries later than his supposed exploits. Hence some historians frankly reject his historical existence: he has been called "a hero of romance, a pure myth," to whom the exploits of the real Ambrosius have been wrongly transferred. (Ramsay, *Foundations of England*, i.) His origin has been sought in the remotest antiquity, he is a Celtic "culture hero" or early divinity, brought down into historical times by some strange error of tribal memory. Or he is "the ideal champion of his race, belonging to all the Celts who spoke a Brythonic language from Morbihan to the Caledonian Forest". He is called "a popular creation, localising himself readily here, there, and everywhere, in the domain of the race in whose imagination he lives." (Rhys, *Celtic Britain*.) His name has been resolved into something mythological, and he disappears into a sun myth or a racial totem—Art-ur, the "bear-man"—in the writings of certain exponents of folk-lore.

I must confess that I am not convinced by these arguments, and incline to think that a real figure lurks beneath the tale of the *Historia Brittonum*. The name was undoubtedly Roman, like that of most British princes of this period: leaving out of count the numerous Artorii in the *Classical Dictionary* who had no connection with this island, we know of one who held high command in Britain in the third century, and went, at the head of "*Vexillations*" of horse and foot, from the legion at York and other garrisons, to put down an insurrection of the Armoricans. (Besides Augustus's physician, and the person censured by Juvenal, there are a considerable number of Artorii. in C. I. L. inscriptions.) This C. Artorius Justus, whose monument has been discovered in Illyria, may have left numerous relatives or freed men in Britain.

At the same time, any Celtic-speaking provincial may have confused the purely Latin name with the Art = bear root in his own language. It is to be found several times in centuries later than the fifth: there was a South-Welsh prince named Arthur, son of Peter, whose name appears in the Harleian genealogies, during the seventh century. As to the fact that Arthur is not mentioned by name in Gildas, we may point out that the same is the case with Constantine, the last usurping emperor in Britain, with Germanus, Vortigern and Hengist. Indeed, the only two names that occur in the fifth century portion of the *Liber Querulus* are those of Aetius ("Agitius" as Gildas prefers to call him) and Ambrosius Aurelianus. It is even possible that Arthur is alluded to in that hysterical work, though he is not named, in one of its most obscurely-worded paragraphs.

★★★★★★

Gildas, as Mr. Nicholson of the Bodleian pointed out to me, calls one of the contemporary princes whom he abuses, a certain Cuneglassus, "*ab adolescentiae annis multorum sessor, aurigaque currus receptaculi Ursi.*" Can this possibly mean that Cuneglassus, who is spoken of as no longer young, had been in earlier days the charioteer, or, to use late-Roman phraseology, the *comes stabuli* of some king whom Gildas calls the "bear" = Arth? It is puzzling, however, to see that Cuneglassus is also himself called "Urse," unless that word be a mistaken duplication from the immediately following Ursi.

★★★★★★

Nor is this enigmatical hero to be found in the *Historia Brittonum* alone. His name is associated with very many sites both in North and in South-Western Britain, and, though this fact may not prove his existence, it certainly does not disprove it. It is safer, on continental analogies, to look for a real personage dimly remembered, distorted, or even wrongly localised, behind such place-names, than to deny his historical character. The memories of Brunehaute, Charlemagne or Roland, even when attached to spots or works with which those undoubtedly real personages had apparently no connection, testify to a genuine memory of their existence and greatness. Probably Arthur's Seat and "Arthur's Oon" and such like, must be considered as bearing similar evidence.

It may be added that Arthur is repeatedly mentioned in the earliest Bardic poems of Wales—whatever may be the date of the shape in which they survive. When Celtic scholars will agree to assign a fixed age to those ancient relics, we shall be better able to judge of their value as corroborating the *Historia Brittonum*, Meanwhile, the allusions to Arthur which occur in them seem to belong to the earliest stage of their compilation, and have no trace of the later Arthur-legend which grew popular in days after Nennius, and was ultimately put into literary shape by that most unconscientious person Geoffrey of Monmouth in the twelfth century.

As in the *Historia*, he seems to be merely *dux bellorum*, a military chief, not a king—still less a supreme high-king of all Britain, such as tradition afterwards made him. Meanwhile historians still await a satisfactory estimate of the exact worth of these poems from a competent critic, who must be at once a Celtic philologist and a sound historian. If the decision is in favour of an early date, we cannot hesitate to accept the Arthur of the *Historia Brittonum* as a well-established historical person. If it places the poems very late, we are thrown back on what information we already possess concerning him, and I am inclined to think that this alone suffices to take him out of the region of myth.

CHAPTER 2

The Settlement of the Conquerors: The Early Kingdoms (515-570)

When the first triumphant inrush of the Teutonic invaders of Briton was arrested by the resistance made by Ambrosius Aurclianus, and finally checked at the Battle of the Mons Badonicus, the survivors settled down, not into one single State, like the Franks in Gaul or the Visigoths in Spain, but into many. The same phenomenon was seen four hundred years later, when the Danes of the "Great Army," who had been acting for many years as one compact war-band, broke apart into many sections, after they had been taught by Alfred's sword that all England was not to be theirs.

******

We might add, as a parallel in a nearer time, the fate of the Lombards in Italy, who broke up into the states of Benevento and Spoleto, besides the larger northern kingdom, after failing to conquer all Italy.

******

The moment of settlement was a moment of political disruption.

The first invasions must have been led by many chiefs in succession, of whom Hengist was the first and very probably Aella the second. The tradition preserved by Bede that an "*imperium*" over all the bands of the invaders, from the Humber southward to the Gallic Sea, was possessed by Aella the founder of the South Saxon kingdom, then by Ceawlin a West Saxon, then by Aethelbert of Kent, then by Raedwald the East Anglian, is clearly a memory of the fact that the Saxons, Jutes and English worked together against the Britons. The view that each war-band stuck to the narrow piece of coast on which it had landed, without paying attention to what was going on to right or left, is an erroneous deduction from the entries of the *Anglo-Saxon Chronicle*. They do not necessarily bear such an interpretation, and, if they did, it must be remembered that they come from a document of the late ninth century, which (as we shall presently see) has little authority for the history of the sixth.

It is incredible that the "*imperium*" of Bede means a territorial domination over all the newly established insular states, held by chiefs who owned such small realms as Sussex, Kent, or even East Anglia. But taking the word in its classical military sense, a sense which Bede was scholar enough to appreciate, there is no reason to doubt that a league of war-bands might be, from time to time, captained by a chief whose own following was not the largest contingent in the host. The settlement that he occupied as a permanent holding might, therefore, be comparatively small.

Down to the check at the Mons Badonicus it is quite probable that we ought not to speak of separate Teutonic kingdoms as existing in Britain. The fluid mass of invaders may have crystallised into solid units only when there was, for a time, no more land to be won, so that it became necessary to take stock, so to speak, of that which was still at their disposition. The disruption of the conquering host into petty kingdoms with definite boundaries is a phenomenon of the early sixth century, and was practically complete by its end. Concerning their foundation, we have in some cases a certain amount of information, but in others none. Exactly similar was the history of the Danish "Great Army" in the ninth century, of which we shall tell in due course.

One thing is clear: the invaders had been no homogeneous mass of "Saxons," as we should have gathered from the narratives of Gildas and the *Historia Brittonum*, Their own account of their origin, as given by Bede, must be accepted, for this is one of the matters on which tribal tradition does not go astray in a mere two hundred years.

> The immigrants came from three very powerful nations of Germany—Saxons, Angles and Jutes, From the Jutes are descended the people of Kent and the Isle of Wight, and those also who, dwelling in the province of the West Saxons, are to this day called the Jute-folk, seated opposite to the Isle of Wight. From the Saxons, that is from the land which we now call Old Saxony, came the East Saxons, the South Saxons and the West Saxons. From the Angles, that is from the region which is now called 'Angulus,' and which is said to have remained from that day till now depopulated, lying between the boundaries of the Jutes and Saxons, came the East Angles, the Mid Angles, the Mercians, and all the race of the Northumbrians who dwell north of the River Humber, and the remaining English tribes.

The Saxons, Jutes and Angles are old acquaintances of those who have read Tacitus's *Germania* and Ptolemy's *Geography*, The former had dwelt in the second century to the north of the river Elbe, in what is now called Holstein, "on the neck of the Cimbric Chersonesus," as Ptolemy puts it. They owned also "the three islands off the mouth of the Elbe," whatever that may mean. Tacitus, oddly enough, makes no mention of the Saxons, and from Ptolemy to the third century they escaped the notice of Roman historians, because they were far away from the wars of the Rhine frontier. But in that third century fell the period of the building up of the great confederacies which formed the later German nations.

And just as the Franks on the Lower and the Alamanni on the Upper Rhine suddenly appear as new composite units, superseding many older and smaller tribal entities, so it is with the Saxons farther north. They evidently coalesced with the Chauci, the most numerous of the North German races, who occupied all the land between the Elbe and the Ems, in the modern province of Hanover. The confederacy took the Saxon not the Chaucian name, and we find Zosimus calling the Chauci "a part of the Saxons," in the fourth century. Apparently, the Saxons, though the smaller tribe, had, by conquest or by peaceful means, taken the greater part in building up the union, and imposed their name on it.

From 286 *A.D.* onwards we find them perpetually mentioned by the Roman historians as pirates infesting the North Sea, as we have seen already when dealing with the history of Carausius and Stilicho. Hence came the establishment of the two naval governments of the *Littus Saxonicum per Brittanias* and *per Gallias*, whose fleets and harbour-forts were destined to cope with the marauders. With the break-up of the Roman power in Britain and Northern Gaul, during the miserable reign of Honorius, the defence of the North Sea and Channel ceased, and the Saxons could not only ravage for the future but settle down where they pleased.

It was not only in Britain that they won themselves a holding; a section of them seized part of the north coast of Gaul, between the mouth of the Seine and the Peninsula of the Côtentin, where they are found the fifth and sixth centuries under the name of the *Saxones Bajocassini* (from Rajocae, now Bayeux, the chief centre of the settlement). (*Gregory of Tours*, v.) They were presently subdued by the Franks, and incorporated in the Merovingian realm. It seems likely that there was another small Saxon settlement on the coast of the Dover Strait behind Calais, where a group of place-names of purely Saxon type covers a small compact region. But no traces of these colonists appear in historical records; unlike the *Saxones Bajocassini* they did not attract the notice of Gregory of Tours.

The Jutes are the second Teutonic tribe named by Bede as taking part in the conquest of Britain, and to them belonged, by common repute, the exiled chief Hengist, who hired himself out with his warband to Vortigern, and afterwards led the first great raids of the piratical confederacy. The Jutes are a much more obscure people than the Saxons. They are apparently first found in Tacitus, as the Eudoses, one of a group of seven small tribes (of whom the Angles and Varini were others) dwelling together somewhere far to the north beyond the

Langobardi. The historian has nothing of interest to say about these races, save that all seven joined in the common worship of an earth-goddess named Nerthus, whose sanctuary was on an island, (Alsen off the east coast of Schleswig?; see Furneaux's note to the *Germania*)—but whether it lay in the North Sea or the Baltic there is no indication.

Indeed, all Tacitus's geography in this part of the *Germania* is vague to a degree. Since, however, the Varini and Angles, who are mentioned along with the Eudoses, were certainly seated in the Cimbric Penin-sula, there can be little doubt that the Jutes also were already dwelling in Jutland, the land where they have left their name, as early as the year 100 A.D. Ptolemy, however, has no mention of them, and it is not indeed for several centuries that we again come upon them, under the names of Eutii, Euthiones, or Eucii, in connection with the Franks. Venantius Fortunatus, the last Roman poet of Merovingian times, tells us that his patron Chilperic had defeated the Dane, the Euthio and the Saxon, and some forty years earlier a letter of King Theudebert to Emperor Justinian states that the Saxons and Eucii had recently submitted to him. (Or perhaps the Saxones Eucii, the phraseology is obscure. It is quite possible that the Merovingians considered the Jutes as Saxons, just as the Britons most certainly did.)

That the Frankish power ever reached to Jutland in any effec-tive way seems unlikely: but since Fortunatus mentions the "*Euthio*" between the Saxon and the still more remote Dane, there can be no doubt that the races had been in collision. And since we know that Danes under Hygelac (Chrocolaicus) invaded the Frankish northern borders by sea in 515, and were defeated by the son of King Theu-deric, we may perhaps suppose that the Jutes also had been attempt-ing settlement in the same direction. If they came to Britain, they could far more easily come to the lands of the Rhine-mouth. Objec-tions have been raised on philological grounds to the identification of Bede's *Jutae* with the Euthiones or Eutii, owing to the initial J of the name. But the balance of opinion seems to be in favour of regarding them as a North-German folk, closely akin to the Angles, who were afterwards subdued by the Danes, and amalgamated with their con-querors, so that their language and customs ceased to be German and became Scandinavian.

That the old English had no doubt that the Jutes of Kent and the Wight came from Jutland, is sufficiently shown by the fact that the chronicler Ethelweard says, that the Cantuarii and "Uuhtii" of Eng-land derived their origin from the Gioti, and that the Angles dwelt between the Saxons and the Gioti. King Alfred in his translation of Bede, calls the Jutes of the earlier writer Geatas, but in his *Orosius* renders "*provincia Jutorum*" by Eotaland. Eotas, Gioti, Geatas and Jutae were clearly in the minds of Alfred and Ethelweard interchangeable forms. But the G initial and the form Geatas were apparently caused by a confusion of the inhabitants of Jutland with the Goths of Sweden. The older Scandinavian name for the Jutlanders seems to have been Iotar or Jotar, the later Danish form was Jyder—neither of which should be identified with the Gautar across the water in the Scandinavian Peninsula, who were the real Geatas or Goths.

The Angles give less difficulty to the inquirer. They are named by Tacitus along with the Eudoses and Varini, among the seven tribes who lay beyond the Langobardi, *i.e.,* north of the Elbe, and worshipped Nerthus in common. They were therefore already in the Cimbric Peninsula at the end of the first century *A.D.* Ptolemy mentions them as the Angeiloi, but apparently makes a hopeless confusion as to their geographical position, since he says that they are an inland tribe lying to the east of the Langobardi, and stretching northward to the Middle Elbe. Apparently, his points of the compass have got wrong, and having once placed them east of the Langobardi instead of north, he is forced to consider them as lying in Brandenburg instead of in Schleswig. Their real position is clearly given by Bede—as above quoted—lying between the Saxons and the Jutes, and also by King Allied when he says that "north of the Saxons lies the land called Angle, and Sillende (another district of the modern Schleswig) and some part of the Danes." Ethelweard is still more definite:

> Old Anglia is situated between the Saxons and the Gioti, having a chief town which in Saxon is called Sleswic, but in Danish Haithaby.

Here lies to this day (1919) the square peninsula called Angeln, between the Schleswig and Flensburg *fiords.*

It must not be supposed, however, that the territory of the numerous race who settled all the north-eastern coast of Britain was limited to the narrow bounds of the modern Angeln. It undoubtedly extended over all Schleswig, some of the Danish isles, (certainly Funen at least, see Bremer, *Germanischen Stämme*), and possibly also over part of Jutland in the fifth and sixth centuries. It is not unlikely that the Angles may have amalgamated with themselves some of the other small tribes whom Tacitus mentions as leagued with them in worship of Nerthus—the Reudigni Aviones, Suardones and Nuithones. The Angles must have been sharing in the maritime expeditions of the Saxons in the fifth century, for, though their name is not on record in the historians, yet we find a corps of Angles among the Teutonic mercenary regiments of the *Notitia Dignitatum*. Evidently, therefore, they had gone south in considerable numbers, and were occasionally enlisting in the imperial army—which can only have happened through sea voyages.

It seems possible also that somewhere about the sixth century they had settlements on the Lower Rhine—just as the Saxons had on the north coast of Gaul. The evidence for this, however, is only an early code of laws called the *Lex Angliorum et Werinorum, hoc est Thuringorum,* which has been attributed to various dates between the sixth and ninth centuries. The Thuringi of this code are evidently the people on the Lower Rhine, more generally known as Thoringi, who, as we know, were annexed to the Frankish empire in the sixth century. The Werini are the Varini of Tacitus, neighbours of the Angles in the Cimbric Peninsula, who had apparently shared in this southward move of some part of the race.

Conceivably this settlement on the Lower Rhine may have been the stepping stone of the Angles on their way to Britain, though it is equally possible that all the colonists came directly from their Cimbric home to our island. We have independent evidence for the existence of the Varini in the Netherlands from Procopius (*circ.* 550), who tells us a long tale concerning their relations with the Franks "from whom they are separated only by the Rhine". But he unfortunately makes no mention of the Angles as being settled with them in that region. We have therefore no other evidence for their existence in the Low Countries than the title of the code cited above.

******

Some authorities wish to place the Angles and Varini of the code in the Thuringia of Central Germany, not the Thoringi a of the Netherlands, where names similar to those of Angles and Varini "Engelin" and "Werinofeld" are found as small districts on the Unstrut and Saal. See Chadwick, but *cf.* for the other view Bremer, whom I follow.

******

Bede is apparently correct when he says that the old home of the Angles in Schleswig was completely deserted in his own day. The Anglian name disappears from the Cimbric Peninsula just when it becomes widely spread in Britain, and we have little trace of any inhabitants save Danes and Saxons in this region after the sixth century. Very nearly the whole race had migrated to Britain. Thus only, indeed, can we account for such a phenomenon as the conquest of the entire coastland from the Firth of Forth to the mouth of the Stour by a tribe whose original home was of such limited dimensions.

Along with the Jutes, Saxons and Angles it can hardly be doubted that fragments of other tribes reached Britain. The invaders were a mixed multitude led by chiefs of several races, and there is good reason to believe that their hosts must have included small bands from the neighbouring tribes of the coastland of the North Sea—especially from the Frisians. Procopius, in his curious account of Britain, speaks of the invaders recently established there only as Angles and Frisians, omitting not only the Jutes but also the Saxons. Yet none of the historical kingdoms of England traced themselves back to a Frisian ancestry. It is probable that stray Varini and Heruli, if not Franks also, may have been among the settlers, since all were more or less sear faring, and all were at hand to profit by the weakness of the Britons, after the removal of the Roman fleet from the Channel.

That the settlements of the Teutonic invaders developed into many small states, and not one powerful kingdom like that of the Franks in Gaul or the Ostrogoths in Italy, is easily to be explained. The settlers were of at least three separate races, and each racial element was composed, not of a king migrating at the head of the whole body of his subjects, like Alaric or Theodoric, but of many war-bands under many chiefs. These obeyed, no doubt, the general whom they had chosen from time to time to head their confederacy, the Hengist or Aella of the moment, but they were not a compact or homogeneous host. Even the Angles, who appear to have migrated practically *en masse* to England, seem to have been led, not by any single prince representing the old royal house that had ruled in Angeln, but by many chiefs of varying descent.

In the pedigrees of the kings of the later states of East Anglia, Bernicia, Deira and Mercia, (all to be found at the end of the *Historia Brittonum*), which are undoubtedly the oldest surviving fragments of Anglian historical memory, we do not find that all the founders of the states start from the same series of ancestors, as would have been the case if all had deduced themselves from the old kings of the Angles. On the contrary, though all ultimately get back to the god Woden, the inevitable forefather of all Teutonic kings in Britain, whether Anglian or Saxon, they reach him by four separate lines of descent, which have no single name in common, save that the Deiran and the Bernician lines both purport to start from Baeldag, son of Woden.

It is curious to note that the West Saxon royal house, which one would have supposed likely to own a perfectly distinct descent from any Anglian line, claimed three ancestors, Woden, Baeldag and Brond, identical with the initial names in the Deiran list as given in the *Historia Brittonum*. But Woden and his immediate descendants being clearly mythical, we can only deduce that the Anglian royal houses had no real connection with each other that could be traced. Otherwise they would have had a number of common ancestors, ending in the generation falling before the date of the invasion of Britain.

The kingdoms which were certainly in existence about the year 550 seem to have been the following:—

(1) Kent, whose kings claimed to descend from Hengist, though their family name of Oiscings was taken not from him but from Oise, who is called his son both by Bede and the *Saxon Chronicle*, though the *Historia Brittonum*, says that Octha was the son of Hengist, and Ossa (apparently a corruption of Oise) was the son of Octha The settlers in this region were wholly or predominantly Jutes, which accounts for the fact that the Kentish dialect had marked peculiarities, which differentiated it from the speech of the Saxons to the west and the Angles to the north.

The kingdom of the Oiscings never extended over any tract of territory much larger than the modern county of Kent, but it is likely that parts of Surrey may have belonged to it in the sixth century, since the dialect of that region shows some, if not all, of the Kentish peculiarities. Yet the name "Surrey," the "southern region," must surely have been imposed on this thinly-peopled and much-wooded district by invaders who entered it from the North, rather than from Kent.

But the strength of the Oiscings in early days must have depended, not on the exact amount of territory occupied by their own Jutish war-band, but on their personal influence as generals of the combined Teutonic invaders of South Britain. It is thus alone that we can account for the fact that Aethelbert (560-617) was reckoned by Bede to have held the *imperium* of all Britain south of Humber, and was certainly granted homage and tribute by his immediate Saxon neighbours, and even by remoter Anglian dynasts farther to the north.

(2) A State even smaller than Kent was founded upon the narrow

sea-coast between the chalk ridge of the South Downs and the woods of the Weald on the one side, and the water of the Channel on the other. This, the least important of all the Teutonic states of Britain, was inhabited by a people who claimed to be of Saxon descent, and to trace their origin from the war-band of a chief named Aella who had landed in this island a whole generation after Hengist and the Jutes.

Yet Aella, according to Bede, had been reckoned the first of all those princes who held the *imperium* of Britain; we must conclude, therefore, that he had been the chief commander of the whole Saxon swarm in the last quarter of the sixth century, and probably was the leader who had to face the rally of the Celts under Ambrosius Aurelianus. As was the case with Kent, the smallness of the personal war-band which followed the predominant chief of the moment did not prevent him from holding authority over confederates who brought larger forces to the field. But when Aella was dead his descendants became unimportant, because none of them was vigorous enough to assert a predominance over his contemporaries. To win such a position became, of course, a task increasingly difficult for the master of a very small war-band, as the other states of Britain crystallised into permanent units.

(3) To the north of the estuary of the Thames we find in the second half of the sixth century the kingdom of the East Saxons, occupying very much the same territory that had once been held by the British Trinovantes, but in addition Middlesex and probably the Eastern holders of Hertfordshire. Neither the royal lists in the *Historia Brittonum* nor Bede give us any tradition concerning the origin of this kingdom nor the name of its founder. But later genealogies, preserved in writers of a much less remote antiquity, show us that the Kings of Essex had compiled an ancestry for themselves going back to Woden through his son Seaxneat—a Saxon war-god.

★★★★★★

But the lists at the end of Florence of Worcester and Henry of Huntingdon undoubtedly represent genuine Saxon traditions, and date back four or five centuries before these chroniclers.

★★★★★★

It is notable that the first king of the East Saxons in Britain is made to be a certain Aescwin, who was the grandfather of Saebert, the undoubtedly historical personage who was reigning when St. Augustine landed in Britain in 597 *A.D.* Working on some rough computations of generations, the pedigree-makers placed the date of Aescwin's assumption of the kingship in 527. This puts the origin of the kingdom so late that we are tempted to conclude that it only formed itself out of certain sections of the general swarm of Saxon invaders, when the defeat of the Mons Badonicus had brought invasion to a stand, and forced the surviving warbands to divide up among themselves so much territory as they still retained. For the fertile and thickly-peopled lands along the coast, between the great Roman towns of Londinium and Camulodunum, must have been among the very first conquests of the Saxons in the middle of the fifth century.

Whether Middlesex, the land of the Middle Saxons, was ever a separate State we cannot tell; it certainly was under the power of the East Saxon king Saebert in 604, when London was chosen as the site of the bishopric founded to serve his dominions. Surrey, "the South region," must also have formed part of the first Saxon settlement in this direction—as has already been observed—though its later history was not connected with Essex but with Kent and the West Saxons. East Hertfordshire was a part of the Essex bishopric of London from the tenth century onward, and was probably included in it from the first; but it is not absolutely certain that the boundaries of the See of London may not have been varied in the confusion that followed the Danish invasions.

(4) Another realm which must have been created on the breakup of the great confederacy of Saxon invaders which followed the disaster of the Mons Badonicus was that of the West Saxons. The early history of this realm, as has been remarked in the last chapter, seems to have been wholly confused by the entries between the years 495 and 530 in the *Anglo-Saxon Chronicle*. These meagre and inexplicable paragraphs inform us—firstly, that two "ealdormen," Cerdic and his son Cynric, came to shore with five ships at the place called Cerdics-ora in 495, and there fought against the Welsh on that same day. Secondly, that in 501 Port, with his sons, Bieda and Maegla, arrived with two ships, at the place that is called Portsmouth, landed there and slew a young British prince of high nobility.

Next, in 508, Cerdic and Cynric fought and slew a king whose name was Natan-leod, and who had 5,000 men with him. Since then the district has been named Natan-lea as far as Cerdicsford. We are then surprised to find that:

In 514 the West Saxons came to Britain with three ships, at the place that is called Cerdicsora, and Stuf and Wihtgar fought

43

with the Britons and routed them.

In 519 Cerdic and Cynric:

> Obtained the kingdom of the West Saxons, and in the same
> year they fought with the Britons at the place called Cerdics-
> ford: and from that time the royal line of the West Saxons has
> reigned.

In 527 Cerdic and Cynric fight against the Britons at the place
called Cerdicslea. In 530 the same two kings conquered the Isle of
Wight, and slew many men at Wihtgarabyrig. Finally, in 534, Cerdic
died and his son Cynric became sole king: and they gave the whole
Isle of Wight to their two nephews, (*nefan*, however, is a vaguer word
than nephew), Stuf and Wihtgar. Finally, Wihtgar dies in 644 and is
buried at Wihtgarabyrig.

The first strange fact that we note in this narrative is that there is
apparently a duplication of the incidents. Cerdic and his son arrive
in 496 at Cerdicsora, but in 514 "the West Saxons" arrive at the same
Cerdicsora under Stuf and Wihtgar. In 509 Cerdic and Cynric slay
Natan-leod in the district near Cerdicsford: in 519 they fight again at
Cerdicsford and "obtain the kingdom". When we reflect that Cerdic
lands in 495 with a son who is full grown and able to act as his colleague, *i.e.*, at an age that cannot be less than forty, and probably is
more, and that he then proceeds to fight and conquer for a period of
thirty-five years (495-530) we cannot but be confirmed in our suspicion that there is something wrong with the chronology. The whole
of the incidents are confused and suspicious.

But this is not all: the Port who lands at Portsmouth betrays to the
first glance that he is an eponymous hero created from the name of
the Roman harbour, *Portus Magnus*. Similarly, Wihtgar is clearly the
eponymous hero of the people of the Isle of Wight, the Wihtgaras;
but the name of the isle has been Icht, or, in Latin, Vectis, for centuries
before the Saxon invasion began. The prince got his name from the
isle, not the isle from the prince.

******

Wihtgar certainly and Port possibly are real Saxon names. But
the coincidence of the two being made to come to the locali-
ties Portsmouth and Wight, whose Roman names were Portus
Magnus and Vectis, is wholly incredible. But see Stevenson in
Eng. Hist. Rev., xiv.

******

Finding ourselves in the company of mythical persons of this sort we begin to notice that Cerdic, too, is only mentioned in connection with places whose titles are compounded with his name, Cerdicsora and Cerdicsford and Cerdicslea. Can it be possible that he is a creation of the same species as Port and Wihtgar?

The next development of the puzzle is even more serious. Many modern philologists tell us that Cerdic (Ceretic, Certic) is not a Teutonic name at all, but Celtic.

✶✶✶✶✶✶

But see Stevenson's article, quoted above. The assertion that the Welsh name Ceretic (or Coroticus) could not lose its stressed second syllable, seems to be disproved by the fact that Cerdic of Elmet has lost it in the *Historia Brittonum* written by a Celt, as also by the modern form Cardigan for Cerétigiaun.

✶✶✶✶✶✶

We know of three or four British characters of the name. The first is a person in the *Historia Brittonum*, who is said to have been Vortigern's interpreter, "and no one save he among the Britons could understand the tongue of the Saxons". The next is one of the many descendants of the great Cunedda, from whom the district along the West coast of Wales got its name of Ceredigiaun—the modern Cardiganshire. A third is Cerdic, Prince of Elmet, in the early seventh century, who was conquered by the Northumbrian King Edwin. A fourth is that Coroticus, to whom St. Patrick wrote—for the name is the same, and in the genealogies this dynast appears as Ceretic Guletic. What right has a Saxon ealdorman descended from Woden to this purely Celtic name? It may be urged that one of the historic kings of Wessex bore a Welsh name, Ceadwalla, in the late seventh century.

But at that time the Saxons had been two centuries in Britain, had become Christians, and had begun to intermarry with the Welsh kingly families. Cerdic, the invader of 495, if he ever existed, must have been born about 450, in days when such intimacy with the Britons and the borrowing of a name from them seems almost incredible. A wild suggestion has been made that the founder of the Wessex dynasty may have been a Briton, no less a person than Vortigern's Saxon-speaking interpreter, the Cerdic of the *Historia Brittonum*. It is suggested that he may have known the tongue of the invaders because he consorted much with them, being perhaps a kinglet who made himself strong by hiring a Saxon bodyguard. If he sided with the Saxons in the long wars, he might have survived, and started a lineage and

45

a kingdom that was at once Celtic and Teutonic.

A parallel might be cited in that Domnal Kavanagh, the son of Dermot McMurrough of Leinster, who adhered consistently to the Norman invaders of Ireland in the twelfth century, and founded a great baronial family, which for all intents and purposes became Anglo-Norman and ceased to be Irish. But this is pure speculation. It is safer to regard the existence of any Cerdic as founder of the West Saxon realm with deep suspicion.

There remains the most fatal objection of all to the early history of the kingdom of Wessex, as related by the *Anglo-Saxon Chronicle*. The lands where Cerdic, Port, Stuf and Wihtgar are found as conquerors in this narrative are described by Bede, an authority far older and better than the *Chronicle*, as not Saxon at all but Jutish. We are distinctly told by him, as has been already pointed out, that the Isle of Wight and the lands opposite it on the mainland had been settled by Jutes, and that even in his own day the people on the mainland north of the Solent were called the Jute-folk (*Jutorum natio*). If this was so, we have no room for West Saxon conquerors, such as the alleged Cerdic and Cymric, in this direction.

Moreover, Bede's statement that Wight was originally independent of the West Saxons is borne out by the first definite mention that we get of it in genuine history. Wulfhere, King of Mercia, about the year 681, gave to Aethelwalch, King of Sussex, "two provinces, *viz*., Wight and the land of the Meonwaras, which last is in the realm of the West Saxons. (South-East Hampshire, where the name is still preserved in the hundreds of East and West Meon and Meonborough.)

Some years after Ceadwalla, King of Wessex, slew Aethelwalch and conquered Wight, which, we are told, was down to that time "entirely given over to heathenism," though the West Saxons had been converted to Christianity forty years before, in the time of King Cynegils and the Bishops Birinus and Agilbercht. Ceadwalla made a horrible massacre of the inhabitants of Wight, and settled the island again with men of his own nation. Moreover, he took pains to exterminate its royal house, by hunting out and executing the brothers of Arwald, king of the island, who had hidden themselves in the "*provincia Jutorum*," *i.e.*, the Hampshire coastland, opposite to Wight.

All this narrative seems to prove that the island was originally unconnected with the West Saxons, and had a people of a different race from them, as well as a royal house of its own. Nor need we doubt that the case was originally the same with the Jutes of the Hampshire coast, though Bede is ready to regard these "Meonwaras" and other Jute-folk as forming a part of Wessex in 680. Probably they, unlike the people of Wight, had been annexed by some earlier king of that realm.

But if Cerdic is a doubtful figure, and if the coastland of Eastern Wessex was Jutish soil in the sixth century, whence came the origin of the West Saxon state? We are almost compelled to conclude that the original nucleus was formed from those parts of the earliest Saxon swarm which did not coalesce into the other kingdoms of Sussex and Essex, from war-bands seated west of Middlesex, in Berkshire and North Hampshire, and perhaps holding also some small settlement north of Thames. We shall see reason to believe that Ceawlin, the first historical king of the West Saxons, started from this centre, since his first recorded actions were the driving off of the men of Kent from Surrey, and the conquest of the regions about Buckingham, Bedford and Oxford.

When the first "bishop-stool" was created in West Saxon territory, after the conversion of King Cynegils, it was placed at Dorchester-on-Thames, in Oxfordshire, and in nearly every other case in Britain we find that the first bishop was established close to the court of the king. (This is not a necessary deduction. But certainly, the king mast have had much royal demesne about Dorchester.) The deduction would seem to be that the royal dynasty of Wessex may have had its favourite residence on the Thames rather than in the South. Winchester may have taken the place of Dorchester only when South Hampshire and the Wight had become West Saxon soil.

It may be noted that the name West Saxons suits a people seated on the Middle Thames quite as well as a people seated in Hampshire, according to the accepted tradition. It gives also a far better meaning to Middlesex, which on this hypothesis is actually between the East and the West Saxons, while most maps show it lying between the East Saxons and Anglian tribes seated in the South Midlands. (For the arguments for and against this hypothesis see Sir Henry Howorth in *Eng. Hist. Rev.*, xiii., answered by Mr. Stevenson in the same periodical, xiv., and a summary in Chadwick's *Origin of the British Nation*.)

Ceawlin, as has been already said, is the first King of the West Saxons of whose existence we can be sure. Bede mentions him as next after Aella among those monarchs who held an "*imperium*" over all Britain south of Humber. The Wessex genealogy which makes him son of Cynric and grandson of Cerdic may have been compiled at a very much later date. The *Anglo-Saxon Chronicle* fixes his accession at

560; whether this be correct or no, he was certainly the leader who renewed the attack on the Britons which had ceased since the disaster at the Mons Badonicus in 516. Gildas wilting apparently in 545, says that his countrymen had lost no more territory to the Saxons since that fight, which was about thirty years back when he wrote the *Liber Querulus*. Apparently if he had written a generation later, he would have had to unsay his boast. Ceawlin's victory at Deorham—only ten miles from Bath (577)—undid the work of the earlier battle, and marks the commencement of the second great advance of the Saxons. Of this more *anon*.

The West Saxons had a tribal name besides the more ordinarily used appellation drawn from their geographical position. This was Gewissae; it does not seem however to have been an early designation brought by them from Germany, but merely means the "allies" or "confederates," a sufficiently good name for a body of war-bands, leagued together originally for some temporary need. We might even suspect that it implies a mixed origin in the composition of the host, which may have included other elements besides the purely Saxon. An ancestor called Gewis was inserted in the pedigree of the Wessex kings to act as the eponymous hero of the tribe. (Mullenhof, *Beowulf.*)

(5) North of the settlements of the East Saxons and the West Saxons we find the Angles established, all along the east coast of Britain, before the year 550. The southernmost of their kingdoms was that of East Anglia, a State composed of two sections, the North-folk and the South-folk. There are indications that this division may have implied the existence of two original petty kingdoms; but they seem normally to have acted as a single unit, and to have obeyed a single king, in later times, and the royal house of the Wuffings ruled over both.

The state must have come into existence among the earliest of the Teutonic kingdoms of Britain, but we know nothing about its early history. Wuffa was the grandfather of Raedwald, who was reigning in East Anglia about 600-618, so that his date cannot be put earlier than 550-70. The genealogies at the end of the *Historia Brittonum* state that Guecha (Wehha) father of Wuffa was the founder of the kingdom:—if his existence may be accepted, the East Anglian settlement must have coalesced into a State somewhere about 520: this is one of the many indications which tend to make us fix the epoch immediately after the Battle of the Mons Badonicus as that of the crystallising into permanent units of the Anglian and Saxon war-bands.

The territory of the East Angles was compact, and well-marked by natural boundaries;—like that of their predecessors in the land, the British Iceni. It extended westward only to the edge of the great marshland which then, and for many centuries after, surrounded all the lower course of the Ouse from Huntingdon northward to the sea. The Isle of Ely, in the midst of this fen, was reckoned part of East Anglia. (Bede.) Cambridge on the other hand seems to have been considered outside the borders, and to have belonged to another Anglian tribe. Southwards the boundary was formed by the East Saxons, whose march lay along the estuary of the Stour.

The only East Anglian king who ever attained to importance during the early history of the state was Raedwald, who according to Bede held the *imperium* over South Britain for a few years in the first quarter of the seventh century, having superseded Aethelbert of Kent in the position of dominance, though the latter survived his loss of power for some years.

(6) North and west of the East Angles lay three or more kingdoms inhabited by men of the same race—those of the Lindiswaras, the Middle Angles, and the Mercians. The settlement of the former, in the lands between the Wash and the Humber, around the old Roman city of Lindum—which gave the district its modern name of Lindsey— must have belonged to a date as early as that of East Anglia or Essex. But the same may not necessarily have been the case with the inland kingdoms of the Mercians and Middle Angles.

Indeed, the question as to how far the first devastating rush of the invaders carried them in this direction, during the second half of the fifth century, is the hardest point to settle in early English history. The East Midlands, the Valleys of Trent, Ouse, and Nen, had been one of the less important and less populous districts of Roman Britain: there was apparently no important town west of Verulamium or Lindum, or east of Corinium, Viroconium and Deva. The resisting power of the Britons must have been very weak in all this region; on the other hand, it might be argued that the thickly wooded and often marshy plain may not have been so attractive to the intrusive Angle as certain other lands.

If we could only trust the early entries of the *Anglo-Saxon Chronicle*, we should be obliged to conclude that the Midlands fell at a very late date into the hands of the invaders, for Cuthwulf, the West Saxon, is described as fighting with Britons at Bedford in 571, and capturing immediately after "Lygeanbyrig and Aeglesbyrig, Benesingtun and Egonesham," which are undoubtedly four places in Oxfordshire and Buckinghamshire, *viz.*, Lenbury and Aylesbury, Bensington and Eynsham. I must confess that this entry seems to me wholly untrustworthy. That the Britons could have been holding as late as 571 places like Bedford and Aylesbury, which are distant only thirty-five or forty-five miles from London, which were not old walled towns of the Roman time, and which are protected by no natural defences of any kind, seems contrary to all probability.

But this is not all: we are not merely dealing with probabilities; Gildas, writing about 545 *A.D.*, over twenty years before the alleged conquests of Ceawlin in this direction, gives us a picture of a Celtic Britain which does not extend anywhere towards the east coast, and indeed would seem to stop short at the eastern watershed of the Severn Valley. We are forced to conclude that the existence of British principalities in the South-East Midlands about the year 571 is simply incredible. Yet Ceawlin is undoubtedly a historical personage. Bede vouches for him—as a great conqueror, and the practical founder of the West Saxon kingdom. One way out of the difficulty alone remains, Ceawlin may have fought at Bedford, and have subdued Aylesbury and Eynsham, but the idea that his enemies were *Britons* may have been a misconception of the Wessex annalist who compiled the *Chronicle* in the ninth century.

So many entries begin with "This year King X fought with Britons at Y," that for once the words "with Britons" may have slipped in unadvisedly. The preceding entry in the *Chronicle* introduces Ceawlin contending, not with Britons, but with Teutonic neighbours, as beating King Aethelbert at Wibbandun and driving him back into Kent in 568. Granting that this means that he was endeavouring to establish a hegemony over all the Teutonic principalities, what is more likely than that his next move would be to turn northward against smaller Saxon or Anglian communities, seated beyond Thames, on the Thame and the Ouse and the Evenlode? They are added to the West Saxon league of "Gewissae"—confederates Perhaps they even give the conquering nucleus that new name.

It is when they have been attached to Ceawlin's original war-band that the king becomes strong enough to require homage from East Angles or East Saxons, and to acquire, in Bede's phrase, the "*imperium*" of South Britain. Only when this is his own does he start campaigning against the Britons in 577, and put an end to the comparative peace from external invasion which they had been enjoying for more than half a century.

It may therefore be permitted to us to attribute the overrunning and settlement of the whole of the Midlands, north and south, to a date nearly a century earlier than the conquests of Ceawlin. And Bensington and Eynsham, Bedford and Aylesbury, may be taken as the central villages of small Saxon or Anglian communities, rather than as Welsh strongholds. Their names certainly suggest that this must have been the case: not one of them was an old Roman town, such as might have been the capital of a British king. Indeed, Bensington is but three miles from an old city—Dorchester-on-Thames—whose name shows its Roman origin, and whose walls would certainly have been the residence of a British prince if such a person had existed in Oxfordshire about 571.

A Teutonic settler, surely, would have been the only person who would have deserted this site for the adjacent Bensington, whose name shows its origin. The name of the whole group of settlers was "Chilternsaetas," men of Chiltern, in the seventh century. (This tribal name, though not found in Bede, occurs in the celebrated "Tribal Hidage," which is undoubtedly a seventh century document.)

We may suspect Saxons just north of Thames, but farther away, in Bedford, Cambridge and Northamptonshire, as well as in all the land that lies beyond them, the first colonists were Angles. In Bede's time the whole of the region from the borders of Essex as far as Leicester was known as the land of the Middle Angles, while the lands in the basin of the Trent, from the boundary of Lindsey as far as the Welsh frontier, were called Mercia, the "march land". The former would include the modern shires of Cambridge (minus the Isle of Ely), Huntingdon, Bedford, Northampton, Leicester: the latter was composed of Nottinghamshire, Derbyshire, Staffordshire, part of Warwickshire, and the eastern strip of Shropshire.

The Middle Angles apparently consisted of a group of sub-tribes, of whose names that of the Gyrwas (Gyrvii), on the borders of the Fenland (Cambridgeshire, North Northamptonshire, South Lincolnshire) is the only one that survives in written history. But it is pretty certain that a number of other small units, whose names recorded in the curious early document called the "Tribal Hidage" (see Mr. Corbet's article in *Proceedings of the Royal Historical Society* for 1900), also belonged to the Middle Angles—such as the Arrosaetna, on the Warwickshire River Arrow, the Faerpings and the Spaldings.

Bede calls the land of the Middle Angles a kingdom, but we have no trace of its having a king, or indeed of its having formed a homogeneous unit of any sort, till Penda of Mercia made his son Peada ruler of the whole district about the year 653. It is quite probable that down to that date it was but a loose confederation of neighbouring tribes, each with a local prince. (The Gyrvii had certainly such a ruler in the seventh century, see Bede, *E. H., iv.*)

The Mercians, on the other hand, seem to have coalesced into a monarchy at a comparatively early date, and we have for them a royal genealogy of the usual sort, going back to Woden and his son Wihtlaeg. The progenitor whose name was preserved in the patronymic of the house was a certain Icel, from whom they were called Icelings. Icel was said to be the fifth in ascent from Penda, the first king of Mercia concerning whom we know anything tangible.

As this prince reigned from 626 to 655, the founder of the family ought, if there is anything of truth in the pedigree, to have been living somewhere about the year 500 or a little earlier. The date is sufficiently probable, but we have no external evidence to support it, save that it is possible that a Crida whose death is recorded in the *Anglo-Saxon Chronicle* under the year 593 may be the Mercian King Creoda, who was great-grandson of Icel and grandfather of Penda.

But the *Chronicle* is of no great authority in the sixth century, and moreover its Crida may not be the Mercian Creoda. (There is a mysterious Creoda in the West Saxon royal pedigree in certain versions. See Plummer's A. S. C., ii. But his date would not suit.) The Mercians are described by Bede as being divided into two subtribes—the North and South Mercians—by the river Trent; but there is little reason to think that there were ever two distinct kingdoms among them. (The only reason for thinking of such a possibility is the mention by Bede of a Cearl king of the Mercians who does not appear in the royal genealogy.) On the other hand, the Pecsaetan—or dwellers in the land of the Peak—in North Derbyshire, seem to be treated in the "Tribal Hidage" as a separate unit from the Mercians proper, though their region is always counted a part of Mercia in historic times.

It may only have been annexed by King Penda at the same date that he conquered the various sections of the Middle Angles on the other—the southern—side of his realm. The Pecsaetan are, however, the only tribe whom we seem to find owning a separate identity in the North-Western Midlands, and the Mercians under the house of the Icelings were probably from the first one of the more considerable

Anglian States. Their realm must have included all the lands bounded by the Mountain of the Peak district on the North, and the Forest of Arden on the South, and extending to the Severn Westward. But Chester itself (Deva) was still in the hands of the Britons, and was first taken from them in 616 not by the Mercians but by an invader from another quarter, the Northumbrian king, Aethelfrith.

It may be convenient to state at this point, before passing on to consider the settlements of the Angles north of Humber, what we know of the Celtic kingdoms of Southern and Western Britain, at the time (550-70) at which we have arrived while dealing with their Teutonic enemies. Here we have to help us the works of Gildas, an absolutely contemporary writer, since he composed his *Liber Querulus* while Maglocunus (Mailcun) was the most prominent British king, and that prince died in 547 of the "yellow plague," the famous pest which, starting in Persia in 542, devastated the empire of Justinian in 543-44, and then spread slowly westward all over Europe.

In 545, when Gildas seems to have composed his book, the British kingdoms are described by him as being still practically unmolested by the Saxon or Angle, as had been the case ever since the battle of the Mons Badonicus. But they are not therefore prosperous; city life had almost ceased:

> The towns of my fatherland are not inhabited as of old, but to this very moment they lie deserted and ruinous, though foreign wars (if not civil war's) have ceased.

The kings are entirely given over to family feuds and inter-tribal strife. Since the generation which helped Ambrosius Aurelianus to check the Saxon died out, all ideas of public duty have been forgotten both by the lay and the ecclesiastical rulers of Britain. The bishops and clergy are given up to simony and self-seeking; the kings, when not occupied in murdering their relatives, or robbing their neighbours, are prone to commit every crime in the calendar, from marriage with a deceased wife's sister to harbouring highway robbers, and giving flagrantly unjust decisions in their courts of law.

> Britain has kings, but they are tyrants; she has judges, but they are godless: they strike down and prey upon the innocent alone. They give shelter and patronage—but only to robbers and criminals. They have many wives—but all of them adulteresses or prostitutes. They often take oaths, but always break them. They make vows but almost immediately perjure themselves.

53

They wage wars, but only unjust wars on their own country-men. They may hunt down thieves in the countryside, but they have thieves at their own tables, whom they love and load with gifts. They distribute great alms, but heap up a greater mass of crimes in their realms. They sit in the seat of judgment, but rarely seek for the rule of right decision.

The quotation might be continued to a weary length. The important thing in Gildas, however, is to note the names and dominions of the five kings on whom he descants in detail, when he has finished his long general preface.

The first is Constantine of Damnonia, who has divorced his legitimate wife, and has planted a "slip of the vine of Sodom" in his heart. He has also lately murdered two young boys, his near relatives, in a church, before the very altar, though a certain abbot cast his cloak around them to give them protection. The second is Aurelius Caninus, (or Conanus, apparently the well-known Celtic name Conan, famous in Brittany), apparently the descendant and successor of Ambrosius Aurelianus, whose heirs (as Gildas has previously observed) still lead out the Britons to war, though they have sadly degenerated from the virtues of their ancestor.

This young prince has "rolled as deeply in the mud of parricide and adultery as Constantine, or even deeper." His territories are not named, but must certainly be that portion of South-West Britain which was not embraced in Damnonia—the as yet unconquered regions between the Severn mouth and the Dorsetshire coast, where the West Saxons had not penetrated in 545. Perhaps Bath, Gloucester and Cirencester, which yet existed in some diminished shape as inhabited towns, were his strongholds. They are mentioned thirty years later in the *Anglo-Saxon Chronicle* as British "chesters". The third king censured is Vortiporius, ruler of Demetia (South Wales), "a man spotted like the leopard with crimes and evil living," the worthless son of a good father, whose hair has grown grey in a long reign of craft and cruelty.

The fourth is Cuneglassus, who is described in the curious terms, already referred to in a previous chapter, as having been in his youth "the driver of the chariot of the den of the Bear." He has lately driven away his wife in order to wed her sister, who had taken vows as a nun, thus doubly violating the precepts of the Apostle. His dominions are not specified, but he is certainly the Cinglas, son of Eugenius and descendant in the fourth generation from Cunedda, who occurs in the oldest Welsh genealogies. (See Zimmer, *Nennius Vindicatus*.) His realm must be sought for on the borders of Mercia, in the northern parts of the basin of the Severn, in what was later called the region of Powys.

Lastly, we have the greatest king of all, Maglocunus (Mailcun), "the dragon of the island," as he is called by Gildas, because he ruled his North-Welsh kingdom from a royal residence in Anglesey. This prince was evidently the dominating personage in Britain when Gildas wrote; as many paragraphs are devoted to him as to all the other wicked kings taken together. He has deprived many other tyrants of their lives as well as of their realms. He started by dispossessing his own uncle, and after him made havoc of many more. But when incontestably the greatest lord of Britain, he was suddenly struck with penitence, devoted himself to religious studies, abdicated his throne, and became a monk, after what Gildas owns to have been a real spasm of remorse and consciousness of sin.

> Oh, what an abundant flame of heavenly hope would have been kindled in the hearts of desperate sinners, if thou hadst but remained in that blessed estate.

But a short experience of monastic life had disgusted Maelgwyn: he "returned like the dog to his vomit," resumed his crown, called back his follower and started on a second career of conquest, accompanied with much evil living. He is particularly reproached with having murdered his nephew and taken his widow to wife, after clearing a way for her by slaying the spouse whom he had married before his monastic episode. It breaks the heart of the preacher to see the renegade monk once more the greatest and the most boisterous of kings:

> First in mischief, strongest in malice as well as in power, more liberal than others in giving, more licentious in sinning, strong in arms but stronger in working his own soul's destruction.

He is threatened with all the torments of the damned, in language of a violence which would surely have secured Gildas's instant execution if he had shown himself within the realm of North Wales. Indeed, the virulence of his denunciation in dealing with all the five kings whom he takes to task is so extraordinary, that we might well believe that the *Liber Querulus* was written, as tradition relates, outside this island, while the author was residing in the monastery in Brittany of which he was the founder.

That Britain had not yet lost all traces of her Roman civilisation is shown by the fact that Gildas quotes Virgil and Philo, and seems to show a knowledge of Claudian and Juvenal, as well as of Jerome, Orosius and other Christian writers with whom we are not so surprised to find him acquainted. His style is obscure and euphuistic, after the manner of Cassiodorus and other sixth-century writers—indeed it is often quite hard to make out what actual meaning his bombastic phrases are intended to convey.

But he has no historical perspective, and all that he narrates of events beyond his own memory needs careful study before it can be accepted. Yet for the affairs of 545 his book, so far as it goes, is of absolutely primary and incontestable authority. He is the only source from which we know of the cessation of the Teutonic invasion between 516 and 570, after the Badonic battle, and from him alone can we judge with some degree of certainty what was the boundary between Briton and Saxon about the year 545, and what was the internal state of the British kingdoms.

One of the most extraordinary gaps in the narrative of Gildas is his omission to say what was going on to the north and south of the limited area on which he sheds a fitful light. One of the great phenomena of the fifth century had been a wholesale emigration of Britons to Gaul. Gildas gives no hint of this save in the single sentence in which he says that:

Some sought regions beyond the sea, groaning under the sails, by way of Rowel's' song, 'Thou has given us as sheep to the slaughter, O God, and scattered us among the Gentiles'

But the Britons appear in Gaul by no means in the character of scattered sheep, but rather as warlike bands seeking settlement by force of arms. If the *Historia Brittonum* can be trusted, the first emigrants were the British auxiliaries of the usurper Magnus Maximus:

Who gave them many lands from the pool that is on the crest of Mons Jovis (the great St. Bernard) as far as the city which is called Cantguic (Quentovic, south of Boulogne), and they are now at the Western Promontory, that is Crucoccident (Cape Finisterre, in Brittany), For the Britons of Armorica, who lie beyond the sea, who went forth on the expedition of Maximus the tyrant, since they could not come home, devastated all Western Gaul, slew off all the males, and took their widows and daughters as consorts.

This is, of course, like all the early narrative of the *Historia Brittonum*, very doubtful stuff. There is no reason why the first British settlement in Armorica should not have begun as early as 383, with the arrival of the troops of Magnus Maximus in that region. But at the same, time we have no trace in contemporary continental sources of such immigrants. On the other hand, we have clear proof from the Roman writers of the late fifth century that, from about 460 onwards, Britons were numerous north of the Loire. The first tangible mention of them seems to be that a certain Mansuetus, "bishop of the Britons," attended a council at Tours in 461. There is no indication that he was a Briton of the island, and as, immediately after, we find great masses of his countrymen on the spot, it seems safe to conclude that he was their representative.

In 469 we find in the letters of Sidonius Apollinaris, (*Epistolae*), the statement that one Arvandus had been accused of treason before the Emperor Anthemius, for having incited the Visigoths to attack "the Britons situated beyond the Loire". In the same year we find that Anthemius solicited aid from these Britons, and that their King Riothimus came to join the imperial army with a force of 12,000 men. (Jordanes, §45.) This number, even if exaggerated, shows that there was a large colony already established in Armorica, Riothimus reached Bourges, and was apparently at that city for some time, as Sidonius wrote several letters to him, complaining of the conduct of his soldiers, who had been tempting away the slaves of the neighbouring Gallic proprietors. (*Epistolae*). But the Visigoths finally came up against Riothimus and defeated him at Deols in the department of the Indre, so that he was forced to fly.

★★★★★★

Jordanes, 45; Gregory of Tours, ii. 18. From Jordanes' mention of ships and disembarkation with regard to Riothimus, some modern authors would make him an insular Briton. But see La Borderie, *Histoire de Bretagne*, i.

★★★★★★

He thereupon disappears from history, but his countrymen remained seated in Armorica, as is shown by plenty of later notices.

It seems probable that, whether the soldiers of Magnus Maximus made the first settlement in Armorica or not, the development of a British colony in that peninsula was mainly caused by the great Saxon assaults in Britain about the middle of the fifth century. That the exiles came largely from the South-British lands affected by the ravages of Hengist and Aella seems probable. But there also must have been many West-Britons among them to account for the transference of names like Domnonie (Damnonia) and Cornouailles, from the island to the continent; and that this was the predominating strain among the immigrants is made clear by the fact that the Britons of Armorica spoke Celtic and not Latin. If they had mainly come from the south-eastern regions, they would have spoken Latin and not Celtic.

It is always unsafe to lean too heavily on dates or facts drawn from the lives of saints, written long centuries after their death. But it is worthwhile noticing that the period assigned by legend to the coming of the British monastic missionaries to Armorica is the fifth century, and its later half, just as we should have expected from the more trustworthy facts to be gleaned from contemporary secular writers.

St. Samson, who founded the bishopric of Dol, is said to have landed somewhere about 448. St. Machutus (St. Malo) seems datable to somewhere about the year 450. St. Brieuc falls a little later, apparently about 485. St. Paternus, the patron of Vannes, was consecrated between 461 and 470. (See La Borderie, for all this dating.) We may recognise in these holy exiles the fugitives of Gildas, who crossed the ocean to the continent ingeminating psalms. It is a pity that he has told us nothing of their warlike countrymen who, like Riothimus, emigrated with their swords in their hands, and plunged fiercely into the wars of the dying empire in Western Gaul.

But strange as it may be that Gildas says so little about the lands beyond the Channel, it is far more strange that he gives no information as to the condition of affairs in North Britain, in the parts beyond the realm of Mailcun. A struggle was going on between Briton and Angle north of the Humber, while in the south and the Midlands the invasion had come for a time to a standstill. For this northern conflict we are driven to use the *Historia Brittonum*, which begins, about the year 550, to give us information which can be accepted with gratitude, and differs entirely from its wild tales of Vortigern and St. Germanus and other fifth-century worthier With the aid of the *Historia*, supplemented with caution by names from the earliest Welsh genealogies, and with still greater diffidence by entries in the much later *Annales Cambriae*, some sort of a sketch of Northern Britain in the sixth century may be made out.

Our last knowledge of these regions was obtained from St. Patrick's letter to Coroticus. When we once more get a glimpse of the lands between Humber and Forth we find several British states in existence, and still more kings, the lands owned by a dynastic group being apparently shared or held in common by three or four of its members. The main principality, comprising Clydesdale as its central nucleus, but with its capital at Alclyde, north of the Firth, on the rock of Dumbarton, seems to have been in the hands of the descendants of Coroticus, or Ceretic Guletic, aa the genealogies call him.

South of it was another state called Reged, (not to be confounded with the South Wales Reged in Glamorganshire), which seems to represent the modern Cumberland with so much of Northumberland as had not yet been conquered by the Angles. Possibly (see Cadwallader Bates, *History of Northumberland*), the name Redesdale preserves a memory of this forgotten realm. It is probable that the Picts of Galloway—the Niduarii—were subject to their British neighbours but still had sub-kings of their own. The kingdom which centred at Alclyde seems to have included neither the west coast of the Lowlands nor the shores of the Firth of Forth. Kyle, Garrick and Cunningham, the three districts of the former region, may represent ancient principalities—Coel, Carawg and Canawon—which appear vaguely in the earliest Welsh poetry.

On the east the Angles seem to have had an uneasy lodgement upon the shore of Lothian, but the western section of that region, the plain of Manau, was still in the hands of the Picts, who had moved southward into it in the fifth century, and held the lands between the Carron and the Avon. South of Reged there were other British states; we only know the name of Elmet, which comprised all, or great part, of the West Riding of Yorkshire. There must have been at least one more principality west of Elmet, along the Irish Sea, but its very name is forgotten. South Lancashire, on the other hand, seems to have gone along with Chester and the lands by the Dee, which together formed a region named Theyernllwg, and were more closely connected with North Wales than with the kingdoms farther up the Irish Sea.

While Alclyde, and probably a presidency over the other North British States, seems to have been in the hands of the house of Coroticus, there was another many-branched family in possession of much territory. This was the line of Coel the Old, who (if the Harleian genealogies count for anything) lived four generations before 550, *i.e.*, somewhere about the year 430. They held Reged and many other lands. In the war with the Angles that filled the third quarter of the sixth century, we find three "kings" of this house, representing three separate lines, Urbgen (or Urien), Gwallawg, and Morgant, joining with Rhyderch of Strathclyde in resisting the advance of the Angles.

59

But these houses were as prone to civil war as their kinsmen farther south, whom Gildas abused so strenuously.

By the time that the sixth century had passed its middle year the Angles had long been established on the coast line from Lothian to Spurn Head, all along the shore of the two regions which were to be called Bernicia and Deira—names of uncertain derivation, the latter probably adapted from the Celtic Deifyr, the former perhaps originating with the dim ancestor Bearnoch who appears in Northumbrian genealogies. The first landings on the Yorkshire and Northumbrian coast must have started in the very beginning of the Saxon invasion—we may believe, if we like, that there may be something in the tale in the *Historia Brittonum*, that Hengist's kinsmen Ochta and Ebissa were granted land near the border of the Picts, at the same time that the Jutish chief himself was established by Vortigern in Kent. Nothing is more probable, though nothing is more impossible to prove.

Long before, it will be remembered, Saxon allied with Pict had already been trampling down the northern parts of Britain, in the days of the "Hallelujah Victory." We may take it for granted that all the Romano-British towns in the North-east—York, Corbridge, Aldborough and their smaller sisters—perished long before the year 500 was reached—very probably even before the year 430. (Though many of them, like Corbridge, emerged as royal "vills" in the Northumbrian period.)

The genealogies appended at the end of the *Historia Brittonum*, which are shown by internal evidence to have been compiled not long after 685, give us lists of the two Anglian royal houses of Bernicia and Deira, which go back, as usual, to Woden. But in each case the prince who is credited with establishing a kingdom comes long after the first ancestor who is brought to the shores of Britain. The Bernician kingship starts with Ida, whose date is fixed by Bede at 547, a year which works in well with the data in the *Historia*, The Deiran kingship begins a few years later, in 560, with Aella. But in the Deiran genealogy in the *Historia* it is Aella's predecessor in the fifth generation, one Soemil, of whom it is said that "*iste primus separavit Deur a Birneich*".

Taking the usual calculation of thirty years for a life, Soemil must have lived somewhere not long after 410, *i.e.*, in the very first days of the Teutonic ravages in Britain, and his "separating of Deira from Bernicia" must mean the carving out a principality for himself from the loosely compacted Anglian settlement. There is no reason to doubt the real existence of the persons intervening between Soemil and Aella, for two of their names Uxfrea and Iffi are found among later members of the royal house of Deira, the son and grandson of the good King Edwin. (Bede.) Edwin would very naturally bestow the names of his own grandfather and great-grandfather on his descendants. Similarly, in the more northern Anglian settlement where Ida is reckoned the first "king," we must believe that at least his father Eoppa and his grandfather Ossa, and probably remoter ancestors also, were settled in Britain. Ossa Cyllelawr, "Ossa with the knife," appears in the earliest Welsh traditions—whatever their worth may be—as the opponent of British kings in the North, even of Arthur himself.

Be this as it may, there must have been a full century between the first establishment of Anglian settlements on the coast between Forth and Humber and the establishment of the "kingdoms" of Bernicia and Deira. We must suppose that (like the Middle Angles) these original settlers were planted in small communities, ruled by ealdormen who did not attain to the royal title. Indeed William of Malmesbury, late though his date and weak his authority, was practically right when he wrote that the Northumbrians for nearly 100 years were content with "*duces*," who took no kingly title and ruled each in his own corner,— though we may doubt his additional statement that they paid a general homage to the king of Kent.

Ida, according to the *Historia Brittonum*, reigned for twelve years (547-59) and fought long and fiercely with the Britons, whose chief leader at the moment was a king called Dutigern. We are told that Ida joined to his kingdom of Bernicia the great stronghold of Dinguardi, *i.e.*, the rocky promontory crowned by a fortress, which later generations were to know as Bamborough. But as yet it bore only its Celtic name, for Queen Bebba, from whom its new English denomination of Bebbanburh was to come, was the wife of Ida's grandson Aethelfrith. Ida had twelve sons, of whom no less than five succeeded him on the throne. (See the Bernician genealogy in *Historia Brittonum*. But I am unable to follow the order of reigns of the five sons there set forth.)

The list of these short-lived kings, Adda, Frithwulf or Frithwald, Hussa, Theodric and Aethelric is given in different order by the *Historia Brittonum*, the *Chronicle* appended to Bede's history, and the later authorities—a fact which may point to a division of the kingdom between them.

★★★★★★

According to the genealogy annexed to the More MS. of Bede we must add another son, Clappa, who reigned a single year immediately after his father Ida. But he does not appear in the

61

Historia Brittonum or its appended genealogy, though Florence of Worcester and other late authorities give him. The order of succession presents immense difficulties. Our earliest source, the *H. B.,* first gives the order—Adda, Aethelric, Theodric, Frithwald (or Frithwulf), Hussa. But it then goes on to say that Urien fought Hussa, and also fought Theodric and was murdered after he had shut up his enemy in Farne. So according to this version of the tale Theodric is apparently the later of the two; but Aethelric was certainly the last of all, since it was he who annexed Deira after the death of Aella in 588, and passed on the crown to his son Aethelfrith.

★★★★★★

More than one of them, it would seem, fell in battle with the Britons, as might have been guessed from the shortness of their reigns, of which the whole only make up thirty-three years (559-93).

Against the sons of Ida, the British princes fought long and courageously. This seems to have been a time notable for vigour in the Britons of the North. The *Historia Brittonum* tells us that it was then that the great bards flourished, Talhaern and Aneurin, Taliessin and Bluchbard (Lluwarch). Poems attributed to several of them are still extant, and celebrate the exploits of the very princes whom the Historia gives as their contemporaries, Urbgen (Urien Reged) and his son Owen, Rhyderch and Gwallawg. If only we could be sure that the poems had not suffered fatally in transmission, or had not been entirely rewritten at a later age, we should have much lyrical detail for the story of early Northumbria.

Urien Reged was the most notable of the British champions. According to the *Historia Brittonum* he fought against Hussa and Theodric with frequent success. He shut up the latter prince for three days and three nights in the Isle of Metcaud (Lindisfairne), having literally driven the Angles into the sea. But while he was on this expedition, he was murdered by contrivance of King Morgant, his kinsman, from envy, "because he excelled all other British chiefs in warlike capacity". Later tradition had much to tell concerning the assassination of Urien, by the traitor Llovan Llawdivro, the tool of Morgant, on the sands of Aberllew.

★★★★★★

The poem xii. in the Red Book of Hergest, whatever its date, is full of details of Urien's murder. Aberllew is apparently on the Low, the stream that enters the sea opposite the Isle of Lindisfarne.

★★★★★★

Owen, son of Urien, took his father's place, as leader against the Angles, but with less success. He was slain by Theodric "the burner" (Flamddwyn) as the Britons called him. After this the defence seems to have slackened, and the Celts retired to the interior, leaving the kingdom of Bernicia a stronger state than it had ever been before.

Aethelric, the last survivor of the sons of Ida, not only ruled Bernicia but got possession of Deira also on the death of Aella, whose daughter Acha he married to his son Aethelfrith. Aella had no male heir save his infant son Edwin, who was carried off into safety and exile by faithful adherents, and was harboured first by Cadvan, King of North Wales, if Welsh tradition may be trusted, and afterwards, as it would seem, by English neighbours south of Humber. Aethelric reigned for five years over Bernicia and Deira united, and left the double crown of Northumbria to his son Aethelfrith (593-617).

With this prince we may be said to emerge from the twilight of history, in which we have hitherto been wandering. For the future we have Bede to guide us, instead of the meagre and confused notices of the *Historia Brittonum*. Aethelfrith was already reigning at the moment when Augustine's mission to Kent began, and his story is intimately associated with that of Edwin, the first Christian hero of Northumbria, of whom the *Ecclesiastical History* has so much to say. Of him more must be told in a later chapter.

CHAPTER 3
Conquests of Ceawlin and Aethelfrith (577-617 *A.D.*)

Some twenty years before the union of Bernicia and Deira under Ethelfrith had enabled the Angles of the North to commence a new series of conquests, the Saxons in the South had at last found the leader who was to enable them to resume the westward march which had been stayed two generations back, at the Mons Badonicus. This leader was Ceawlin, the third king, according to Bede, who asserted an *imperium* over the whole of the petty States that had been established by the first invaders.

His domination was evidently created by force of arms the first fact recorded of him is that in conjunction with his brother, Cutha (or Cuthwulf, to use the longer form), he fought in 568, with Aethelbert, King of Kent, a young prince who had come to the throne three years before, defeated him at Wibbandun, and drove him back into his own realm. (Cutha is only a shortened "hypocoristic" form of Cuthwulf. Later chroniclers, not knowing this, made them distinct persons.)

The battle-place is apparently the suburban Wimbledon in Surrey; the victory must have put that region for the moment into the hands of the West Saxons. It is probable that it may also have forced the men of Kent, and perhaps those of Sussex too, to become subject-allies of Ceawlin. The next exploit of the West Saxons was an invasion of the regions north of Thames in 571; Cuthwulf, the king's brother, fought a battle at Bedford, and immediately afterwards conquered the four towns of Aylesbury, Lenborough, Bensington and Eynsham. We have already seen in the last chapter, that these successes must almost certainly have been won over Teutonic and not over British neighbours, despite of the mention of the latter as enemies in the *Anglo-Saxon Chronicle*.

The result of the campaign was to make the "Chilternsaetas," the people of the Chilterns, subjects of the West Saxon state. They remained united to it for more than a century; probably they were by race Saxons, not Angles; so that the union would be easy and natural. We may suppose that Essex and East Anglia yielded, not long after, the homage which gave Ceawlin the *"imperium"* of which Bede speaks. At any rate, he was able six years later to begin a great invasion of Western Britain. Presumably it was at the head of a confederate host, not of his own tribesmen only; a large force must have been required to undertake an enterprise which no Saxon king had essayed for sixty years.

Ceawlin struck at the point where the belt of British states lying across Western Britain was narrowest, between the Upper Thames and the Bristol Channel. Advancing, as we may presume, by the old Roman road from Silchester to Bath, he met the united forces of three British kings at Deorham (Dyrham) a few miles to the north of the last-named city. His adversaries are named by the *Anglo-Saxon Chronicle*—Conmail, Condidan, and Farinmail.

******

Condidan is apparently the Roman name Candidianus in a Celtic form. His identification with a Cynddylan whose elegy is found among the Bardic poems (Skene, i. 311) is not properly made out, and the poem is too late. Farinmail (Fernmail, Fernvael) is a known name in Welsh genealogies; a prince of the house of Vortigern bearing it was reigning on the Upper Wye some generations later, and is mentioned in the *Historia Brittonum*. Conmail is apparently equivalent to Cynvael, also a known royal name. But the Welsh records do not give us any trace of dynasts bearing these names about the year 577.

******

One of them was, no doubt, the ruler of the British realm immediately attacked, that which occupied parts of Gloucestershire, Somersetshire and Wiltshire, and which had lately been the holding of the heirs of Ambrosius Aurelianus, whom Gildas mentions thirty years before. His allies must have been kings either of Damnonia or of the British states along the Severn or immediately beyond it. (There is no reason to suppose that the three kings ruled each over one of the three cities, Bath, Gloucester and Cirencester, as is often assumed.) Whatever may have been the dominions or the military strength of his enemies, Ceawlin defeated and slew all three (577). The consequence of his victory was the complete conquest of the land between the Somersetshire Avon and the Forest of Arden, with its three cities of Bath, Gloucester and Cirencester, all of which seem to have been surviving in some sort of decayed existence at the moment.

The region was at once settled up by Teutonic colonists: they appear in subsequent history as the race of the Hwiccas, whose name still remains on their eastern and western boundaries—in Wychwood, the forest that divided them from the Chilternsaetas, and the Wych—the northernmost pass of the Malvern Hills.

******

This at least seems the easiest and most probable way of accounting for the appearance of the Hwiccian tribe. Their dialect seems to be Saxon rather than Mercian. But we have no definite mention of them till a century later.

******

Their territory embraced all Gloucestershire east of the Severn, most of Worcestershire, and the southern and larger part of Warwickshire. They were probably a mixed multitude, mainly Saxon but partly Anglian, as was Ceawlin's army. They were so far from being homogeneous with the West Saxons that they never became amalgamated with them, and within two generations after their first settlement appear as a distinct sub-kingdom with reguli of their own. Whether the seventh and eighth century rulers of the Hwiccas claimed a descent from the West Saxon royal house we cannot tell—the early links of their genealogy are lost.

******

Their names such as Eanfrith, Osric, Oswald, Eanhere, mentioned by Bede, and living 650-700, and the later Oshere, Ae-

65

thelhere, Aethelweard, Aethelric, for the most part suggest a Northumbrian rather than a West-Saxon origin. Aethelweard, however, is a name of the West Saxon house.

★★★★★★

This was the greatest conquest that the Saxons had made for three generations, and it must have exalted Ceawlin's power to a high pitch. We are told that he continued his campaigns against the Welsh, presumably pushing up the Severn, or across it in the direction of South Wales. But seven years after the victory of Deorham he seems to have met with a decisive check; he and his brother, Cuthwulf, fight with the Britons in 584 "at the place which is called Fethanleag." There Cuthwulf was slain, and Ceawlin "after taking many towns and spoils innumerable, returned wrathful to his own land". Fethanleag cannot be identified; nothing serious can be urged in favour of putting it at Faddiley in Cheshire, or at Frethern in Gloucestershire, the two sites that have been suggested. It is probably the name of a wood or a district rather than a place.

Then occurs a gap of six years in West Saxon history, after which we get, to our surprise, the notice that in 590 Ceolric, (called in a tiresomely syncopated form Ceol in most MSS. of the *Anglo-Saxon Chronicle*), the son of Cuthwulf, was set up as king, and that in 591 "there was a great slaughter in Britain at Woddesbeorge, and Ceawlin was expelled". This seems to mark the end of his *imperium*, since Aethelbert of Kent was held to be the dominant king in South Britain very soon after. The obvious suggestion is that first some of Ceawlin's own people revolted against him and chose his nephew as king, and that his subject-allies then aided the rebels in crushing their former lord. We can hardly doubt that Aethelbert must have been the mainspring of the movement.

There is no reason to subscribe to the view that Ceolric had been proclaimed king by the newly settled Hwiccas, or that the Britons had anything to do with the affair. The locality of the battle Woddesbeorge, or Wodnesbeorge as some manuscripts have it, was apparently Wanborough near Swindon in North Wiltshire. But to argue from its position that Hwiccas or Britons must have been involved in the slaughter is most dangerous. (The narratives of Ceawlin's fall in Guest and J. R. Green, are pure hypothesis. Mr. Stevenson doubts the identity of Woddesbeorg and Wanborough.)

Ceawlin, though his imperium had certainly been shattered, though his vassals had all fallen away, and though he may even possibly have been deprived of his kingship over the West Saxons themselves—for the word "expelled" (*utadriven*) suggests even this—survived two years more and perished in 593, probably in civil war with Ceolric. The crown passed away for nearly a hundred years from his house, and stayed from 593 to 685 with the descendants of Cuthwulf; Ceolric (591-97) and his brother and successor Ceolwulf (597-611) can have made no attempt to maintain Ceawlin's lofty position.

******

Terrible confusion is caused in the early West Saxon history by the fact that the shortened form Cutha was often used in the chronicles for Cuthwulf, brother of Ceawlin. Many later writers supposed them to be different persons, and gave Ceawlin two brothers. But Ceawlin had also a son, Cuthwine, whose name was likewise shortened to Cutha, and got in that shape into some of the West Saxon royal genealogies (as in that of Ceadwalla under the year 685 in the *A. S. C.*). To make things worse it seems that Cuthwine had a son, Cuthwulf, and he too appears as Cutha in a still later genealogy, that of Aethelwulf (under the year 855 in the *A. S. C*), unless, indeed, Cuthwine and the third Cutha in this passage are a stupid reduplication.

******

They were more or less subject to the *imperium* of Aethelbert of Kent, and probably retained only those conquests of their uncle which were made before 577. The Hwiccas even may already have broken loose and started a principality of their own. All that is recorded of these kings is that in 607 Ceolwulf fought with the South Saxons—a weak enemy—with no recorded result and the utterly impossible statement that he also "fought and contended incessantly against Angles, Welsh, Picts and Scots," an entry which looks as if it rather belonged to the name of Ceolwulf of Northumbria (729-37), for how could a king of Wessex have fought with Picts or Scots in the early seventh century?

The son of Cuthwulf was clearly an unimportant subject-ally of the King of Kent. He would have left more of a name behind him if he had ever conducted great northern campaigns. Perhaps the confusion arose because Ceolwulf of Northumbria was, like his Wessex namesake, the son of a "Cutha". (He is so called in his genealogy in the *A. S. C.*, *sub anno* 731. As a matter of fact, his father was named Cuthwine, like the son of Ceawlin.)

Aethelbert meanwhile was now at the height of his power:

He had extended his dominions as far as the great River Humber, by which the southern Angles are divided from the northern. (Bede.)

That is to say that he was undisputedly *suzerain* over all the Teutonic states of Britain save the united realm of Bernicia and Deira, now held by Aethelfrith, the one king who could vie with him in power. His name was so great that, first of all the insular sovereigns, he had been granted the hand of a daughter of the famous Merovingian house—Bertha, the child of Charibert, King of Paris—and this though he was a heathen. The house of Hengist was once more predominant in Britain, as it had been at the moment of the first invasions, and Ceawlin's western conquests seemed only to have been made in order that his supplanter's empire might be the broader.

Meanwhile the King of Northumbria was adding to the Anglian territory as much as Ceawlin had won for the Saxons of the South. Aethelfrith was a great and ruthless conqueror. As Bede relates:

In that day, he was the strongest of kings, and the most greedy of glory. He harried the race of the Britons more than all the other chiefs of the English: so that he might be compared to Saul, King of Israel (who was a head and shoulders taller than all his contemporaries) but for the fact that he lacked knowledge of the true faith. He conquered more lands from the Britons than any other ealdorman or king, and either drove out their inhabitants and planted them afresh with English, or subdued them and made them tributary. (593-617).

It seems clear that the accession of strength which had come to the house of Ida by the annexation of Deira had given the Northumbrians a preponderance over the Celtic neighbours which they had never enjoyed before. Aethelfrith pushed his conquests right across the Pennine range to the shores of the Irish sea, overrunning the kingdom of Reged and driving the petty kings of the house of Coel to the north and west. It seems that the Britons in their despair called in fresh aid from the north, for in the year 603 we find Aedan, son of Gabran, King of the Dalriad Scots, the newly established kingdom of Irish settlers on the coast of Argyle, marching against Northumbria with a very great army.

Anglian tradition said that he was called in by Hering, son of Hussa, the Bernician king who had reigned thirty years back. (*Anglo-Saxon Chronicle, sub anno* 603.) Very possibly Hering had been rejected because of his tender age, according to Teutonic custom, when his uncles, Frithwulf, Theodric and Aethelric, were successively elected kings, in the thirteen years that followed Hussa's death (575-88). Now he is said to have brought down the Scots to back his claim, promising, no doubt, the aid of a faction among his cousin's subjects. But it is almost certain that Aedan must also have been invited to march against Aethelfrith by the vanquished Welsh princes, who had suffered from the new conquests of the Angles. For he is said to have collected "immense" forces, which could surely not have been furnished by his own small realm on the coast of Argyle, even though he was also, as we know, aided by adventurers from Ireland.

It must be remembered that Aedan was a Christian; he had been baptised and anointed by St. Columba, who had come from Ulster to Iona about 565, and had completed the conversion of the Dalriad Scots, which had been begun by earlier Irish missionaries. Aedan appears to have been a very vigorous and enterprising prince. He had cast off the connection with Ireland, which his ancestors had kept up, and with it the tribute that they had been wont to pay. He had fought long and successfully with the Picts, and had even directed maritime expeditions against the Orkneys and the Isle of Man.

In 603 he must have been far advanced in age, as he had been reigning since 574, and in 596 had many sons old enough to take the field in war. Clearly, he was the one prince in Northern Britain to whom all the enemies of Aethelfrith, whether Northumbrian malcontents or Celtic kinglets, might look for succour.

But the attempt of the Scot to beat down the rising power of the grandson of Ida was doomed to failure. The hosts faced each other at Degsastan, apparently Dawston in Liddesdale, on the frontier of the Bernician realm, and on land which the Angles can only lately have won.

★★★★★★

Mr. Plummer suggests, however, in his edition of Bede, ii., that Daegsastan may be only a corruption of "aet Aegdancs Stane," at Aedanstone, in which case we may have to look elsewhere for the battle-site.

★★★★★★

The fight was hard, and Aethelfrith's brother, Theodbald, fell with his whole following. (For the narrative of the battle, see Bede, i., and the entry in Tighernach's Irish Annals.) But the fortune of the day was with the Northumbrian king; the allied princes of the North were smitten with a great slaughter: the few put to flight the many, and Aedan fled homewards with only the wreck of an army, leaving dead on the field his ally Maeluma, son of Baedan, King of Ulster, and many other chiefs. Bede wrote in 730:

> This fight of Aethelfrith's, was in the year 603, after the incarnation of Our Lord, after he had completed the eleventh year of his reign, which in all covered twenty-four years. It was also in the first year of the Roman Emperor Phocas. And from that day onward no king of the Scots in Britain has ever dared to come to open battle with the race of the English.
>
> ★★★★★★
>
> Note: Quite correctly dated, as it would seem, for Phocas came to the throne in November, 602, so that the fighting season of 603 would fall into his first year. But the Ulster annals give 605 and Tighernach 606 for the battle. Welsh legend ascribed the defeat to Aedan's treachery or cowardice, and he is recorded in the Triads as one of "the three great traitors of the Isle of Britain"—which seems hard.
>
> ★★★★★★

The victory of Dawston must have confirmed Aethelfrith in the possession of the upper valleys of the Tweed and its tributaries, as far as the watershed of the Clyde, and, no doubt, of the land round Carlisle and the west end of the Roman Wall also. (It has been suggested that the "Catrail," the long boundary ditch, from the Tweed southward across the lands toward Solway, may mark this delimitation between the Angles and the Britons. But this is very doubtful.)

It is curious to find that he did not then proceed to make an end of the British kingdom of Elmet, in the hills and woods of the West Riding, for this state, as we know, survived into the next generation. It is, however, highly probable that Aethelfrith may have compelled its king Cerdic to do him homage and pay him tribute. But his last and greatest expedition was directed further to the south, against a region broader and more fertile than the mountain valleys of Elmet—the lands between Ribble and Dee, which were still in the hands of the Britons.

These formed, in the early seventh century, part of the kingdom originally known as Theyrnllwg, of which the later Powys was the surviving remnant. It then extended from the Ribble to the Upper Wye, and from the Clwyd to Cannock Chase, and had been for a century the connecting link between the Britons of the North and those of the West.

******

According to Welsh tradition the limits of Theyrnllwg were "from the Forest of Derwent to the Aerfen (Dee)." (See Guest's *Origines Celticae, ii.* 49).

******

Its ruling sovereign at the moment was Brocmail, son of Cincen, a descendant of that Catell, who appears in the *Historia Brittonum* as first founder of this kingdom, in the days of Vortigern and St. Germanus. To aid Brocmail in the defence of this all-important central isthmus of the British territory came his neighbour and overlord, Cadvan, King of Gwynedd, and Selim, son of Cynan, a prince whose dominions it is impossible to identify, but who may have been a kinsman of Brocmail, and a sub-king of some part of Powys. According to the Harleian genealogy he was Brocmail's grandson.

******

According to the legend (*H. B.*, 35) he was a serf who was given the blessing by the saint that he should become a king, and that kings should never fail from his seed. In the Triads, he is one of "the three kings in Britain who were born serfs."

******

The forces of the invader and of the Welsh princes met near the site of the old Roman Deva, the "city of the legions," which may already have been the "waste Chester" that we read of in ninth century annals. For there is no sign that it was a living city, or the capital of Theyrnllwg, as we should have expected. No story of the sack of a great and wealthy town ends the history of Aethelfrith's campaign in Bede, or is hinted at in the later legends of the Welsh. Indeed, the chief incident that is recorded concerning it seems to imply that Deva, though the strategical centre of the district, was no longer its spiritual centre. Bede says:

> Aethelfrith, being about to give battle, saw the priests of the Britons, who had come together to pray to God for their soldiery, standing apart in a place of safety. He asked who they were, and for what they had assembled in that place. Now the most of them were from the monastery of Bancor, in which there is said to have been so great a number of monks that, the monastery being divided into seven parts, with a ruler over

71

each, none of those parts contained less than three hundred persons, who all lived by the labour of their hands. A great part of them came to this battle, after having celebrated a fast of three days, to pray along with the rest, having Brocmail appointed as their escort, to guard them from the sword of the barbarians while they were intent on their prayers.

And when Aethelfrith heard of the cause of their coming he said: 'If they cry to their God against us, they too are our adversaries, though they bear no weapons, since they oppose us by their imprecations'. So he ordered them to be first attacked, and then destroyed the rest of that unlucky army, not without much loss in his own ranks. About 1,200 of those monks who came to pray are said to have been slain, and only fifty to have escaped. Brocmail and his men had turned their backs at the first charge, and left those whom he should have guarded unprotected to the mercy of the sword."

This tale seems to be corroborated, at least in part, by the fact that the Irish annals call the battle "the slaughter of the Saints". Selim and another king called Cetula (Catell?) are said to have been slain in the fight, though Brocmail escaped ingloriously. (613 *A.D.*).

★★★★★★

The tale of the monks of Bangor (of course Bangor Iscoed, not Bangor-on-Menai) is told by Bede *apropos* of the prophecy said to have been made by St. Augustine, that if the British clergy would not join in preaching Christianity to the English nation they would be punished by receiving death at English hands.

★★★★★★

It might have been expected that the victory of Chester would have given permanent possession of the lands between Ribble and Dee to the Northumbrians. This, however, was not to be the case: Aethelfrith probably annexed the region, but it did not stay with his successors. He was destined to fall in battle only four years later, and if the conquered region did not then revert to the Britons, it certainly did so at the death of his successor Edwin in 633, when Cadwallon of Gwynedd destroyed for a moment the whole power of Northumbria, and ravaged it as far as Hadrian's Wall and the Firth of Forth. The lands about Chester and the mouth of the Dee were destined to form part of Mercia, not of the more northern English realm, and their permanent occupation was by settlers from the valley of Trent, not from the valleys of the Ouse or Tyne.

Meanwhile we must leave Aethelfrith, the last but one of the great heathen kings of the English race, in order to turn back to the history of Aethelbert of Kent, to whose court the missionaries of Roman Christianity had come when the Northumbrian conqueror was but commencing his eventful reign. The heir of Hengist had already bowed his knee before the Cross when the heir of Ida was slaughtering the servants of Christ in ignorant hostility before the walls of Deva. The second epoch of the history of the Teutonic settlers of Britain had begun before the first was well finished. The period of the conversion of the English overlapped that of their great conquests. But Ceawlin and Aethelfrith between them had finished the more important paid: of the work of settlement. The lands which were to be added to the area of permanently settled Saxon or Anglian soil after 613 were but of limited extent compared to those which had already been occupied.

CHAPTER 4

The Conversion of the Anglo-Saxon Kingdoms (597-671 *A.D.*)

With the year 597, when Aethelbert of Kent had already enjoyed for some years a predominance over all the kingdoms south of Humber, while Aethelfrith, ruler of the united realm of Deira and Bernicia, was supreme north of that estuary, begins the second period of Anglo-Saxon history.

Sometime in the spring of that year there landed in the Isle of Thanet, at Ebbsfleet or possibly at Richborough, the mission of some forty persons headed by the priest Augustine, which Pope Gregory the Great had sent forth from Rome about ten months before. It is impossible to omit the pretty tale which explains Gregory's interest in the English race, though Bede, its first narrator, gives it only as an *opinio*, a tradition or ancient report. (There is a letter of Gregory's to one of his agents in Gaul, ordering the purchase of English slaves. See Haddon and Stubbs, *Councils, iii.* 4.) Long before Gregory had been consecrated to the Roman bishopric, perhaps about 585-88, he had seen in the slave-market beside the Tiber a group of youths exposed for sale, notable for their fair complexions, their attractive faces, and their abundant hair.

When he saw them, he asked from what region or land they

had been brought. He was told from the Isle of Britain, whose inhabitants were all of that aspect. Again, he asked whether these islanders were Christians, or still wrapped in the errors of paganism. He was informed that they were heathens. Then he drew a long sigh and exclaimed: 'Alas! that beings of a such a fair countenance should be in the grip of the Author of Darkness, and that such a graceful exterior should enclose minds destitute of grace within!' So, he asked again what was the name of this nation. The reply was that they were called Angles.

'Good', he answered, 'for they have the faces of angels, and such should be co-heirs with the angels in heaven. But what is the name of the province from which they have been brought?' He was told that it was Deira. 'Good again!' he said, '*De ira eruti*—snatched from God's wrath, and called to Christ's mercy. And how is the king of their land called?' The answer came that he was named Aella. But Gregory, playing with the name, exclaimed: 'Then ought Alleluia, the praise of God our Creator, to be sung in the realm of Aella'.

The legend tells that he immediately went to his bishop (Pelagias II.) and offered himself as a missionary for the conversion of the English, but that he was unable to carry out his desire "because the citizens of Rome could not bring themselves to allow him to depart to such a distance from their city." (The date of the legend is fixed to the years 585-88 by the fact that Gregory only returned from a very long stay in Constantinople in the former year, while Aella died in the latter.)

When, however, he was elected bishop himself a few years later (590) he was able to start by proxy the work which he was prevented from discharging in person.

The mission to England was but one of many enterprises which Gregory the Great took in hand. The activity of the founder of the medieval papacy was all-embracing: his emissaries strengthened the hands of the pious Reccared, newly converted to orthodoxy, in Visigothic Spain. They won peace from Agilulf the Lombard, who seemed at this time destined to make an end of the Roman empire in Italy. Gregory was the familiar correspondent and adviser of the able if unscrupulous Austrasian queen, Brunhildis, who was vainly endeavouring to maintain the crumbling royal power among the turbulent Franks. He started the as yet half-conscious attempts of the Roman See to free itself from the political supremacy of Constantinople, by his contest with the Emperor Maurice and the patriarch John the Faster. (Yet we must allow he does not always show independence in his correspondence with Maurice, and addresses the cruel usurper Phocas in adulatory terms.)

The papacy was to be the heir of the empire in the West, and the missionary invasion of England was in a very true sense the reclaiming for the world-power which was to replace the empire, of the province which had been lost under Honorius. Apostolic zeal is none the less real though it be combined with statesmanship, as it was in this case.

A glance at the internal condition of Italy in 590-96 suffices to explain why the mission of Augustine only went forth six summers after Gregory had been elected to fill the papal throne. The period of the commencement of his episcopate was one during which the Lombards were ravaging the remnant of imperial Italy with special vigour and success. They had closed in on Rome itself, and actually laid siege to the city in 593: though turned back, they continued to occupy Tuscany and much of Umbria; it was still possible for some time that they might reappear, to sack Rome, or to turn it into the residence of a duke or a royal "*gastaldus*".

The twenty-seven years during which—as Gregory complains in one of his letters—Rome had lived in terror under the shadow of the Lombard sword, were only just over when the missionary band destined for Britain was despatched. Indeed, formal peace was only obtained in 599, when Gregory negotiated with King Agilulf a *modus vivendi* not only for his own city but for all the surviving imperial territory in the peninsula. Augustine and his party must have passed in 596 through towns and fields still black with recent burning, and have suffered perils by the way from half-hostile Lombard war-bands, for though King Agilulf had ceased to advance he had as yet consented to no definitive treaty.

The character of Gregory, saint and statesman, is sufficiently well known to us, not so much from his biographers, as from his own books and letters. Augustine is a more shadowy figure: he was a man of mature years and had been a monk in the monastery of St. Andrew on the Caelian Hill, of which he was prior at the moment of his despatch to Britain. Gregory says (*Epistles*), that he had been well trained in monastic discipline, "was filled with a knowledge of Holy Scripture, and endowed with good works by God's special grace." The story of his mission shows that he was zealous, persuasive, untiring and ascetic, but suggests at the same time weak points in his temperament—the two opposite faults of a certain want of self-reliance and of an occasional lapse into self-assertion.

Of the latter we shall hear more hereafter. The former seems to be indicated by the curious fact that he and his party actually halted at Aix or Arles on their way to Britain, "seized with a sudden fear at the idea of proceeding to a barbarous, fierce and unbelieving nation". Augustine returned to Rome, bearing the request of his companions that they might be excused so dangerous and uncertain a mission. But the resolute Gregory sent him back, with orders to proceed at all risks, and letters commendatory to many Gallic prelates who were to help the travellers on the way (July, 596). Very early in the following year the whole band crossed the Channel, apparently from Boulogne: they had, as it seems, passed through Autun and Metz on their northward progress.

They landed in Thanet:

An isle of about 600 families according to the English manner of reckoning, separated from the mainland by the River Wantsum, which is about three furlongs broad, and is fordable only in two places.

Ebbsfleet is the traditional point of their coming ashore, though something may be urged in favour of Richborough, despite of the fact that the site of that old Roman port cannot be described in strict accuracy as lying in the bounds of Thanet; it was apparently in those days isolated on a little island of its own. (See the excursus on Augustine's landing-place in Mason's *Mission of St. Augustine*.) The party was permitted to land without hindrance, and Augustine was allowed to announce his arrival to Aethelbert, who bade him remain in Thanet till he himself should have leisure to take counsel concerning him.

English heathenism does not seem to have had any firm hold on its votaries. Apparently, it had lost vitality on being transplanted from its original continental birthplace. Religions which are bound up with local ceremonies and institutions, such as those which Tacitus describes as being common to the Angles and their neighbours, are indeed wont to grow weak when they are divorced from their old connection. A very few generations had sufficed to destroy the faith of all the other Teutonic races, which had taken part in the great migrations of the fourth and fifth centuries. If the invaders of Britain adhered longer to the faith of Woden and his fellows than did other kindred races, it was because their conditions differed from those of the Frank or the Goth.

They had well-nigh exterminated the earlier Christian inhabitants, instead of receiving the whole provincial community to surrender and homage. Their religion, like their language and their social customs, had survived in a way that was unknown on the continent. They had erected temples containing rude idols in spots specially consecrated; we hear now and then of priests, though there is no evidence that the class was numerous or powerful. There is absolutely no indication that they formed an organised body, able or willing to combine in defence of the old faith. Indeed, on the only occasion where a heathen priest is recorded to have taken a prominent part in religious discussion with the Christian missionaries, he was on the side of innovation. The speech of this Deiran high priest, recorded in Bede, seems to hint that his position was not a very important one. He is made to say:

No one has applied himself more diligently to the worship of our gods than I; and yet there are many who receive greater favours from their king, and are more preferred than I, and more prosperous in all their undertakings. Now if the gods were good for anything, they would rather forward me, who have been more careful to serve them. If on examination we find the new doctrines which are now preached to us better and more efficacious, let us receive them without any delay.

It seems probable that in matters religious the king, as the general representative of the nation in its dealings with the powers of heaven, was more important than any priest of any individual god.

Nothing can be more striking in the narrative of the conversion of England than to note the toleration displayed to the emissaries of Christianity, even by those rulers who remained themselves impervious to its teaching. Penda of Mercia, who was to a certain extent the champion of the old religion, and put down the Northumbrian kings who had abandoned it, was yet no persecutor.

He did not obstruct the preaching of the Word among his people, if any were willing to hear it, but on the contrary hated and despised those who, when they had once received the faith, he saw not living up to its works. He would say 'these are wretched and contemptible men who despise the commands of the God in whom they believe.' (Bede.)

It is a notable fact that in the long history of the English missions, which lasted for three-quarters of a century between Augustine's landing and the conversion of the last heathen in the Sussex Weald, there is not a single record of martyrdom. The preachers of the new faith were sometimes hunted away, but never, as far as we know, put to death. If any had suffered, it is absolutely certain that their fates would have been recorded in moving words by the conscientious Bede. This contrasts strongly with what happened in Frisia and continental Saxony, where several notable martyrdoms took place.

It appears probable that the English had been impressed by the fact that their powerful neighbours across the Channel, the Franks, had long ago abandoned their native heathenism. This was the only race with whom they had much to do in the way of friendship and commerce, and it seems clear that the insular kings looked up to the Merovingian royal house, and that Aethelbert had been considered fortunate to win the hand of one of its daughters. It must not be forgotten that close kinsmen of the English, the Saxons of Bayeux and on the Picard coast, were subjects of the Franks, and had shared in their conversion. Nay, some of the Merovings had even claimed a certain *suzerainty* over the English in general, (Procopius, iv.) though we have no proof that it was ever admitted. Augustine brought with him Christian interpreters from the Frankish realm; it is almost certain that they must have been descendants of some of the Saxons settled beyond the Channel.

That any predisposition which the English may have felt towards Christianity came from their connection with the Franks, and not from intercourse with the Britons, is certain. The English had from the first spared a certain number of the conquered Britons, who became the base of the servile class among them, those of whom Gildas speaks as:

Coming in, worn down by famine, to hold out their hands to the enemy, accepting perpetual slavery that they might not be slain forthwith—the best terms that they could obtain.

But it is certain that they were but a remnant, and exercised no influence on their masters; it is not even clear that they preserved their Christianity after a generation or two. The unconquered Britons of the West and North made no effort to convert their adversaries, a refusal not very unnatural in itself, which is perpetually used as a source of reproach to them by Bede, and other English writers. Even 150 years after the first invasion they were still as bitter as ever against the incomers; the only reference to the English that can be detected in the surviving notes of the proceedings of British church-councils is a clause in the canons of the Synod of Lucus Victoriae (569 *A.D.*), imposing a penance of thirteen years on any man who shall have acted as guide to "the barbarians," or a penance for life if the barbarians, so helped, shall have done any serious damage on their raid.

It is certainly strange that no improvement of the relations between the two races, resulting in missionary effort on the part of the British clergy, should have taken place during the long halt of the Saxons, between the battle of Mount Badon and the advance of Ceawlin—a period of sixty years. We find that exiled Anglian princes were during the period of their paganism occasionally entertained at the courts of British kings, as happened with Edwin, the son of Aella, and his nephew Hereric. And the Celts were even politically leagued on occasion with Angles, as in the case of Hering, the son of Hussa. But such communication as these relations involved does not seem to have led to any attempt at conversion.

Not one solitary legend survives to hint at such an endeavour; the British Church, as a whole, contrasted strongly throughout its independent history with the daughter Church of Ireland in its lack of missionary enterprise. It appears to have exhausted the greater part of its energy in the multiplication of monasteries and the practice of minute asceticism. Those who are interested in the details of the monastic life may find many strange ordinances in the fragments of Gildas's tract *On Penitence* and the canons of the *Sinodus Aquilonalis Britanniae.*

If we may judge from these documents, no amount of rules and no seclusion from the world was wholly sufficient to prevent strange lapses from the rules of ordinary morality among the British clergy. The common punishment for all offences, great and small, was a longer or shorter diet of bread and water and the repetition of a smaller or greater number of Psalms. (See the texts in Stubbs and Haddan's *Councils and Ecclesiastical Documents,* vol. i.)

The Welsh Church seems to have been in its organisation a legitimate descendant of the Roman provincial Church of the fifth century: it had regular diocesan bishops, whose dioceses were coterminous with the kingdoms, and was not ruled by tribal abbots and non-territorial bishops like the Irish Church. The earliest indications seem to show that there were probably five bishoprics west of Severn, four of which survived as the Sees of Bangor, St. David's, St. Asaph and Llandaff; a fifth at Llanbadarn, which took in the greater part of the modern Cardiganshire and Brecknockshire, was merged in St. David's not long after 700.

In South-Western Britain there were at least two more, one probably comprising Cornwall, the other the more eastern parts of Damnonia. Farther north, St. Ninian's bishopric of Whithern (Candida Casa),
for the Galloway Picts, goes back to the fifth century, and St. Kenti-
gern's bishopric of Glasgow to the sixth. But it is extremely probable
that there were other British Sees between Clyde and Mersey whose
memory has perished.

Aethelbert of Kent was certainly acquainted with the existence
of Christianity, and not indisposed to give its missionaries a friendly
welcome, but this was due to the fact that he had been wedded for
many years—as has already been mentioned—to a Christian spouse,
Bertha, the daughter of Charibert, the Merovingian King of Paris.
She had brought over with her many dependants of her own religion,
including a certain Luithard, a bishop, (said to have been Bishop of
Senlis), who acted as her chaplain, and her husband had permitted her
to utilise the old Roman Church of St. Martin, on the east side of his
royal town of Canterbury, as her chapel.

Pope Gregory, in a letter to her, which has been preserved, (Gregory's *Epistles*), gives her a gentle admonition that she might have done
more for the faith; but at least she appears to have predisposed Aethelbert in its favour, and when Augustine appeared in Kent she exercised
all the influence that she had in his favour.

A few days after the arrival of the mission the king came to Thanet,
and bade Augustine appear before him and state the cause of his coming. The interview, as Bede tells us, was held in the open air, because
there was an old superstition that witchcrafts and deceptions might be
practised within four walls, but not beneath the sky. But the strangers
were permitted to approach in processional order, singing litanies, and
marching under a silver cross and a banner consisting of a panel-
picture of the Saviour. Augustine was invited to seat himself and to
explain his mission. He spoke, through his interpreters, with great
fervour, setting forth the blessings of Christianity in this world and the
next. The king replied that:

> His words and promises were fair, but because they were new
> and unproved, he could not give his adhesion to them, aban-
> doning all the beliefs that he and all of his race had held from
> time immemorial. Yet since the missionaries were evidently
> desiring to communicate to others things that they sincerely

believed to be good and profitable, they should be given a fair trial. They should receive daily food from the royal store, and might preach where they would, nor should any hindrance be put in the way of their making converts.

Probably Aethelbert was already prepared to go farther than he said, and gave this cautious answer, rather for the benefit of his chiefs and councillors sitting around, than because he himself had any objection to a faith of which he must long have known the main characteristics by means of his wife.

At any rate Augustine was treated with a kindness much greater than had been promised him. He was invited to Canterbury, lodged close to the royal dwelling, and permitted to preach, to pray, and to celebrate the sacraments, in the old church which had already been granted as a chapel to the queen. Aethelbert frequently attended at his services, and held private conference with him. There was evidently no resisting power in Kentish paganism: the missionaries were not only unopposed, but welcomed everywhere. On Whitsunday (June 2), 597, less than three months after Augustine's landing in Thanet, the king was baptised, and after him great numbers of his subjects great and small. The royal convert presented to his teacher an adequate residence in Canterbury, and certain permanent endowments.

It is interesting to find that Aethelbert bade Augustine not only to build but also to repair churches wherever he might please. (Bede, *E, H., i.*) This seems to suggest that a considerable number of Roman ecclesiastical buildings must have been standing in a more or less ruinous condition. Had they been used by a subject British servile population all through the last 150 years? Or were they merely wrecks which could be identified as churches by their form? Lacking, as we do, all trace of a Christian subject population in Kent, it is safer to accept the second alternative.

Augustine had been told by Gregory that, if his mission should prosper, he must get himself ordained a bishop, as the first step towards giving the English Church a definite organisation. When all seemed going well, he repaired to Gaul, and was consecrated by Virgilius, Bishop of Arles, probably late in 597. (Not Aetherius, as Bede wrongly says. The latter was Archbishop of Lyons.) He promptly returned to Kent, and then sent two of his companions to Rome, not only to bear the tidings of his success, but to lay before the Pope a number of questions relating to problems which were beginning to trouble him.

Some of them were questions of the same sort which often beset missionaries of today (1919) in Africa—problems as to the recognition of heathen marriages, the distribution of alms, and the punishment of crime among converts.

Others related to ceremonial. But the most important of them all was the request for a definition as to Augustine's position with regard to the Bishops of Britain, by which was clearly meant the Celtic Church of the West. It is not quite certain whether Gregory fully understood the problem, eleven realised that there was an existing Church in Britain, bitterly hostile to the English, converted or unconverted. (See Mason's *Mission of St. Augustine.*) He replied:

> All the bishops of Britain we commit to your charge, that the unlearned may be instructed, the weak be strengthened with persuasion, the perverse corrected by your authority.

But he was at the same moment arranging that Augustine should consecrate an English hierarchy, and it is quite possible that it was to this alone that he was referring. If he had known of the difficulty that was arising as to the relations of the English and the Welsh Churches, he would probably have written at great length on the problem, as he did on several other of the questions that were submitted to him.

It is a clear sign of the inadequate knowledge that Gregory possessed of the state of Britain that when, in 601, he sent over many priests to England to aid in Augustine's mission—among them Mellitus, Justus and Paulinus, all destined in the future to be archbishops—he made them the bearers of a letter in which he set forth a scheme for the division of the island into dioceses, which was wholly impracticable. They bore a *pallium* for Augustine, with which he was to invest himself on taking the title of Archbishop of London; he was to consecrate twelve bishops as suffragans to himself, and a thirteenth as Archbishop of York, who, "when that city and its neighbourhood receive the Word of God," was to consecrate another twelve to be subject to himself.

This arrangement could not be carried out, firstly, because it would have been unwise for Augustine to desert his patron Aethelbert of Kent, and to transfer his residence to a city of the comparatively unimportant king of Essex; secondly, because the mission, satisfactory though its progress was, did not convert all England at one sweep. It was twenty-four years before York saw an archbishop, and nine centuries before the English Church counted as many as twenty-four dioceses—a total not reached till the reign of Henry VIII. Augustine himself only lived long enough to ordain two suffragans, Justus for Rochester and West Kent, Mellitus for London and the kingdom of the East Saxons.

For Kent and its subject state of Essex were the only two realms which seemed sufficiently settled in their Christianity to justify the appointment of a bishop, and even in these—as we shall see—there was a period of reaction. King Saebert of Essex, the nephew of Ae-thelbert, was the only one of that monarch's vassals who followed the example of his *suzerain*, by giving a prompt adhesion to the new religion. He was a zealous convert, and joined with his uncle in the foundation of St. Paul's, London, as the cathedral of Bishop Mellitus; that Aethelbert took part in it shows that his authority over Essex was much more than a nominal hegemony. Raedwald of East Anglia, a more powerful vassal, would not go so far; he was baptised during a visit to Canterbury, but on returning home:

> Seduced by his wife and certain perverse teachers, he tried to serve at the same time Christ and his former gods. For he had in the same temple an altar to Christ, and another small one in which he used to immolate victims to devils. (Bede *E.H.* ii.)

On what logical principle Raedwald worked, whether Christ was introduced into the heathen pantheon, according to the experiment once made by Alexander Severus of old, or whether Woden and Frey were treated as vassals and demiurges of Jehovah, it is interesting but useless to speculate. At any rate, this scandalous trimmer in religion got no bishop granted him from Canterbury.

The only important events which are recorded concerning the later period of Augustine's seven-year archiepiscopate are his unfortunate conferences with the Celtic bishops in the year 603, which started the bitter strife between the English and the Welsh Churches which was to endure for several centuries. When the conditions of the meeting are taken into consideration, it is perhaps hardly wonderful that the Roman missionary and the Welsh clergy could come to no agreement. The question of obedience was the really fatal point. The British Church had governed itself, according to its own lights, for the last 150 years, and during that long period had practically no relations with any other Christian body save the daughter community in Ireland.

When Augustine came, with his letter from Gregory, which placed him at the head of all the insular churches, it was hardly wonderful that the Celts saw no reason to accept as their overlord this stranger, who had been but a few years in Britain, and had made a few thousand converts in districts very far from their own border. The Britons refused to surrender their autonomy, but they made their fight, not on the question of recognising the authority of the Roman pontiff, but on a number of matters of ecclesiastical custom and ritual, which served to mask the real heart of the controversy.

The conferences were held at the place afterwards called Augustine's Oak, "on the confines of the West Saxons and the Hwiccas," apparently Aust on the Bristol Channel, a very convenient place for Welsh delegates crossing from Gwent or Glamorgan by the well-known old Roman passage.

★★★★★★

Bede, *E. H., ii.* 9. Some commentators have argued that the first conference may have been not at Aust, but at some place such as Cirencester or Malmesbury more exactly on the confines of the two peoples. But Aust answers fairly well for both.

★★★★★★

Augustine, as we are told, began by brotherly admonitions to the "bishops and doctors" who had come to meet him, urging that they should undertake in common the labour of preaching the Gospel to the English. But he showed little tact if, as Bede seems to state, he raised at the same time the question of their differences from the continental churches, especially—the head and front of their offence—their habit of keeping Easter at a different date from the Romans and the other Western Christians. The project for mission work among the English provoked no enthusiasm among the Welsh; they disliked the enemies who had robbed them of two-thirds of Britain so bitterly, that they could not feel any deep concern for Saxon souls. But this, of course, it would have been scandalous to state in so many words. The insinuations against their orthodoxy, on the other hand, offered fine fighting ground.

After a long disputation they would not comply with the entreaties, rebukes, or exhortations of Augustine, but preferred their own traditions before all the churches in the world.

The Paschal controversy, on which the dispute mainly hinged, was in its essence a comparatively simple business. Down to the year 458 the whole of the Churches of the West, from Italy to Britain, had calculated Easter in a rather loose fashion, determining the Paschal

Moon by a cycle of eighty-four years attributed to Sulpicius Severus (*circa* 410) but really going back to the Council of Arles in 314. In 458, however, the Roman Church began to use a new system of computation, the 532 years cycle of Victorius of Aquitaine; and this again was replaced in 525 by the decidedly more correct Alexandrine cycle of Anatolius, also of 532 years, a change which had the additional advantage of bringing the Roman reckoning into harmony with that of Alexandria and all the other orthodox churches of the East.

These changes had been gradually copied by all the continental Churches in touch with Rome. But the British and Irish Churches, cut off from the rest of Christendom by the intervening wedge of English heathenism, had continued to employ a form of the 84 year cycle, attributed to Sulpicius Severus. They were now so devoted to it that they utterly refused to make a change, on the authority of Roman or other foreign calculators; they considered their own system good enough after its long hallowing by tradition. They were also, it may be suspected, incapable of following the astronomical and arithmetical arguments against it. It resulted that their system was to count as Easter Day the Sunday which fell next after the Spring Equinox, between the 14th and 20th days of the moon. The latest Roman system took Easter to be the Sunday which fell next alter the Spring equinox, between the 15th and 21st days of the moon.

******

It is clear that the Welsh were not "Quartodeciman" heretics of the old type. Bede expressly acknowledges this (iii. 17), though Aldheim insinuates it, somewhat unfairly. The British Church did not insist on the number 14. See the excursus on the controversy in Plummer's edition of Bede, vol. ii.

******

A considerable discrepancy of dates naturally resulted. That any communities of Christian men should have refused each other communion, on points of dispute of which this mere mathematical problem was the most important, seems sufficiently deplorable. But the root of the matter was not, it is clear, the Paschal cycle, but the determination of the British Church to preserve its autonomy; if it chose to make its calculation on an antiquated system, it would do so, despite all argument. This was patriotic obscurantism, no doubt; but on the whole more blame attaches to Augustine for insisting that the Britons should abandon a system which was, after all, Roman and very ancient, in order to take up the new one.

If only the new English and the old British Churches could be got into friendly communication, for the common purpose of missionary work among the heathen, the greater would of necessity end by absorbing the less. It is clear that the Apostle of England showed himself lacking in tact and pliability, if the Celts were lacking in common Christian missionary zeal.

The first abortive conference at Augustine's Oak was followed by a second, to which there came many more representatives of the British Church, seven bishops (as Bede gives the tradition) and many learned monks, of whom Dinooth, Abbot of Bangor Iscoed was the most notable. But the arguments were as unfruitful as those at the earlier meeting, and the controversialists parted denouncing each other as schismatics. Bede gives a legend—surely British in origin—to explain the breach. Some of the Welsh delegates, on their way to the conference, sought advice of a certain anchorite of great sanctity. The hermit said:

> If Augustine is a man of God follow him, Our Lord said, 'Take My yoke upon you and learn of Me, for I am meek and lowly of heart'. If, therefore, Augustine is meek and lowly of heart, it is to be believed that he has taken upon himself the yoke of Christ, and offers the same to you. But if he shows himself stern and haughty, it appears that he is not of God. Contrive that he arrive first at the place of conference; if at your approach he shall rise up to meet you, hear him submissively. But if he shall show you that he despises you, by not rising up to greet you, let him be contemned.

The story runs that the Welsh bishops tried this plan, and that Augustine, as it fell out, received them sitting on his throne, as a superior meeting inferiors.

> Whereupon they flew into a passion, charged him with pride, and contradicted all that he said. (Bede, *E. H., ii.*)

The incident is, no doubt, mere legend, but it contains this much of truth, that the key to the whole quarrel was that the Roman Church treated other Churches as subjects and inferiors, and that the British Church was proud and sensitive, and rejected all notion of inferiority.

The breach, if Bede may be followed, took the form of an ultimatum by Augustine, requiring the Welsh delegates to reform their custom of keeping Easter, to adopt the Roman details in the sacrament of baptism, and to join at once in missionary work among the English.

★★★★★★

What was the particular divagation of the Welsh Church from common practice in baptism is not clear. Perhaps a neglect of subsequent confirmation, or of the trine immersion. See Plummer's Bede, ii.

★★★★★★

Minor divergencies of ritual he would not insist upon. The Celts answered that they consented to no one of his three points, and that they did not acknowledge him as an archbishop. Thereupon Augustine departed, with a threatening prophecy that:

If the Britons would not preach the Way of Life to the English nation, they were likely to find death from the English sword.

This vaticination was considered to have been fulfilled a few years after Augustine's death, by the great slaughter of the Welsh princes and clergy by the heathen King Aethelfrith of Northumbria, at the Battle of Chester (613 *A.D.*).

From this time onward the breach between the newly founded English Church and the old British Church seemed irreparable, and the relations of the Roman mission with the Irish Church were hardly better. A few years after Augustine's death we find Archbishop Laurentius, his successor, complaining that an Irish bishop, one Dagan, refused when passing through Canterbury not only to eat with him, but even to enter the same dwelling. Three generations later St. Aid held records that the priests of the Welsh not only refused to join in any act of worship with an English cleric, but regarded him as so deeply polluted that they would not use a dish or cup which he had touched, but would break it, or at least solemnly purify it with ashes or sand, and cast any food partly eaten by him to dogs or swine.

The English retorted by treating all British or Irish bishops as schismatic, and called the peculiar Celtic tonsure, in which the whole front of the head instead of the crown alone was shorn, "the tonsure of Simon Magus". So far was the conversion of some of the English kingdoms from having any effect in bringing out better relations between Christian Celt and Christian Teuton, that we shall find the Welsh king Cadwallon deliberately leaguing himself with the heathen Penda of Mercia against the Christian Edwin of Northumberland, and after Edwin's death ravaging Deira with peculiar atrocity, in company with the pagan Mercians. It was to be many generations before a better state of things was gradually reached. National hatred was far too strong to be affected by theoretical brotherhood in Christ.

On Augustine's death (May 26, 604) he was succeeded as Archbishop of Canterbury by Laurentius, one of his original companions, and the person who carried his queries to Gregory and brought back the answer in 601. He had been consecrated as his spiritual father's coadjutor not long before, "lest upon his decease the state of the Church might falter, if it should be destitute of a pastor, though but for one hour". We know little of him, save that he was an indefatigable worker, and made some attempt to renew the negotiation with the Welsh Church, which had failed so lamentably in his predecessor's time. It had, as might have been expected, no effect. In the twelfth year of his archiepiscopate died King Aethelbert (February 24, 616) who had ruled Kent for the long period of fifty-six years, and had raised it, during the central portion of his reign, to a predominance over the other English kingdoms which it was never again to enjoy.

It would seem, however, that in his old age his power was beginning to slip from him, for we are told that, while he yet lived, Raedwald, King of East Anglia, once his vassal, had begun to assert himself, and to claim the primacy for his own tribe. Whether this king, the man who devised the strange compromise between Christianity and heathenism already mentioned, had rebelled against his *suzerain* and freed himself from homage by force of arms, or whether Aethelbert's former hegemony insensibly slipped from him, we do not know. But for a few years Raedwald was reckoned chief king among the English; his domination extended over a wider area than that of his predecessor, for in 617 he overcame and slew Aethelfrith of Northumbria, the victor of Chester.

The cause of their strife was that the East Anglian king had harboured Edwin, the exiled son of Aella of Deira, whose dominion Aethelfrith had long possessed. After striving to get the young prince delivered up to him, first by bribes and then by threats, Aethelfrith declared war on Raedwald, but was surprised, as we are told, before all his army had assembled, and slain with all his follower on the banks of the Idle, in North Mercia. Raedwald then placed his *protégé* Edwin on the Northumbrian throne, not only restoring to him his own kingdom of Deira, but gaining for him Bernicia also, which was properly the patrimony of the house of Ida. Aethelfrith's four sons escaped, and spent many years as wandering exiles. Like Edwin, however, they were destined one day to come to their own.

The period which began with the death of Aethelbert and the

predominance of Raedwald was one very unfavourable to the infant Church of England. Aethelbert's son and successor, Eadbald, had never been baptised, and immediately on his accession scandalised Archbishop Laurentius by wedding his father's young widow, a second wife whom Aethelbert had espoused in his extreme old age, after the death of Queen Bertha. This caused an open breach between the king and the Christian community among his subjects; the archbishop lived for a long time under daily expectation of misusage or exile. But open persecution was never seen in England during the age of the early missions. Eadbald contented himself with ignoring the protests of Laurentius, and signifying his displeasure.

Many fair-weather converts fell away, but the Church was not openly molested. Yet the general outlook was unpromising. Saebert, King of Essex, died very soon after Aethelbert, and his sons, Seaxred and Saeward, were pagans at heart, though during their father's lifetime they had seemed to acquiesce in the establishment of Christianity within his realm. They expelled Bishop Mellitus from London, and proclaimed that the worship of the old gods was once more permitted. Yet here again we hear neither of martyrdom nor of actual persecution. The two princes of Essex in the very next year quarrelled with Cynegils, King of the West Saxons, and were slain by him in battle (617). But Sigebert, the son of Saeward, who succeeded his father and uncle, was also a heathen, and the Church which had been planted among the East Saxons became almost or quite extinct.

The exiled Bishop Mellitus and Justus, Bishop of Rochester, so much despaired of the situation that they fled overseas into France, lest worse things might befall them. Laurentius of Canterbury, so Bede's story runs, would have followed them, if he had not been reproved and chastened by St. Peter in a dream. He resolved to remain, and shortly afterwards things began somewhat to mend. King Eadbald was visited with a succession of temporary fits of insanity, which his uneasy conscience ascribed to his rejection of Christianity and its laws. He put away his wife, abjured the worship of idols, and sought peace with the archbishop, by whom he was shortly afterwards baptised Justus was recalled to his bishopric of Rochester, and the church of Kent began once more to flourish.

But Eadbald did not possess his father's authority over the other kingdoms, and twenty-five years after Augustine's first coming, Christianity was officially recognised in Kent alone. Laurentius died in 619, and was followed in succession at Canterbury by Mellitus (619-24) and Justus (624-27), both elderly men who had worked under St. Augustine. The spread of the new faith seems to have made no progress during their short archiepiscopates. But their successor, Honorius (627-53) was destined to see times of better omen and greater prosperity.

The new advance was due to a political change, which once more placed a convert zealous for the new faith at the head of the English kingdoms. Raedwald of East Anglia died within a year after his great victory over Aethelfrith of Northumbria, and since his son Eorpwald was a man of no mark, the short predominance which he had won for his state passed away, never to return. The most able and enterprising of the surviving princes of England was that Edwin of Deira whom Raedwald had restored to the throne of his fathers, after the destruction of Aethelfrith.

In the course of a few years he asserted over the rest of the English states that same sort of loose *suzerainty* which Aethelbert and Raedwald had enjoyed before him. We have no details of his earlier wars, but it is certain that before 626 he had reduced the Mercians and East Angles to homage, and was about to assail Cynegils and Cwichelm the joint kings (father and son) of Wessex. Nor was it the English alone who felt his sword: he had taken up the task which had been begun by his predecessor and enemy, Aethelfrith, of harrying the Britons of the North and West. He annexed the little Celtic State of Elmet or Loidis, in the Yorkshire West Riding, which had probably already been made tributary by Aethelfrith, and expelled its king Cerdic. It is quite possible that other expeditions of Edwin against the less remote British States may belong to his earlier years, though, if we accept Bede's rather vaguely worded narrative of his conquests, we must place them all in the time after 626.

It is certain, however, that the period of his greatest activity and power was after his conversion to Christianity. How this came to pass is narrated at great length in Bede's *Ecclesiastical History*. Edwin having lost his first wife made overtures to King Eadbald of Kent, to ask for the hand of his sister, Aethelberga. From the apolitical point of view, the match offered many attractions to Eadbald, since it would ally him to the most powerful monarch in England. But he doubted whether he ought to give a Christian princess in marriage to a heathen. The Northumbrian, however, promised that his wife should be allowed to keep her own faith, and to bring with her priests, along with any other retinue that she might desire. This concession settled the matter, and Aethelberga was accompanied to the North by one Paulinus, who was to act as her chaplain. In the hope that much might come of his mission. Archbishop Justus ordained him a bishop before his departure (July, 625).

Paulinus was a man of tact as well as of zeal, and while labouring among the queen's court found means to commend himself to the king. Edwin cannot have been wholly ignorant of Christianity, since, during his years of exile, he had spent a certain time at the court of Cadvan, King of North Wales. He was apparently already well disposed to listen to the missionary, when a narrow escape from death brought his hesitation to a crisis. On Easter Day, 626, he received an ambassador from Owichelm, King of Wessex, whom he was apparently threatening with war. The envoy, one Eumcr, was a desperate and devoted follower of Owichelm, who had suborned him to assassinate Edwin. When received in state by the Northumbrian king, Eumer, while pretending to deliver his message, suddenly drew a dagger and dashed at Edwin, who would have perished if a faithful thegn, named Lilla, had not thrown himself between them and received the thrust.

"Yet the wretch struck home so fiercely that he wounded the king through his retainer's body." (Bede, *E. H., ii.*)

He was then cut down, fighting so hard that he slew another thegn ere he was finally despatched.

On the same night Aethelberga bore to Edwin her first-born child, a daughter. The king at first gave thanks to his own idols, but afterwards listened to Paulinus, when he assured him that his own and his queen's happy deliverance were both the results of Christian prayers. He vowed that if the god of Aethelberga would grant him that his wound might heal, and that he might take vengeance on Cwichelm, he would accept the new faith. And as a pledge of his promise he allowed Paulinus to baptise his little daughter, whom he consecrated to Christ. This child, Eanflaed, was afterwards destined to wed King Oswiu, and to be the ancestress of the second Northumbrian royal house.

When healed of his wound Edwin conducted a furious campaign against the two kings of Wessex, whose land he devastated till they craved his pardon and did him homage. That he did not pursue them to the death was perhaps the first mark of Christian pity in his heart. On returning victorious to his own land he informed Paulinus that he would redeem his word, but that he must first confer with the council of his wise men, and hear their opinions. The narrative of the proceedings of this meeting, as given by Bede, gives clear proof of the weakness of English heathenism. The outworn creed had come to be despised by its votaries, because it did not satisfy their moral aspirations, or their sense of divine justice, or their desire for knowledge of the other world. One old councillor said:

> The soul of man, is like a sparrow, which on a dark and rainy night passes for a moment through the door of a king's hall: entering, it is for the minute surrounded by light and warmth and safe from the wintry storm; but after a short spell of brightness and quiet, it vanishes through another door into the dark storm from whence it came. The life of man is a moment visible; but what goes before, or what comes after, we know not. And if this new doctrine can tell us something about these mysteries, by all means let us follow it.

Less poetic in imagery and less noble in thought, but more practical in its appeal to common-sense, was the curious speech of the pagan high-priest, Coifi, which has already been alluded to in an earlier paragraph. The ancient gods, he said, have no care for those who have served them most faithfully. Their loyal worshippers fare no better than other men. He had himself been for a whole lifetime their most diligent servant, but had won neither special favour from his king nor worldly prosperity. The more carefully that he sought for truth in his old religion the less did he find it.

> And I freely confess that in the new preaching I seem to find the truth I sought, when it promises us the gifts of life, salvation, and eternal bliss. Wherefore I advise, O king, that we abjure and give to the flames those temples and altars which we have hallowed without receiving any fruit from them.

In short, the whole witan gave an active or passive assent to the king's wishes, and Coifi the priest himself took the lead in destroying the great temple at Godmundingham, the chief sanctuary of Deira, which lay not far from York to the east, beyond the River Derwent. The king, with many of his nobles and a countless multitude of the commons, was baptised on the following Easter Day, and the oratory which was built for him became the first church of York, and the cathedral of Paulinus, who assumed his episcopal title from that town, as Gregory had ordained in his letter to Augustine a quarter of a century before.

So great was the fervour of the first conversion that Paulinus is recorded to have spent thirty-six continuous days at Adgefrin (Yeavering, near Wooler) in baptising in the river Glen the multitudes of Bernicians who flocked to him, desirous of admission to the king's new faith. Among the Deirans also the conversions were very numerous; tradition records similar great baptismal gatherings at Catterick (the old Roman Cataractonium) on the Swale.

Edwin was anxious that his vassal kings should join him in casting away heathenism, and his efforts were very successful. Eorpwald, King of East Anglia, the son of his old benefactor Raedwald, was the first to conform (628). He was murdered shortly afterwards by a pagan; but his cousin Sigebert, who finally succeeded to his throne, was a very zealous Christian. He had spent some years among the Franks across the Channel, where he had been baptised, and called in a bishop, Felix of Burgundy, whom he established at the port of Dunwich, which became the religious centre of East Anglia. There Felix taught and baptised with much success for seventeen years.

In the sub-kingdom of the Lindiswaras, south of the Humber, which seems at this moment to have been directly subject to Edwin, Paulinus himself made a long missionary tour. He set up a stone church in Lincoln city, and baptised there Blecca, who was its high-reeve (*praefectus*). The report of his good work made such an impression at Rome, that Pope Honorius raised him to the dignity of archbishop, and sent him a *pallium*, thus making him the equal of his own namesake, Honorius of Canterbury, to whom he sent the same gift shortly after.

While Edwin was aiding and forwarding these missions, he was at the same time extending his political power. The six years after his conversion appear to have abounded in offensive wars: the most striking of his expeditions was an attack by sea on Man and Anglesey—the last naval enterprise but one that is recorded on the part of any king of the Heptarchic period. He is said to have reduced them both to homage. (Bede, *E. H.*, *ii.*) The expedition against Anglesey seems to be connected with a general assault on North Wales; we are told in the Welsh chronicles that in 629 he besieged Cadwallon, King of Gwynedd, in the isle of Glannauc (*Annales Cambriae, sub anno 629*)—Priestholm, opposite Beaumaris—and there are some indications that Cadwallon was shortly afterwards an exile in Ireland. (See Rhys's *Celtic Britain*.)

If this were so, it would seem that Edwin drove him out, and set up for a time in his stead princes who were prepared to do homage to Northumbria. By this supposition we can best account for Bede's very clear and definite statement that:

> Edwin received under his dominion all the borders of Britain that were provinces of the English or of the Britons—a thing which no king had ever done before.

We may connect with this general expansion of his kingdom the building, or rebuilding, of his great castle on the rock, far to the north in Midlothian, the Edwinsburgh which was to be the nucleus of the future capital of Scotland. We have also to fit into his general policy a campaign in the south. The *Anglo-Saxon Chronicle* records under the year 628 that Penda, King of Mercia, who was at this time one of Edwin's vassals, fought with the West Saxon kings, Cwichelm and Cynegils, at Cirencester, and came to a treaty with them after the battle.

This seems to show that the two kings of Wessex had tried to re-assert themselves, after their discomfiture by Edwin in person before his baptism, but were defeated by the Mercian: the treaty probably involved the cession of the lordship over the Hwiccas of the Lower Severn Valley, which may have passed at this moment from Wessex to Mercia. At any rate, this is the last mention for many years of the appearance of any kings of the house of Cerdic in Gloucestershire.

To Edwin's last years, 630-33, we may refer the picture of the prosperity of Britain which Bede records.

> There was such perfect peace that, as was said in the proverb, a woman with her new-born babe might walk through the island, from sea to sea, without receiving any harm. Moreover, the king took such good care for the good of his people, that at every fountain by the highway he set up stakes, with brass cups chained to them, for the convenience of travellers. And no man would touch them save for their proper use, either for the dread that they had of Edwin or for the affection that they bore him. His dignity was so great that banners were borne before him, not only in battle, but when in time of peace he rode with his officers through town and countryside. And when he walked on foot through the streets of towns that sort of ensign which the Romans called *tufa* was in like manner carried before him.

Some have seen in this ceremonial a claim of Edwin to take up the old Roman dignity of the *dux Britanniarum*, or even of the emperor himself, which might be claimed, without too much presumption, by a monarch whose *suzerainty* was owned over every foot of land which had once formed part of the old province of Britain.

But Edwin's greatness was to have a disastrous end. Cadwallon of Gwynedd returned from Ireland and raised rebellion against him. He was joined by Penda of Mercia, the greatest of the English vassal kings, and one who was a staunch adherent of paganism. This prince was a man of marked character; he had succeeded to the Mercian throne at a very advanced age—he was fifty, we are told—in the year 626, but had from the first shown himself able, ruthless and ambitious. He had no scruple in joining with the Welsh, the old enemies of his nation, and in their company advanced towards York.

Edwin, apparently cut off from the succours of his other subject allies, gave him battle at Heathfield (Hatfield, near Doncaster), but was utterly defeated and killed, along with his eldest son Osfrid (Oct. 12th, 633). All his army was slain or scattered, the city of York fell into the hands of the victors, and for many weeks the whole of Deira was cruelly devastated. The Christian Cadwallon, we are told, showed himself a more pitiless enemy than the heathen Penda He aimed at nothing less than exterminating the whole nation of the Northumbrians, and his Welshmen spared neither women nor children, and took no captives. Indeed, he intended to make the whole land Celtic soil once more, and cared nothing that the tribe whom he was trying to extirpate were Christians.

Aethelberga, the wife of Edwin, fled to her native Kent, accompanied by his infant family and Archbishop Paulinus. Their two sons died young, but Edwin's daughter Eanflaed survived to wed his worthy successor, Oswiu. The Deirans rallied for a moment under Osric, the cousin of Edwin, and his nearest adult male relative; but the Bernicians called back from exile Eanfrid, the eldest son of Aethelfrith, and the representative of the house of Ida, which Edwin had driven out. Both Osric and Eanfrid reverted to paganism, though the one had conformed during his cousin's reign, and the other had been baptised by the Irish monks of Iona during his exile. Apparently, they judged that the conversion of Edwin had brought him ill luck, and that the Northumbrians would fight better against the Christian Cadwallon in the name of their old faith.

Indeed, the conduct of the Welsh king had estranged many new converts and led to a widespread reversion to paganism. Hardly one of Paulinus's missionaries had remained behind, when their leader fled, and Christianity seemed almost extinguished in the land. (Bede only mentions one, James the Deacon, of whom he has much to tell.) But the days of the two apostate kings were few and evil. Osric, at the head of his Deirans, beset Cadwallon as he lay encamped at York; but he was slain in a sally of the Welsh after a reign of only six months. Eanfrid that same autumn (634), after being defeated in battle, came with twelve of his thegns to offer homage to the conqueror, but Cadwallon refused to grant him grace, and ordered him to be beheaded.

The Bernicians, thereupon, saluted Oswald, the next brother of Eanfrid, as their king. This prince, unlike his predecessor, was a devout and zealous Christian; he rallied his countrymen for one more battle, and set up as his standard a great wooden cross, under which, on the banks of the Deniseburn, near Hexham, he gave battle to Cadwallon.

★★★★★★

The spot of victory was called the "Heavenfield" (*coelestis campus*) by the Northumbrians, Bede, iii. 2. The Deniseburn has been identified by mention in a Hexham charter: it runs into the Tyne south of the Roman Wall.

★★★★★★

He was completely victorious, though his army was a mere remnant, much outnumbered by the enemy. The Welsh king was slain, and with him perished the hope of the Celts that they might once more recover the north. Many reckoned him the last high-king of Britain, and dated the end of the Celtic supremacy at his death.

The victorious Oswald not only became undisputed monarch of all Northumbria, but claimed to succeed to Edwin's superiority over the other English kings. Bede reckons him the sixth who enjoyed "*imperium*" over the whole land. But there is surely exaggeration in this view of his position, for during the eight years that he reigned (634–42) he never succeeded in making an end of Penda of Mercia, though he may possibly have concluded a truce with him for a time. That ancient heathen, indeed, seems to have been very powerful during Oswald's earlier years, since we know that in 635, he fell upon East Anglia, and slew in battle its two kings, the pious Sigebert and his successor, Egrice.

Sigebert, we are told, had retired to a monastery after three years of reign, handing over his kingdom to Egrice, his cousin. But on the approach of Penda, his former subjects insisted that he should lead them to battle, though he refused to bear arms, and would carry no more than a wand, lest any man's blood should be upon his head. His prayers availed them nought, and both he and Egrice were slain.

Whatever may have been the case with Mercia, however, it is certain that Oswald exercised a certain supremacy over the West Saxons, for it is related that when the aged king, Cynegils, was baptised, Oswald was present at the ceremony, and confirmed the gift of the town of Dorchester-on-Thames to the Church, which the ruler of Wessex made as the first-fruits of his conversion. Since Wessex and Mercia were generally at war, it would have been very natural for Cynegils to seek the aid of Northumbria, though it could only be obtained by doing homage, or even by embracing Christianity.

The missionary who baptised the King of Wessex, and received Dorchester as his place of abode, was one Birinus, of whom we only know that he came to Britain by the advice of Pope Honorius, having vowed to work in some region where no other preacher had been before him: wherefore he went neither to Canterbury nor to York, but selected Wessex, as a virgin field. Whether he was an Italian or a Frank we do not know. He is recorded as a zealous teacher, and a consecrator of many churches, during his sixteen-years' episcopate. But his time was troublous, since not only was Wessex often wasted by war in his days, but Coenwalch, the younger son of Cynegils, had not been baptised with his father, and when he came to the throne (643) remained for some years a heathen, till he learnt Christianity, in the moment of defeat and exile, at the court of the pious Anna, King of the East Angles. On his restoration he took Birinus as his teacher, and when he died (650) placed at Dorchester in his stead a Frankish bishop named Agilberct.

The glimpse of Oswald's activity in the south fits in well with all that we know of his life. He was busy for the faith in every direction. But his inspiration came not from Rome, like that of Aethelbert and Edwin, but from Iona, where he seems to have assimilated the enthusiastic, ascetic, and emotional Christianity of the Irish monks. His main guide and helper was the Scot Aidan, who had come down to his aid, when the first bishop sent to him from Iona proved a stumbling-block to converts, on account of his tactless severity. Aidan won all hearts by his humility, sweetness, and lack of self-assertion; he was the most charitable of all men both in act and in thought, and found in the king a kindred spirit. Bede's touching story of their friendship is well worth quoting.

The Lenten fast was just over, and Oswald and Aidan were sitting together, about to commence their Easter feast, when the official charged with the king's alms came in to whisper that he had distributed all his resources, but that many starving poor were still waiting outside the royal gate. The king, without a moment's hesitation, sent out his untasted meat to be distributed among them, and then ordered the great silver dish which had stood before him to be cut up into pieces, and distributed among the most necessitous. Aidan, moved to tears, seized his master's right hand, and cried, "May this hand never perish!" Northumbrian tradition added that the saint's blessing took such effect that when Oswald's hand was lopped off, in the battle which brought him death a few years later, it remained incorruptible, and was preserved entire and unshrunken for centuries in the church of St. Peter at Bamborough. It may he noted that even Welsh tradition remembered the king as "Oswald Lamngwyn," "Oswald of the fair hand," in the days when the *Historia Brittonum* was compiled.

But Oswald's piety and zeal did not save him from the same fate which his predecessor Edwin had encountered. He fell in strife with Penda of Mercia, who was apparently once more leagued with the Welsh—for the site of the battle was Maserfelth, better known in later history as Oswestry (Oswald's tree) on the border of Powys, north-westward from Shrewsbury; and in the Welsh records the field bears the name of Cocboy. (The local traditions and dedications of Oswestry seem to corroborate the statements of the *Vita Oswaldi* as to the identification.)

It seems quite clear that such a spot can only have been the meeting-place of the armies if the Welsh were concerned in the matter; either Oswald must have been marching against the Welsh, and have found Penda already joined with them on their frontier, or he must have heard that they were about to concentrate, and have hurried forward to give them battle, before they should attack his own dominions by way of Cheshire and Lancashire. No ordinary struggle between Northumbria and Mercia could conceivably have been fought out at such a spot as Oswestry (Aug. 5, 642).

The Northumbrian king's death was in unison with his life; it is recorded that when he saw the battle lost, and the remains of his host surrounded, his last thoughts were for them, and not for himself, "Lord, have mercy on the souls of my army," were his dying words. The victory was apparently an expensive one to the Mercians, as we are told that Penda's brother Eowa, the ancestor of many later kings, fell there with countless others.

The first result of the disaster of Maserfelth was to break up the Northumbrian realm; the same result followed that had been seen after Edwin's fall at Heathfield. The Deirans, once more reverting to the house of Aella, took as their king, Oswin, the son of that Osric who had been slain by Cadwallon in 634. The Bernicians acknowledged Oswy (Oswin) the younger brother of Oswald as their lord. This state of things lasted for seven years, and while it endured Northumbria was powerless before King Penda. The situation, however, differed from that of 633-34, in that both the new kings were zealous Christians; there was no reversion to heathenism, and Aidan and his priests did not have to flee away, as Paulinus had done after Edwin's death, the Irish mission seems to have bitten more deep into Northumbria than that which had started from Kent. Bede, though deploring the fact that Aidan was in communion with the schismatic Church of the West, and not with Rome, cannot find terms sufficiently high to praise his character and his influence.

For thirteen years after his victory over Oswald, Penda of Mercia seems to have enjoyed as great a pre-eminence over all the other kingdoms as Aethelbert or Edwin had ever possessed, yet he is not reckoned in the list of kings who owned the *imperium* by Bede, perhaps because he was a heathen and an enemy of those Christian kings whom the historian so much admired. But the recital of his acts shows that his power extended into every corner of England. He repeatedly harried all Northumbria, as far as Bamborough, whose walls were only delivered from his assault, according to tradition, by the prayers of Bishop Aidan. He fell upon his old enemies of Wessex, over whom Coenwalch, the son of Cynegils, was now reigning (645), and drove the king out of this realm, setting up in his stead petty chiefs who became his vassals.

The East Anglians suffered equally at his hands; he descended upon them in 654, and slew in battle their king Anna, the third Christian prince of the house of Wuffa who perished at his hands. Aethelhere, the brother of Anna, was compelled to become his vassal and tributary. It seems probable that Oswy also must have made submission to him during some part of the early years of his reign. For thus only can we understand the fact that the Mercian king's daughter Cyneburh was wedded to Oswy's son, Alchfrid, while Peada, Penda's eldest son, took to wife, Alchflaed, daughter of Oswy. This double marriage must have marked a temporary peace between the Christian and the heathen princes, which can hardly have come about on any other terms than that the former should do homage to the latter.

It is noteworthy that Penda's political supremacy by no means put an end to the rapid spread of Christianity during the middle years of the seventh century. He himself was so far from being a persecutor that he made no objection when his son Peada was baptised, under the persuasion of his Bernician bride. He was wont to say that he despised not Christians but bad Christians, and, though he rejected the new faith himself, did not count all its adherents as his necessary enemies. The final and definite conversion of several of the English kingdoms falls into his day of supremacy.

Coenwalch, King of Wessex, when he won back his kingdom, in 648, after three years of exile, openly adhered to Christianity, though he had rejected it in the day of his father Cynegils. He brought over the seas a Frankish bishop named Agilberct, whom he installed in the See of Dorchester, which his father had created, and afterwards set up another bishop of Saxon birth, named Wini, at Winchester. Essex, where the Church seemed to have been extinguished by the expulsion of Mellitus in 617, and where several heathen kings had reigned since the death of the pious Saebert, was won back to Christianity in the reign of Sigebert the Good (650-60), who was converted by the personal influence of Oswy, whom he used—as we are told—often to visit in Northumbria, presumably to concert common political action against Penda.

He brought back with him to London, as his bishop, Cedd, a brother of the better known St. Chad, who was consecrated by Oswy's bishops of the Irish line (653). Of Sigebert the curious tale is told that he was ultimately murdered by two nobles of his own kindred:

> Who being asked why they slew him, had nothing better to answer than that they hated him, because he was too apt to spare his enemies, and easily to forgive the wrongs that had been done him. (Bede, iii.)

Christian ethics did not appeal at once to all the English; it is indeed marvellous that they took so strong and early a grip upon the majority of them.

It will be noted that more than one of the bishops named above was of English blood. The surest sign of the firm establishment of the Church was that it had become possible to fill its higher ranks with well-trained and learned native priests. The first bishop of English parentage was Ithamar, consecrated to Rochester in 644, a Kentishman; the second, Thomas, a Gyrwa by birth, bishop of the East Angles in 647; the third, Cedd, already named; after that year native bishops became the rule and not the exception, and Canterbury, the highest

See of all, received in 655 its first archbishop born within the isle, Fri-
thonas, or Deusdedit as he renamed himself, a South Saxon. Between
him and the first Norman archbishop in the eleventh century, Robert
of Jumiéges, there was only one primate who was not an Englishman.
(Odo, Edmund's archbishop, was however an Anglo-Dane.)

This, however, was one of the greatest of all the archbishops, that
Theodore of Tarsus (668-90) of whom we shall have much to tell
hereafter. Whether trained in the school which St. Augustine had
started at Canterbury, or in the monasteries of the Scots, the early native bishops of the seventh century seem to have kept a high level of
life, and to have been most worthy pastors of the new Church. There
is only one of them, Wini of Winchester, of whom any evil is told; he
is said to have lapsed into the sin of simony, by purchasing for money
the See of London from King Wulfhere. (Bede, iii.)

This happened, however, some years after the date which we have
reached—the time when Penda was exercising his domination over
most of the English kingdoms. That hegemony probably extended
over the Britons of Wales also, since we find that Welsh princes are
named among his auxiliaries; But whether Cadwallader, the son of
Cadwallon, and the rest, marched as the allies or the vassals of Penda,
it is not possible to determine with certainty. Oswy's first endeavours
to maintain his independence from the Mercian were certainly unsuccessful. In 651 he slew Oswin of Deira, under circumstances that
reflected no great credit on himself, but he did not thereby succeed in
uniting Southern Northumbria to his own Bernician realm.

******

Oswy, we are told (Bede, iii. 23), invaded Deira in such force
that Oswin dared not face him, but disbanded his army and hid
himself. He was betrayed to his rival by a treacherous host, and
promptly put to death. This was considered the sole blot on
Oswy's otherwise blameless reign.

******

The Deirans chose as Oswin's successor Aethelwald, son of St. Oswald, and refused to submit to Oswy. The new king called in Penda,
and by doing homage to him preserved himself from his uncle Oswy.

What was the cause of the last war between the Mercian and the
Bernician kings we do not know, but possibly Penda resented Oswy's
religious dealings with Essex and his other southern vassal states, and
detected a political meaning beneath them. At any rate, in 655 he
marched against Bernicia at the head of all his auxiliaries, English and

Welsh—thirty kings or kinglets are said to have been seen in his host. Their strength was so overwhelming that Oswy fled to the far North, took refuge in the insular castle of Giudi or Judeu, on the Firth of Forth, and sent his royal treasure as a peace-offering to the invader, a sum so great that it was remembered in Welsh legend as "the ransom of Judeu". But Penda refused to accept it, saying that he had come to make an end of Oswy and his men, not to take tribute. (So, Bede, iii. 24; but the *Historia Brittonum*, cap. 65, says that Penda took the treasure, distributed it among his auxiliaries, and went on nevertheless to fight.)

Whereupon the Bernician vowed that if the pagan would not accept his gift, it should be offered to one who would accept it, the God of battles. He marched out to fight, with his son Alchfrid, at the head of an army which did not amount to one-third of the forces of the confederacy opposed to him, and met Penda on the banks of the River Winwaed, whose identification is not quite certain.

★★★★★★

If Giudi or Judeu is the castle on the Firth of which Bede speaks elsewhere (i. 12)—Inchkeith, or less probably Dunbar or Edinburgh—it is very strange that the battle should have taken place at Winwedfield, near Leeds, the place usually identified with the Winwaed. We should have expected it to be within the bounds of Bernicia, and probably very far north, on the Tweed or in Lothian. Yet Bede says that Oswy "concluded the war in *regione Loidis*," which seems to bring us to Leeds. Possibly, when his overtures were rejected, he took the offensive in despair, and advanced into Deira to meet Penda and his auxiliaries.

★★★★★★

There was division and treachery, however, in the Mercian host. Catgabail, one of the Welsh kings, withdrew his contingent in the darkness of the night before the meeting, "whence he was afterwards called Catgabail Catguonmed" (battle-eager battle-shunner), (*Historia Brittonum*), and Aethelwald of Deira drew apart, and did not engage at the moment of the general advance. Evidently Penda's auxiliaries, Welsh and English, had endured his domination long enough, and had little heart for the fray. This may account for his unexpected defeat; he fell himself in the forefront of the battle, and with him Aethelhere, King of East Anglia, and many Welsh princes. So ended this vigorous and warlike old heathen, who is said to have been nearly eighty years of age when he died the warrior's death.

He is often treated as a mere hindering force in the evolution of

English history; but this seems a misconception. It is useless to assert that he prevented Northumbria under Edwin and Oswald from establishing a permanent hegemony over all the English states. The same chance was given to the northern realm under their successor Oswy, and after initial successes, as notable as those of the two earlier kings, he failed in the task, just as they had done, though no Penda opposed or slew him. The fact was that the English states were not yet ripe for close union. But Penda accomplished something positive, in that he at least built up a larger Mercia, as a permanent unit which survived him. The attempts of Oswy and other kings to break it up, and resolve it into its former component parts, failed, because a cohesion had been created which defied the destroyer. This cohesion was undoubtedly the result of the quarter of a century of victorious campaigns fought out in company, to which Penda had led his subjects.

For a few years after the battle of the Winwaed Oswy was supreme in England. He re-annexed Deira to Bernicia, (what became of Aethelwald, last separate King of Deira, we do not know), and added also to his immediate dominions not only the lands of the Lindiswaras about Lincoln, but North Mercia—the region north of Trent in the modern Derbyshire and Nottinghamshire. To his son-in-law Peada, the Christian son of Penda, he left Southern Mercia, south of Trent; but when this pious prince was murdered—by domestic treachery it is said—in 656, it would seem that Oswy annexed this remnant of the original Mercian realm, and held it for three years.

He must at the same time have been enjoying a *suzerainty* over all Eastern England: Sigebert of Essex was certainly his vassal, and no doubt also Aethelwald of East Anglia, who had succeeded Penda's friend Aethelhere, who fell with his master at Winwaed field.

Nor is there any reason to suppose that Coenwalch of Wessex, an old enemy of Mercia, refused his homage. Indeed, the wars of this prince against the West Welsh of Damnonia, which cover a period that begins before Penda's fall and ends long after it, may be closely connected with an alliance with Oswy, since all the Welsh were certainly Penda's allies. In 652 Coenwalch fights at Bradford-on-Avon; in 658 "at the Pens" (*aet Peonnum*), *i.e.*, at Pen-Selwood, in the same direction, on the borders of Wilts and Somerset.

The second battle must have been a considerable victory, as we are told that the Britons were driven beyond the Parret (Pedrida). Yet it does not seem that the borders of Wessex were extended to that limit, the conquest of Mid-Somersetshire being reserved for one of Coenwalch's successors. The kingdom does not seem to have made much permanent or considerable growth westward between the conquests of Ceawlin and those of Ine.

There is much greater difficulty in making out the political condition of the country north-west of Wessex in Oswy's day. We have seen that the land of the Hwiccas, on the Lower Severn, was probably taken from King Cynegils and annexed by Penda in 628, after the battle of Cirencester. What was its fate when that great king fell and his realm was broken up? We have no definite statement on the point in Bede or elsewhere; but we find *reges*, or *subreguli*, of the Hwiccas starting at a date not later, and probably somewhat earlier, than 661. They have purely Northumbrian names—Eanfrith, Eanhere, Osric, Oswald, Oshere, Aethelric—a fact which makes it highly probable that Oswy set up a younger branch of his own house in Hwiccia in 655, which was sufficiently well established there to survive the ultimate extinction of his power as overlord in Central England.

This cutting short of the Northumbrian supremacy began in the year 659, with the rebellion of the Mercians, under Wulfhere, a younger son of Penda, who had lived in exile or obscurity till this moment. He is said to have been proclaimed king by the three *duces* (ealdormen) of the Mercians—Immin, Eafa and Eadbert—and to have recovered all his father's dominions, even as far as the Humber, for Lindsey was certainly in his power a little later. His reign of seventeen years seems to have been occupied in a long war with Oswy, who strove strenuously, but without success, to maintain or recover his grasp on the Midlands.

But so far was he from success that Wulfhere not only reconstituted the old Mercian realm, but won a supremacy over all the minor kings of the South and the East. He is found in 665-66 not only recognised as *suzerain* by the rulers of Essex, but actually appointing a Bishop of London without their consent being asked. As to Wessex, he wrought terrible havoc upon it, and did his best to destroy its unity. Aethelwalch of Sussex, the remotest of all the Saxon kingdoms, is recorded as his vassal a few years later.

The strife between Mercia and Wessex is said in the *Chronicle* to have begun in 661, two years after Wulfhere's accession. The young king began the campaign by defeating Coenwalch at Posentesbyrig, which seems to be Pontesbury in Shropshire, not far south of Shrewsbury. The locality of the battle seems to suggest that Coenwalch must have been advancing, in company with Eanfrith, the King of the Hwiccas, to execute a diversion in favour of their ally or *suzerain*

Oswy. For unless the host of Wessex had advanced across Hwiccia, it could not have reached the neighbourhood of Shrewsbury.

The defeat must have been complete, as Wulfhere is found immediately after devastating Ashdown, the ancient name for the region of West Berkshire. A nephew and a cousin of Coenwalch are recorded by the *Chronicle* to have died at this conjuncture, perhaps slain in opposing the invader. But the advance of the Mercian army was not stayed; in the same year, 661, it is recorded that Wulfhere laid everything waste as far as the shore of the Channel.

He then, to cut short the power of Wessex, made a present of the Jutish land of the Meonwaras, on both sides of Southampton Water, to Aethelwalch, King of Sussex, who was his vassal and godson. This region must have been, since Ceawlin's time at least, attached by direct or indirect subjection to Wessex. At the same time, Wulfhere made Aethelwalch *suzerain* over the *subregulus* of the Wight, where the Jutish royal house was still subsisting. (See *Chronicle, sub anno* 661, and Bede, iv. 13. Bede's "not long before 681" seems to mean twenty years.)

This blow at Wessex was followed by a depression of the power of the house of Cerdic that lasted for a whole generation; it was not for twenty-five years that the lost land on Southampton Water was recovered. Apparently, the West Welsh of Damnonia were encouraged to make strenuous attempts to win back what they had lost; in 667 we hear of a second Battle of Mount Badon, between Coenwalch and the Britons, and fighting at Bath implies that the Celts were in Saxon territory.

★★★★★★

The second Battle of the Mons Badonicus is only recorded in the *Annales Cambriae*. It is placed under 665, but the *Annales* are one or two years in arrears at this time, as is shown by the fact that they place the Great Comet of 678 under 676, and the plague of 684 under 682. The death of Oswy in 670 is put to 669, one year wrong only.

★★★★★★

Nor was this all; when Coenwalch died in 672 his realm seems to have lapsed into anarchy. The *Chronicle* tells us that Seaxburh, his widow, reigned for one year after his death. Such an event, unparalleled among the old English dynasties, seems only explicable on the idea that she must have ruled as regent for an infant son whose name has perished. Bede, on the other hand, says that on Coenwalch's decease the *subreguli* of Wessex "took upon themselves the kingdom, and dividing it among them held it for ten years." (Bede, *E. H., iv.*) We have during this period a mention of two kings—Centwine, brother of Coenwalch, and Aescwin, his distant cousin, a representative of the house of Ceolwulf—who may have been either rivals or else two royal ealdormen, who in a time of general confusion successively took upon themselves the kingly title.

It is impossible to reject Bede's distinct statement that Wessex reverted for ten years to a state of divided rule, recalling the earlier anarchy that seems to have prevailed after Ceawlin's fall in 591. Possibly Wulfhere supported one claimant against the others: at any rate the *Chronicle* relates that he fought with Aescwin in 675 at "Biedanheafde" (a spot that cannot be identified), and apparently defeated him. Obviously, it would be to the Mercians' interest to keep Wessex weak and divided. A few years later (682) we hear of Centwine fighting with Britons, and driving them "to the sea": presumably this implies that the Damnonians had again taken advantage of the weakness of Wessex in order to invade it, but were driven back to the shores of the Bristol Channel. Certainly, no advance of the Saxon border is implied, as some historians seem to have inferred. This was a time of chaos, not of growth.

The last eleven years of Oswy (659-70), after the rise of Wulfhere, must have been a time of diminished power for Northumbria, but it does not appear that its internal strength and prosperity had much suffered. Oswy seems still to have been considered the greatest king in Britain, even though he was no longer its undisputed master. There is no sign that his realm suffered, like Wessex, from Mercian invasions. Allied to Earconbert of Kent, and to Coenwalch of Wessex and his successors, he was strong enough to keep Wulfhere in check, though not to subdue him. The most important event of his later years had nothing to do with battles or with secular politics, yet was of the highest moment for the future history of England. This was the celebrated Synod of Whitby (664), at which he and the whole Northumbrian nation abandoned their connection with the Church of Iona, and put themselves into communion with Canterbury and Rome.

Oswald and Oswy, as will be remembered, had been themselves converted and baptised at Iona, and had brought down with them to Northumbria, when they became kings, Aidan and Finan, the Scottish preachers to whom the second and effectual evangelisation of Bernicia and Deira was due. The survivors from Edwin's earlier Roman mission were few. What Bede calls "the episcopacy of the Scots among the English" lasted for thirty years, and Oswy "having been instructed and baptised by them, and being perfectly skilled in their language, thought nothing better than what they taught." In his old age, however, he fell under other influences; his wife, Eanflaed, the daughter of Edwin, had been reared in Kent, and steadfastly adhered to the Church in which she had been brought up: and his son, Alchfrid, whom he had made under-king in Deira, was of the same persuasion, owing to the teaching, as we are told, of Wilfred, Abbot of Ripon, who had been trained at Lyons and Rome, and held the Scots in contempt.

The queen and prince had sufficient influence with Oswy to induce him to put aside his predisposition in favour of his original teachers, and to undertake a serious inquiry into the relations of the Irish and the Roman Churches. He was, as we are told, a sincerely religious man, and had long been vexed by the continuous friction caused by the divergent views of the two bodies of mission workers, both of whom he readily supported. For he was on friendly terms with the East Anglian and West Saxon kings and bishops, who held to the Roman allegiance, though his own clergy in Northumbria, and the teachers whom he had sent out into Mercia and Essex, were of the other confession. At his own court the absurd sight of two Easters kept in continuous weeks was sometimes to be seen:

> For on the day when the king, having ended his fasting, was keeping the Paschal Feast, the queen and her retainers would be still fasting, and celebrating Palm Sunday. (Bede, *E. H., iii.*)

It is quite possible that Oswy had already made up his mind to conform to the ceremonial and accept the *suzerainty* of Rome, in order to secure unity for the English Church, before he summoned the Synod of Whitby. But he allowed a prolonged discussion of the points at issue before he declared his decision. On the one side appeared his own bishop, Colman the Scot, and Cedd, who had been consecrated in Northumbria bishop of the East Saxons, with many of their clergy. On the other, was Wilfred, Abbot of Ripon; Agilberct, Bishop of the West Saxons, who chanced to be on the spot as a visitor; James, the last survivor from Paulinus's mission, and several others. The discussion was of a polyglot sort, for neither Agilberct nor Colman had a mastery of the English tongue, and Cedd had to act as interpreter.

The main topic over which the arguments ranged was, according to Bede, the usual point in dispute between Rome and the Western Churches—the much-vexed question of Easter, though no doubt the tonsure and the other minor divergencies had their place. Colman is said to have claimed for the Irish and British usage an immemorial antiquity, derived originally from the practice of St. John the Evangelist, and hallowed by the sanction of Columba and other saints. Wilfred, who spoke for the other side, quoted the authority of the Council of Nicaea, and contrasted the dignity and learning of the Apostolic See and the Continental Churches with the "rustic simplicity" of a small community in a remote island, which lacked the culture needed to understand the new calculations which had been adopted everywhere else. Rome was greater than Iona, Peter than Columba, and Wilfred concluded by quoting the oft misused text—

> Thou art Peter, and upon this rock I will build My Church, and the gates of hell shall not prevail against it, and to thee I will give the keys of the kingdom of heaven. (Bede, *E. H., iii.*)

Oswy, we are told, found a way to end the discussion by asking Colman whether the text was correctly quoted, and when the Scot owned that it so ran, declared that "if the keys of heaven are given to Peter, and he is the door keeper, I will not oppose him, but obey his decrees, lest when I come to the gate of heaven there be none to open to me, the guardian of the keys being my adversary The king's words are not to be taken literally, or counted a mark of naive superstition and barbarous cunning, but were rather a humorous way of putting the fact that the authority of the whole Western Church weighed heavier than that of the Celtic remnant in the far West. He closed the controversy by announcing that he should conform to the Roman usage, and place himself in communication with the Church of Rome.

Cedd, and the majority of the English priests of Northumbria, followed the example of the king, and conformed. But Colman, with his Scottish clerks, shook the dust of England from their feet, and retired to Iona. Oswy replaced him by one Tuda, "a good and religious man, who, though educated and ordained bishop among the Scots, yet kept the Catholic time of Easter."

Thus, ended the chance that Teutonic Britain might be permanently divided into two Churches, the one in communion with Rome, the other with the Celtic peoples of the West. Nor can it be doubted that Oswy's decision was in every way beneficial to the English. The connection with the Papacy was fraught with dangers and difficulties in the future; before the next generation was over the first of those innumerable appeals to Rome, which were to cause so much trouble throughout the Middle Ages, had been made. But for the present the advantages of the decision made at Whitby were clear and decisive. It was more profitable for the infant Church of England to be in touch with the bulk of Western Christendom than with the Scots alone, if it was to be an active and useful limb of the great Christian community. The Celtic Church produced many great saints and many devoted missionaries, but it was always lacking in order and organisation.

Fervour and ascetic self-sacrifice are essential virtues for those who have to build up a Church, but for those who have to administer a Church already solidly constituted, tact, practical wisdom, and a broad charity of spirit are also necessary. The Celtic Church put before it as its highest aim the extension of the monastic ideal, as is sufficiently shown by the fact that the great tribal monastery was the centre of religious life, while the bishop was a comparatively unimportant personage, inferior to the abbot in status, and only necessary because he alone could make priests or consecrate sacred edifices.

But all mankind, even in the most ideally pious nation, could not be swept into monasteries. Nor is the perfection of the individual soul by ascetic rules the sole aim of Christianity. As an organisation for the spiritual government of a mixed community the Celtic system left much to be desired. Its influence for good was much diminished by its narrow ideal.

Most of all was it noticeable that it had no effect whatever as a unifying force for the nations among which it prevailed. The greatest blessing for Ireland would have been political consolidation, to put an end to its innumerable tribal wars. Absolutely nothing in this direction was accomplished by its Church; instead, the great monastery of each sept became a centre of its local particularism. Ireland, for want of a proper episcopal organisation, was from the ecclesiastical point of view a group of disconnected and independent monasteries. How invaluable, on the other hand, the Roman organisation proved to England as a unifying influence will be shown in the next chapter. It was in Church Synods that the representatives of the English kingdoms first learnt to take peaceful counsel together; a common obedience to the primate taught them in due time the reasonableness of a common obedience to a single high-king.

Almost the first historical notice that we get in England after the Council of Whitby marks a laudable common interest between North and South as to the state of the Church. Only a few months after its end a great pestilence swept over the island, in which died both Archbishop Deusdedit, the first native primate, and Earconbert. King of Kent, a very religious prince who showed his zeal for the faith by destroying the few surviving idol temples in his realm, and fining men who would not keep the Lenten fast. We are told (Bede, *E. H., iii.*) that the appointment of a successor for Deusdedit was a common concern to Oswy and to Ecgbert, the new King of Kent, and that "with the consent of the Holy Church of the English nation" (presumably after a Synod of some sort) they chose in common one Wighard for primate, and sent him to Rome, to receive consecration and the *pallium* from Pope Vitalian.

But the archbishop-designate died not long after he had delivered his credentials, a victim to a pestilence which raged in Italy no less than in England (665), and the Pope sent back in his stead the last and greatest of the foreign primates, the celebrated Theodore of Tarsus, who did not reach Canterbury for more than three years after his predecessor's death. Of him there is much to tell hereafter.

Oswy's later years are said to have been troubled by dissensions with his eldest son, Alchfrid, whom he had made under-king in Deira. But whether they came to open war, and whether Alchfrid died before his father, or was thrust into exile, we are not informed. It is only certain that when Oswy died, on February 15, 671, he was succeeded by his second son, Ecgfrith, and not by his natural heir. It would seem that we must connect with this strife between the old king and Alchfrid the beginnings of an ecclesiastical dispute, which was to vex Northumbria for many a year. Tuda having died in 664, Alchfrid designated as bishop his teacher and confidant, Wilfred, Abbot of Ripon, the successful controversialist of the Synod of Whitby, and sent him overseas to be consecrated by his old friend, Agilberct, once bishop of the West Saxons but now established at Paris.

Wilfred was duly ordained to the office, at Compiegne in a great meeting of Frankish prelates, but he tarried sometime before returning. Whereupon Oswy, either because he had now quarrelled with his son, or because he was irritated by Wilfred's long absence, nominated another bishop, Chad (Ceadda), the saintly brother of Cedd, the bishop of the East Saxons.

★★★★★★

Eddius, Wilfred's biographer, says that Oswy was worked upon by secret enemies of Wilfred, old allies of Colman, who told him that the Church would suffer from the unreasonably long absence of its designated pastor.

★★★★★★

This holy man was consecrated by Wini, the bishop of Coenwalch of Wessex, assisted by two Celtic prelates who had conformed to the Roman method of keeping Easter. (Presumably Damnonian bishops, certainly not Welsh.) Thus from 665 onward there were two rival bishops of Northumbria, but Chad was in possession, while Wilfred tarried at Canterbury, where he made himself useful by performing episcopal functions during the long vacancy of the See that fell between the death of Wighard and the arrival of Theodore of Tarsus.

Of Oswy's end we know no more than that, two years before his death, he was reconciled by Theodore of Tarsus to Wilfred, and allowed him to return to his See (669), while Chad, who showed wonderful humility of spirit, and refused to stand out for his own cause "judging himself never to have been worthy of the episcopal office," was compensated by being transferred to the bishopric of Mercia, then vacant. This transaction proves that Oswy and Wulfhere must at the moment have been at peace, for otherwise the southern king would never have allowed a Northumbrian prelate—however great his personal sanctity—to be thrust upon him.

The reconciliation of Oswy and Wilfred seems to have been complete, since we are told that in his last year of life the king determined to make a pilgrimage to Rome, and begged the bishop to accompany him. All arrangements had been made, and a large treasure spent, when Oswy's failing health prevented the expedition from starting, and not long after he died. He still seems to have been regarded as the most important king in Britain, though he had never recovered the lands beyond Humber, which Wulfhere had torn from him. On the other hand, we are told that he was still, when he died, supreme not only over Deira and Bernicia, but over a great part of the Picts. By this, Bede seems to mean not only the Niduarian Picts of Galloway, but some at least of the northern Picts beyond Forth.

The connection seems to have come from the marriage of Oswy's brother, Eanfrith, to a Pictish princess, in whose right "Tolargain Mac Anfrith," the Northumbrian king's nephew, reigned for some years over Pictland.

★★★★★★

It must be remembered that the Picts adhered to the ancient, but in these latter days abnormal, custom of preferring the female line of succession to the male in the kingship (Bede, *E. H., ii*). There does not seem in the whole series of Pictish kings to be a case of son following father; the succession would normally go to nephews on the female side.

******

On Tolargain's death in 657, Oswy seems to have asserted and maintained a domination over the lands immediately north of Forth, though another Pictish prince, Gartnaid, son of Donnel, reigned in the farther Highlands. A certain Bernhaeth, who appears as Ealdorman (*dux*) or *subregulus* about 670-72 was probably Oswy's lieutenant for the part of Pictland which he retained under his power. Along with this region there can be no doubt that Oswy was also supreme over the Welsh kingdom of Strathclyde—perhaps it was actually annexed to Bernicia, since no names of kings of Alclyde appear between 658 and 694, and we are distinctly told that Oswy and his son, Ecgfrith, owned Britons as well as Picts among their subjects. (Bede, iv.)

CHAPTER 5

The Balance of Power. Mercia, Northumbria and Wessex, (671–709)

At the moment of Oswy's death in 671 the future development of the English States was still a matter on which prophecy would have been difficult. It might, however, have been foreseen that a permanent domination of Northumbria over the southern kingdoms was improbable. The failure of Edwin and Oswald to hold the "*imperium*" which they had won counted for comparatively little; but that of Oswy, whose opportunities were greater than those of his predecessors—for all Mercia had been for three years crushed beneath his feet—was conclusive. The shattered Mercian realm had reunited itself under Wulfhere, despite of all difficulties, had reasserted its independence, and won back its border as far as the Humber. Nay more, it had established a *suzerainty* over Essex, Sussex and East Anglia, and had almost annihilated the ill-compacted West Saxon state, which had fallen into chaos and anarchy.

It looked as if the future was with Mercia, whose central position gave it a unique facility for dealing with its enemies in detail. Northumbria had no such geographical advantages, and the other States were too small and weak to vie with the realm of the house of Penda. Moreover, Mercia might still grow at the expense of the Welsh, a chance denied to all the other English states save Northumbria and Wessex. Indeed, it would seem that expansion in this direction was actually taking place in Wulfhere's reign.

In the third quarter of the seventh century we find a new district beyond Severn in the hands of the English, with a *subregulus* who was the vassal of Mercia, and (a little later) a bishop of its own. This was the land of the Magesaetas or Hecanas, which comprised the modern Herefordshire, with South Shropshire and the Forest of Dean. This annexation may have been made by Penda, but it is unlikely, as he was the ally of the Welsh, and had their aid in all his wars, from Heathfield down to the day of his death at the Winwaed. It was more probably the work of Wulfhere, whose brother, Merewald, is recorded to have been the first alderman or sub-king of the Hecanas, the founder of the abbey of Leominster, and the father of the two sainted nuns Mildred and Mildgyth.

★★★★★★

I see no reason to doubt the existence of Merewald, king of the "West Angles," West Mercians, or Hecanas, as he is called in various places. He is not named by Bede, but occurs in the Mercian genealogical table preserved by Florence of Worcester, and is mentioned as the husband of Eormenburh, daughter of Eormered, King of Kent, in the sketch of the Kentish royal house in the same author. But his best warrant is that he is always given as father of St. Mildred, a well-known saint whose convent was in the eighth century the glory of Thanet.

★★★★★★

This sub-kingdom of the Magesaetas was the last considerable patch of territory won from the Welsh of the Severn valley by the English. There were small modifications of the boundary in the eighth century in favour of Mercia, but no great addition was made. The extent of the district is indicated by that of the See of Hereford, whose first bishop died in 688; it included the land between Wye and Severn from the Bristol Channel northward, and at its northern extremity reached the Severn on each side of the Wrekin, though Mercia proper was reckoned to include some small portion of the land south of that river, in the immediate neighbourhood of Pengwyrn, the Welsh town which had changed its name to Shrewsbury (Scrobbesbyrig).

The western boundary of the Magesaetas did not quite reach the modern frontier of Wales and England, but was drawn at the edge of the foot-hills which bound the plain of Severn and Wye, leaving rough districts, like Clun Forest and Ewyas, still in the hands of the Celts. (So at least we may conclude from the boundary of the diocese of Hereford.)

It seems probable that the whole Mercian realm, as held by Wulfhere, consisted of the original nucleus on both sides of Trent with which Penda had started in 626, increased by the subject provinces of the Magesaetas, Hwiccas, Gyrwas and Lindiswaras, each governed by a local prince, whose status is indicated by the fact that his title fluctuates between *subregulus* and *dux, ie.,* between king and ealdorman. (The names of Lindiswara princes recorded in Florence of Worcester's genealogies suggest Northumbrian origin, like those of the Hwiccas.) It remains uncertain whether the West Saxon district north of Thames, the land of the Chilternsaetas, round Dorchester, Aylesbury and Eynsham, was in Wulfhere's hands. The deplorable state of Wessex at the time renders this highly probable. If so, it must have been lost again by Mercia at some subsequent date, since the kings of the house of Ceawlin were in possession of it again in the early eighth century. Surrey was certainly under Wulfhere's influence.

But great and powerful though Mercia was in the year 671, Northumbria was still strong enough to renew the struggle for supremacy, and, if the lands of its British and Pictish vassals north of Solway are taken into consideration, its whole empire was no less in extent than that of the southern kingdom. Ecgfrith, the son and successor of Oswy, seems to have resolved to take up the struggle in which his father had failed. After putting down, in the very commencement of his reign (671-72), a rising of the northern Picts, (this rebellion and the victory of Ecgfrith and his *subregulus* Bernhaeth are told in some detail in the *Life of Wilfred,* by Eddius), he turned three years later to attack Wulfhere, probably leaguing himself with Aescwin of Wessex, whose unsuccessful campaigns against the Mercians have been already narrated, and with Lothere of Kent. (*Bede, E. H., iv.*)

If his ally failed, Ecgfrith himself seems to have been more successful, as he recovered the province of the Lindiswaras, and held it from 675 (or perhaps a little earlier) till 679. We are even told by one almost contemporary writer that the Northumbrian expelled Wulfhere from his whole kingdom, a statement which can hardly be accepted.

★★★★★★

The war between Ecgfrith and Wulfhere must have commenced later than 673, since in that year the Northumbrian king was present at Archbishop Theodore's great Synod, which was held at Hertford. Clearly Ecgfrith could not have been at that spot if he were at war with Mercia, nor could a Synod at which bishops from all the states were present have been held in time of war.

★★★★★★

But it is certain that the Mercian king died in 675, the year of his last Battle of "Biadanheafod," and was succeeded by his younger brother Aethelred.

Apparently, this prince continued the war with Ecgfrith and his allies, for in 676, the year after his accession, we are told that he cruelly ravaged Kent, burning many monasteries and the cathedral and city of Rochester. (*A. S. Chronicle*, 676, and Bede, *E. H., iii.*) But the struggle did not come to a head till a great pitched battle was fought on the Trent in 679. It was evidently a victory for the Mercians, "since a story told by Bede shows us that Aethelred's army had possession of the battlefield, and Aelfwin, Ecgfrith's brother, is recorded to have been slain. (*E. H., iv.* 22. A Northumbrian noble, left for dead on the field, is captured by Aethelred's soldiers and sold as a slave.) But the Northumbrians if beaten were not disheartened, "and there wets every reason to expect more bloody war, and a more lasting enmity between those kings and their fierce nations".

Peace, however, was unexpectedly brought about by the mediation of Archbishop Theodore, who was equally respected by both parties. The Mercians paid a heavy *weregeld* for Aelfwin's death, but Ecgfrith, on the other hand, surrendered the province of Lindsey, so that the balance of profit was on the side of Aethelred. The treaty seems to have included Ecgfrith's allies of Kent and Wessex, "and peace continued long after between the kings and their kingdoms". (Bede, iv., xxi). Indeed, it was to be thirty-five years before we have another record of war between the two chief powers, Mercia and Northumbria——an interval unparalleled since the first strife between the greater English States began, in the time of Edwin and Penda, and not to be repeated again in their later history.

During this long time, we shall find Northumbria entirely occupied with northern wars against the Celts, and Wessex striving both with the Damnonians and with her smaller Teutonic neighbours, Kent and Sussex. But as far as we can judge, a real balance of power had been created, and no king disturbed it by grasping at the "*imperium*" which Edwin or Penda, Oswy or Wulfhere, had exercised over his neighbours.

Into the earlier part of this long peaceful interval fell the major part of the activity of the great primate Theodore of Tarsus (669-90), though, as we have already seen, he had been busy at his work of organisation ever since he arrived in England. To the same period belongs the chequered career of the Northumbrian prelate Wilfred, whose grievances and triumphs fill such a disproportionate space in Bede's history, and are set forth at even greater length by his biographer Eddius.

Theodore, whose career was far more important than that of Wilfred, deserves a careful study. He had been, as it will be remembered, nominated to the primacy by Pope Vitalian in 668, after the death at Rome of the archbishop-designate Wighard. He was a Cilician by birth, and a monk by training: apparently, he had been driven westward, with many other refugees, by the first irruptions of the Saracens into his native district. It seems that Vitalian selected him for a difficult post, which had already been refused by two other notable men, because of his unusual combination of learning, saintliness of life, and practical wisdom. The one doubt as to the wisdom of the appointment was caused by his age—he had reached his sixty-sixth year; but his vigour was unbroken, as was sufficiently shown by the fact that he survived his appointment by twenty-two years, most of which were spent in active and trying work.

Theodore was ordained in 668, and sent off in company with the Abbot Hadrian, an African monk excellently skilled in Greek as well as in Latin literature, who was his helper throughout the whole of his career. It was to the fact that the archbishop was a Greek by birth, and the abbot a Greek scholar, that Canterbury became and remained for some generations a centre of Greek learning, and that the Hellenic tongue was well known in England when it was almost unknown in the other Western Kingdoms. (Bede, *E. H., v.*) Their arrival in England was, however, delayed by the suspicions of Ebroin, the Frankish mayor of the palace, who feared—as we read with some surprise—that Theodore, since he was a Greek, might be acting as an emissary of the Emperor Constans II., and designing to stir up the Kings of England to attack the Merovingian realm for some obscure Byzantine object.

★★★★★★

The idea was not so strange as it seems at first sight. In 668 Constans was in Sicily, and deeply interested in West European politics. He had lately been to Rome, which had not been visited by any emperor since Romulus Augustulus, and was altogether an abnormal and disturbing influence in the West.

★★★★★★

After a long detention in Gaul the archbishop only reached Canterbury in 669.

The work of Theodore's long and green old-age was the organisation of the English Church on a permanent and well-ordered basis. Hitherto it retained something of its original missionary character, though all England was now converted, save the insignificant kingdom of Sussex, and the Jutes of the Isle of Wight, whose remoteness and obscurity was still keeping them out of the movement which had swept over the rest of the island. Even in this last dark corner there were Christian kings and Christian teachers, though the bulk of the people still clung to the old faith.

Down to the arrival of Theodore the English States had (with the exception of Kent) possessed but a single bishop each, and he in all cases retained something of his original status as the kings chaplain: the Sees were generally established in the royal cities, and the bishop was very often at his master's side. Churches in the countryside were comparatively few. The bishop's priests seem to have habitually lived near him, and to have gone out in summer for long tours to baptise and to preach. The piety of wealthy laymen generally took shape in the founding of a monastery, rather than in the establishment of anything like a localised parochial system. Indeed there would seem to have been a great lack of priests in the countryside, the majority of persons who felt a vocation for holy orders preferring to enter a religious community.

Immense districts like Wessex, Northumbria or Mercia could not be adequately served by a single bishop, whose duties at court as a member of the king's council of *sapientes* must often have interfered with his normal avocation as the shepherd of the vast flock entrusted to him. Nor could the people be kept in the daily course of Christian life, in any adequate fashion, by an itinerant clergy whose visits to any particular village must have been few and far between.

The whole Church had entered the Roman obedience in consequence of the Synod of Whitby, but the union had never been brought to practical working, because Archbishop Deusdedit had died just after the union was accomplished, and the primacy had been vacant ever since. Theodore had to start his career by claiming the allegiance of the regions which had been lately in the Irish communion—Northumbria, Mercia and Essex. In all of them the actual condition of the Church was irregular—Chad was holding the See of York, but by a doubtful title, his predecessor Wilfred being in exile at Canterbury. Wini, Bishop of Wessex, had been expelled from his own land, but had bought the See of Essex from King Wulfhere, and was residing in London in simoniacal possession of it. Jaruman, Bishop of Mercia, was lately dead (667) and that immense kingdom had no spiritual head. Rochester was also vacant. Boniface of East Anglia, indeed, was the only bishop in England who was in legal and undisputed possession of his proper See, and he was aged and infirm.

Theodore's first duty, therefore, was to assert his primatial authority, by restoring order among the subject Sees, and filling up the vacancies. His task was rendered easy at the point where most trouble might have been expected: Chad, the meek and saintly occupant of the Northumbrian bishopric, consented without difficulty to resign his place to Wilfred. Nor did he make the least objection when Theodore suggested that his consecration had been irregular (since Celtic bishops had taken part in it), and insisted on re-ordaining him before he transferred him to the vast diocese of Mercia. Chad moved southward in obedience to the orders of his superior, and established himself at Lichfield, which henceforth became the spiritual centre of the kingdom.

Wilfred moved back to York, and presided with great energy over the affairs of the northern realm for the next nine years. Boniface of East Anglia resigned, on account of bodily infirmity, and Bisi was ordained to his place. The vacant Rochester was filled up by the nomination of a certain Putta, "more addicted to simplicity of life than to activity in worldly affairs," whose docility was probably his best recommendation to Theodore. Coenwalch, King of Wessex, was allowed to choose as his bishop Lothere (Eleutherius), a nephew of the earlier occupant of the See, Agilberct, whom he had imported from Gaul. Wini at London seems to have been left undisturbed, though his election had been simoniacal.

Thus, within two years after his arrival, Theodore had restored order to the episcopate; each of the existing Sees had been duly provided with a bishop, and all had acknowledged the primacy of Canterbury. But the great archbishop's designs aimed at something further; he had come to the conclusion that many of the tribal dioceses were far too large for practical administration, and it was his desire to cut them up into smaller and more wieldy units. To this opposition might be expected; the actual tenants of the Sees might object to surrender the importance which they enjoyed through being each the sole spiritual ruler of a kingdom. And the princes might prefer to have at hand a single bishop established at their court, rather than several bishops scattered round their realms.

The unity of the State seemed to be strengthened by the unity of the bishopric; and the appointment of separate bishops for the sub-kingdoms might seem to favour decentralisation and local particularism, which an imperial king of the type of Oswy or Wulfhere might fear. That such objections existed is shown by what occurred at the Synod of Hertford (Sept. 24, 673). This was the first meeting of the united English Church, and was summoned by Theodore to confirm the arrangements which he had already made, and to establish a general system of organisation for the whole island. Its acts, preserved by Bede, give interesting information as to Theodore's aims.

They provide that no bishop shall trespass in the diocese of another, that monks shall not wander at their will from monastery to monastery, that a priest shall not quit his diocesan without letters dimissory, that a convocation of the whole Church should be held once a year at "Cloveshoch"—an unknown locality probably in some central position near London. (Perhaps Cliffe-at-Hoo. Two notable Synods were held at this place in the eighth century.) There were some clauses dealing with the canonical celebration of Easter, and with the rules for lawful marriage and divorce. All this was passed without objection; but Theodore's ninth proposition "that more bishops be made, as the multitude of believers increases" was not ratified, but for the present passed over, evidently because objection, whether from clerical or from lay quarters, was offered.

The projected annual Synods at Cloveshoch were not held, probably because of the outbreak of war between Northumbria and Mercia in 675, which set all England in confusion for some years. But before it began, Theodore had taken the first step in dividing up the great tribal bishoprics. In 674 when Bisi of East Anglia resigned on account of infirmity, two Sees were created, one at Dunwich for Suffolk, the other at Elmham for Norfolk. It is probable that a quarrel between Theodore and Winfrith, the successor of Chad as Bishop of Mercia, recorded in the following year, may have been due to the resistance of that prelate to the carrying out of a similar division in his own vast diocese. The archbishop ended by deposing his suffragan, who retired to the continent—perhaps in order to make an appeal to Rome. (See notes to Plummer's edition of Bede, ii.)

But Sexwulf, his successor, held the undivided Mercian See for some years; the war had broken out, and Theodore probably thought that he had better not meddle with Mercia while it was in progress. But before it was over, he obtained a great triumph in Northumbria. King Ecgfrith had quarrelled with his bishop, Wilfred, and, to revenge himself, espoused eagerly the archbishop's plan for splitting up the broad tribal bishoprics; for no better meeans could be devised for humbling a masterful man, who rejoiced in the breadth of his sphere of authority, than to take from him the greater part of his diocese. The origin of the strife between Ecgfrith and Wilfred is said to have dated for some years back, when the latter had supported and encouraged the Queen Aethelthryth (St. Audrey) in her determination to retire into a nunnery, contrary to her husband's wish.

When she had taken the veil (672) Ecgfrith married again; his second wife, Eormenburh, is said to have been a bitter enemy of Wilfred, and to have stirred up the king against him, accusing him of pride, perversity, and an over great love of getting lands for the Church. There was probably some truth in the accusation, for Wilfred was undoubtedly a great lover of state and dignity, a very stiff-backed adversary, who always stood upon his rights, and a great founder of churches and monasteries. He has been compared in character, and not inaptly, to Becket.

When Ecgfrith invited Theodore to York, and explained that he was willing and indeed eager to fall in with his plans for dividing the Northumbrian diocese, the primate expressed his pleasure, and proposed that it should be split into four parts—Wilfred should keep York and Deira, but there should be two new Bernician Sees at Lindisfarne and Hexham, while the newly conquered district of the Lindiswaras should form a fourth diocese. Wilfred's consent was neither asked nor obtained, but at a meeting of the Northumbrian Council the division was proclaimed as an accomplished fact. The injured prelate protested, and asked that reasons should be shown for his humiliation. The king and primate replied that no personal charge was made against him, but that the change was made for the benefit of the Church—and this was true enough. Wilfred announced that he should appeal to the Pope, and left the kingdom without obtaining permission from either his spiritual or his temporal *suzerain*.

This appeal and departure Theodore regarded as contumacious, and Ecgfrith as treasonable. The primate, though he owed his appointment to Pope Vitalian, was not inclined to welcome Roman interference when his own authority was questioned. He therefore declared Wilfred deposed, and consecrated Bosa as Bishop of York, at the same time that he made Eadhaeth bishop of Lindsey, and Eata Bishop of Bernicia. Ecgfrith is said to have taken measures to secure that Wilfred should never see Rome; according to Eddius he induced his friend,

Ebroin, the Frankish mayor of the palace, to send myrmidons to kidnap or slay the exile.

But Wilfred's ship was driven out of its course by storms, and he landed in Frisia instead of in Neustria, and made his way from that heathen land to Italy among many dangers. In 679 he reached Rome, and laid his complaint before Pope Agatha. The pontiff thought that he had been harshly treated, but at the same time held that Theodore's scheme for dividing up the Northumbrian diocese was wise and necessary. After some delay he sent the exiled bishop back to England, with letters in which a compromise was set forth. Wilfred must be restored to his see, and the intruding bishops must resign; but when matters had been regularised in this fashion, Wilfred must acquiesce in the division of his diocese, and name bishops for Lindsey and Bernicia, whom Theodore should then consecrate. Before his departure from Rome, Wilfred took part in the Council of 680, which denounced the Monothelite heresy; his signature as Bishop of York is appended to its acts.

Returning in triumph to Northumbria, Wilfred presented the papal letters to King Ecgfrith. But to his surprise and dismay the monarch declared that he had probably bought them for money and shut him up in prison. This was exactly the same line of conduct that William the Conqueror or Henry II. would have pursued, in the days when seeking and importing Bulls from Rome had become a well-known offence to temporal rulers. The three intrusive bishops are said to have supported their master. After nine months however, Ecgfrith released his prisoner from the castle of Dunbar, and expelled him from the kingdom. Unable to tarry in Mercia, because the Northumbrian king and Aethelred were now reconciled, Wilfred made his way to Sussex, where the local prince Ethelwalch was a Christian, but the hulk of the tribe were still heathen. (Though, oddly enough, an Arch-Bishop of Canterbury, Deusdedit, and Damian Bishop of Rochester had been Sussex men.)

This king gladly received the exile, and begged him to take up missionary work in his realm. In this task Wilfred was usefully and most successfully employed for six years (681-86). The starting of his career as a preacher is said to have been much helped by the fact that he taught the barbarous people of the coast the art of sea-fishing, with which they were hitherto unacquainted, and by the providential chance that a great drought, which had ruined their crops, ended in a pleasant rain on the day upon which he held his first great public baptism.

By such benefits the bishop gained the affections of all, and they began to expect celestial profit when he preached, because by his ministry they had already received temporal profit. (Bede, *E, H., iv.*)

Within six years the men of Sussex had all been converted, and Wilfred had founded, by the king's liberality, a monastery at Selsey, which became the seat of a new bishopric. Nor did his missionary work end here: in the first days of his exile he had befriended one Ceadwalla, a member of the West Saxon royal house, who had been outlawed and was living the life of an adventurer. When in 686 this prince cut his way to the throne of Wessex, and conquered the Jutes of the Isle of Wight, which was absolutely the last region in England to remain heathen, he made a gift of a quarter of its land to Wilfred, and gave him the charge of converting such of its people as he had not massacred. They were instructed and baptised by Wilfred's nephew Bernwine and his priest Hiddila. Thus, the great bishop's banishment from the North turned to the advantage of the remotest and most barbarous South.

Archbishop Theodore, meanwhile, had, since Wilfred's fall, proceeded most successfully in his design for multiplying the English Episcopate. In 681 he had, with Ecgfrith's approval, established a second Bernician See at Hexham, and a bishopric for the Picts subject to Northumbria, both in Manau and beyond Forth, with its local centre at Abercorn in West Lothian, not far from the end of the Wall of Antoninus. Apparently, he had succeeded in persuading King Aethelred to part the vast diocese of Mercia at an even earlier date, perhaps immediately after that pacification of 679 in which he had borne the part of mediator. But the details of the cutting up of Bishop Sexwulf's unwieldy domain must have taken some time to carry out.

When completed they stood as follows: Sexwulf kept Lichfield and Mercia proper, Leicester became the seat of a bishop of the Middle Angles; the territory of the Hwiccas became the See of Worcester; Lindsey, now just recovered from Northumbria, received a new Mercian bishop who dwelt at Sidnacester (Stow). The land of the Chilternsaetas, recently conquered freon Wessex, as it seems, became another diocese, whose bishop was placed at Dorchester-on-Thames, the original religious centre of Wessex. But when this land was won back by the house of Gerdic the Mercian bishopric ceased. Finally, some years, as it seems, after the establishment of the rest of the new creations, the Magesaetas beyond Severn were organised into the bishopric of Hereford.

★★★★★★

The idea that Putta, the exiled Bishop of Rochester, became first Bishop of Hereford, as early as 676, seems to be a mistake (see Plummer's Bede, ii.) We have no certain Bishop of Hereford before Tyrhtel, consecrated in 688.

★★★★★★

Before the completion of these arrangements, Theodore held the second of his great Synods, at Hatfield, on September 17th, 680, at which not only bishops but abbots and "many venerable priests and doctors" were present. Its object was to acknowledge and confirm the proceedings of the Council held at Rome six months before, by anathematising the Monothelite heresy, and proclaiming the complete adhesion of the English Church to the orthodox doctrine of the West. We are not informed that any notice was taken at the Synod of the difficulties turning on Wilfred's exile: he must at this moment have been crossing Gaul on his way homeward, if he had not already been cast into prison by King Ecgfrith. Theodore, in either case, had no intention of restoring him to York.

Meanwhile secular affairs must once more attract our attention. The peace between Mercia and Northumbria had left Ecgfrith free to turn his attention to the lands over which he exercised, or at least claimed, imperial *suzerainty* in the far North. The trouble in this direction seems to have been caused by a Pictish prince, Bruide (or Bridei), son of the daughter of King Talargain, and therefore a distant kinsman of Ecgfrith, since Talargain was son of Eanfrith, the brother of Oswy, who had married the heiress of the royal line of the Picts. Bruide (672-93), who seems to have held at first only the extreme northern regions about the Moray Firth, was a warlike prince, who encroached on the territories of the southern Picts who had submitted to Northumbria, probably while Ecgfrith was engaged in his four-year Mercian War.

He seems also to have allied himself with Fearcha Fada, a king of the Dalriad Scots, and to have made war with his help on the Strathclyde Britons, who were vassals of Ecgfrith.

Possibly they obtained assistance from the Scots of Ireland also, for thus only is it easy to account for an almost inexplicable action of the Northumbrian king in 684. (The only other explanation suggested is that the Irish were harbouring Ecgfrith's illegitimate brother Aldfrid, whom he had driven out of the realm—see Plummer's *Bede*, ii.) In

123

that year, as Bede and the *Ulster Chronicle* both tell us, Ecgfrith sent a fleet under his ealdorman Beorht (or Beorhtred) across the narrow seas, and ravaged the plain of Breg, the lands between Liffey and Boyne, "miserably wasting a harmless nation, which had always been friendly to the English, insomuch that not even churches and monasteries were spared." (Bede, *E.H., iv.*) This is the last indication that the kings of Northumbria were wont to keep war-ships in the Irish Sea, as in the days when Edwin had conquered Alan and Anglesey half a century back. Indeed, these two notices are the only proof that remains to us to show that the English had not yet wholly forgotten the seamanship of their piratical ancestors.

Chroniclers, Saxon no less than Celtic, were wont to regard the disaster which fell upon Ecgfrith in the following year as the vengeance of heaven for the devastation of the churches of Ireland. In the spring of 685 he entered Pictland, and ravaged all the land till he had passed the Tay. King Bruide "made show as if he fled, and drew him on into the straits of inaccessible mountains," but turned to bay behind a morass called Linngaran "the pool of the cranes," near Dunnechtan (Dunnichen by Forfar). There Ecgfrith fell in battle, with all his nobles and the greater part of his army, on Sunday, May 20th, in the fifteenth year of his reign and the fortieth of his age.

His death is said to have been seen in a vision by St. Cuthbert, the anchorite whom he had drawn from his hermitage only a few months before, to rule over the See of Lindisfarne. Cuthbert, who had warned Ecgfrith not to undertake the expedition, was seized with a trance as he stood admiring the Roman walls of Carlisle, exclaimed that "even now the conflict was perchance decided," and sent to warn the queen to depart at once to York, and await the worst of news, which came only two days later.

The Battle of Nechtansmere, as the English called the fight, was a fatal blow to Northumbria, which on Ecgfrith's death not only lost the greater part of its northern empire, but seems to have started on a permanent decline in strength and vitality. The kingdom showed no signs of recuperative power: it made no serious attempt hereafter to vie with Mercia as the leading power in England, and in the next generation fell into a state of faction and civil war, from which it was never destined to emerge. The immediate result of the disaster was that the Picts of the north recovered not only their complete liberty, but all the lands which Oswy had annexed beyond the Wall of Antoninus, while the Scots of Argyleshire, and great part of the Britons of the Lowlands ceased to pay the tribute which they had been wont to yield. (Bede, *iv.*)

The Strathclyde Welsh, apparently, revolted, but not the dwellers about Carlisle; nor did the Niduarian Picts of Galloway get free, as is shown by the fact that Northumbrian bishops continued to rule the See of Whiterne for another hundred years. Trumwine, however, the Bishop of Abercorn, withdrew to Whitby with many other fugitives from Lothian, so that apparently Manau, no less than the parts beyond Forth, had been evacuated. Bede, writing the fourth book of his history forty-six years after Nechtansmere, makes special note that nothing that was then lost had been recovered down to his own day.

Ecgfrith's successor was his half-brother Aldfrid, an illegitimate son of Oswy, who had long been in exile, first in Ireland and then at Iona. He was a gentle and learned prince, who had been destined for the Church, and though he had refused the tonsure had learned in a monastery to love books and scholars. During his reign of twenty years (685-705) he kept peace so far as he might, leaving Mercia alone, and making no attempt to interfere in the contemporary troubles of the far south, where war was afoot during his early years, though an ambitious king might have sought to turn the struggle in Wessex, Kent and Sussex to account.

It is clear that the Picts must have occupied Aldfrid's main attention; probably the struggle on the borders of Lothian went on during the greater part of his reign, though of it we have only one notice in the *Chronicles*, *viz.*, that in 698 the Picts slew in battle Beorht (or Beorhtred), the ealderman, the leader who had ravaged Ireland fourteen years before at Ecgfrith's behest.

★★★★★★

So, in the *Chronicle* appended to Bede, but the *Anglo-Saxon Chronicle* says 699. Tighernach agrees with the former, calling the ealderman Brechtraig, the son of Bernith (Bernhaeth).

★★★★★★

But that this disaster led to no further loss of territory seems to be shown by Bedels statement that Aldfrid; "nobly retrieved the state of a kingdom that had been ruined, though it was now less extensive than of yore". The best token of his peaceful disposition is that, the moment he was firmly established on the throne, he made peace with Bishop Wilfred, and invited him to return from Sussex to Northumbria. The matter was settled on the lines suggested by the papal letters of 680—Wilfred took the diocese of York, the intrusive Bishop Bosa resigning, but the new Sees of Lindisfarne and Hexham remained in existence, so that Bernicia was never reunited to Deira as to its ecclesiastical organisation.

Archbishop Theodore took a large part in arranging the matter: he had no personal objection; to Wilfred, with whom he was openly reconciled at a meeting in London, but was determined that the old system of unwieldy tribal bishoprics should not be restored. Hence the return of Wilfred to the new and narrower See of York did not displease him. This is the last act of the great primate which is on record; he died: in 690 at the age of eighty-eight, and was buried at Canterbury, in St. Peter's, among his predecessors. He was never formally canonised—most probably because of his long quarrel with Wilfred, who had won the hearts of the clergy both in his own day and in succeeding times. But he had done far more for the welfare of Christendom than many saints, "for to say the truth, the English churches received more advantage during the time of his pontificate than they had ever done before". (Bede, *E. H. v.*)

He has sometimes been credited with the origin of the parochial system of England, as well as of the localised episcopate. This is an exaggeration. No doubt he encouraged the building and endowment of churches by lay landowners, but the system had begun before his time, and was not completed till long after it. His *Penitential*, the only written work from his hand that has come down to us, speaks of local divisions each administered by its own priest, but it is probable that such were still the exception rather than the rule. His real memorials are the Diocesan Episcopate, and the school of Greek learning which he left behind him.

Theodore's last years must have been saddened by the outbreak of war in South Britain, where for a time all had been peaceful after his great pacification of 679. The first stirrer up of trouble was that Ceadwalla who has already been mentioned in connection with Wilfred. He was a descendant of Ceawlin, none of whose house had held the supreme power in Wessex since 592, though his father, Coenbert, is called a *subregulus*. His name, which is purely Welsh, and that of his brother Mul, "the half-breed," seem to suggest that their mother must have been a Celt. At first, we hear of Ceadwalla as an adventurer, lurking with a war-band in the forests of Chiltern and Andred, (Eddius), then as a pretender to the throne of Wessex.

Possibly he may have received aid at first from Lothere, King of Kent, since he was certainly the foe of that princess chief enemy. We read that in 684 Lothere had expelled from his realm the son of his predecessor, Ecgbert—one Eadric—who seems to have been reigning up to that moment as his colleague, or perhaps as sub-king of West Kent. (They issued together a code of Laws, from which we shall have occasion to quote later on.) Eadric took refuge in Sussex, and raised an army there, apparently by the help of King Ethelwalch. He then attacked Lothere, who was mortally wounded in the battle which followed (Feb. 5, 685). The majority of the Kentishmen then submitted to him. But a few months later Ceadwalla burst into Sussex and slew King Ethelwalch, as has already been related. Two ealdormen, Bercthun and Andhun, rallied the South Saxons and drove him off, and then (as it would appear) recognised Eadric of Kent, who had won his throne by the aid of their countrymen, as king of Sussex also.

We next hear of Ceadwalla as attacking his kinsman Centwine, the King of Wessex, and forcing him to retire into a monastery. Having thus won the throne, he engaged in a desperate war with Eadric, being, as Bede says, *strenuissimus juvenis*, and as cruel as he was ambitious. There probably lurks below the meagre tale of his rise much unrecorded fighting, since Ceadwalla had as his enemy not only the king of Sussex and Kent, but probably Aethelred of Mercia also. For when an outlaw in Chiltern he must have been trespassing in that monarch's newly won conquests from Wessex, and when he achieved the kingship, he seems to have won back all the land of the Chilternsaetas. Sussex, too, whose king he had slain, and whose lands he had wasted, had been vassal to Mercia since the days of Wulfhere.

In 686 Ceadwalla fell upon Sussex for the second time, slew Bercthun, the ealdorman, and devastated the whole realm. He then conquered the regions which Wulfhere had given over to Sussex twenty years before—the Isle of Wight and the land of the Meonwaras, to the north of Southampton Water. The former at least of these Jutish districts seems never before to have been in West Saxon hands. The conqueror dealt very harshly with the pagan men of Wight, slaying many, and planting a settlement of West Saxon colonists among them. The cruelty of his tender mercies may be judged from the ghastly anecdote in Bede, which tells how he captured the two brothers of Arwald, King of Wight, and was about to slay them, when a certain abbot, Cynebert, begged that they might not be sent to the other world as heathens, destined to certain damnation.

Ceadwalla thought over the matter, and granted Cynebert a few weeks to instruct and baptise them. They were then beheaded, "joyfully enduring temporal death, through which they did not doubt that they would pass to everlasting life." (Bede, iv.) Having conquered Wight and crushed Sussex, the West Saxon king extended his invasion to Kent, where he apparently tried to set up his brother Mul as king, relying probably on help from the faction which had once backed Lothere and resisted Eadric. Perhaps the brothers counted some Kentish strain among their female ancestors, to justify the claim. And fate seemed at first to favour the project; in the autumn of 686 Eadric died, apparently by natural death, since he is not said to have fallen in battle.

It seems that for a moment Mul was recognised as king by at least some part of Kent. (See Plummer's notes to Bede, ii.) But it was but for a moment; in 687 his subjects beset him by a sudden rising, and he with twelve of his thegns were burnt alive, presumably in some palace or stronghold in which they had striven to defend themselves. Ceadwalla was soon back in arms to avenge his brother; he ravaged Kent cruelly from end to end, and then his devastating career came to an unexpected termination. We read, to our surprise, that in a sudden moment of contrition and agony of spirit, he laid down his bloodstained sword, resigned the throne which he had so hardly won:

And quitted his crown for the sake of Our Lord and His everlasting Kingdom, desiring to go to Rome to obtain the peculiar honour of being baptised in the Church of the Holy Apostles, and hoping that, laying down the flesh as soon as he should be baptised, he might immediately pass to the eternal joys of heaven. (Bede, *E. H., v.*)

It is strange to find that Wilfred's friend had not been baptised already; presumably, like Constantine the Great, he had been deferring a ceremony which would impose upon him moral obligations that he dreaded. Some unrecorded, but horrible, incident of the devastation of Kent may have so preyed upon his conscience that he felt a sudden impulse to put ambition under his feet, and to flee from further blood-shedding. If his conduct with regard to the two Jutish princes from Wight was a fair specimen of his career, such incidents must have been many. His desire was granted him; having abdicated in the autumn of 688 he had reached Rome by the following Easter, was there baptised by Pope Sergius, and died ten days after, on April 20, 689, aged only thirty.

His short and stormy career seems to have left permanent results behind it. Sussex seems never again to have enjoyed complete independence; apparently the race of native kings had ended with Ethelwalch, and the later *subreguli*, whom we occasionally meet, were subject to Wessex, (or to Mercia, when the latter, as in Offa's day, had stricken down Wessex for a time), and sometimes (as it would seem) princes of the royal house of Cerdic. This was certainly the case with Nunna (710), the next South Saxon prince whose name has survived; he was the kinsman as well as the vassal of the King of the West Saxons.

It seems clear that Ceadwalla also left his mark behind him by winning back the land of the Chilternsaetas from Aethelred of Mercia. The Mercian bishopric of Dorchester-on-Thames ceased about 685, and the region is found in West Saxon hands when next it comes into sight. Kent seems to have come very badly out of the wars; there was chaos in the land for two years after Ceadwalla's abdication, and it was not till 694 that Wihtraed, brother of Eadric, appears firmly established as sole ruler, after a struggle with certain "*dubii vel externi reges*," of whom Swebheard, King of Essex, seems to have been one. (But see Plummer's *Bede, ii.* notes. Wihtraed was claiming kingship in 692, but the *A. S. Chronicle* puts his accession in 694, when no doubt he became sole ruler of Kent.)

In Wessex itself, Ceadwalla was followed by Ine, son of Coenred, who was also a descendant of Ceawlin, but a very distant relative to his predecessor. The house of Cuthwulf, which had reigned from 593 to 686 continuously, was apparently extinct, and all the later kings of the Gewissae come from Ceawlin's branch. Ine appears to; have been a man of mark, who not only maintained his realm with the enlarged limits which Ceadwalla had won, but increased it as none of his predecessors had done since the day of the Battle of Deorham. His long reign of thirty-eight years (688-736) contrasts strongly with the ephemeral rule of the five kings before him, none of whom had kept his throne for over nine summers. He was the first prince of his house, since Ceawlin, who gave any promise of winning that supremacy over the neighbouring states which was ultimately to fall to the kings of Wessex, when both Northumbria and Mercia had been tried and found wanting.

But since Ine's reign extends far into the eighth century, we must defer a consideration of it till we have dealt with the careers of the kings of the two great Anglian realms who were reigning when he came to the throne in 688.

Of Aethelred of Mercia there is comparatively little to tell. The later years of his life did not correspond to that triumphant beginning in which he had avenged Wulfhere, and restored the boundary of Mercia on the Humber, by winning back the region of Lindsey. He certainly lost the authority over Southern England which Wulfhere had asserted, and the rise of Ceadwalla permanently cut short his power. As far as we can judge he must have been a peaceful and pious prince; the few notices that we have of him show that he was reckoned a dear friend of Archbishop Theodore, and a founder of bishoprics and monasteries on a large scale, though early in his reign he had been an evil neighbour to the prelates and monks of Kent.

It is therefore surprising to find in the *Saxon Chronicle*, under the year 697, the meagre and inexplicable statement "in this year the Southumbrians slew Ostritha, the Queen of Aethelred," which is slightly enlarged in the epitome appended to Bede, by the note that the murder was done by "the chief men (*primates*) of the Mercians". This would seem to point to civil strife and palace revolutions, of which we have no other trace. Ostritha may have been the leader of a political party, but we know no more about her than that she had shown her piety by translating the bones of her kinsman St. Oswald to the abbey of Bardney. Her death did not involve the deposition of her husband, who reigned for seven years more, till in 704 he abdicated his throne, and retired into the monastery of Bardney, of which he and his wife had both been great benefactors; he died some years later as its abbot.

Sigebert of East Anglia had set the example of resigning the crown for the cowl half, a century before, and Centwine of Wessex had copied it—not apparently by his own free will—in the next generation. But Aethelred appears to have been, like Sigebert and Ceadwalla, an instance of genuine world-weariness, on the part of a conscientious man who felt that he was too old or too weak to cope with the rough political problems of his day.

He was succeeded; by his nephew Coenred, the son of his predecessor Wulfhere, though he had left an heir of his own, Ceolred, who was to mount the Mercian throne a few years later, for Coenred reigned only from 704 to 709. Apparently, he reigned in peace, and certainly he was as pious as his uncle; we have no note of him, save that he did not think it beneath him, to rebuke, and argue, with those of his servants who lived an evil life. (Bede, *E. H., v.*) Bede merely, tells of him that:

Having for some time nobly governed the kingdom of the

Mercians, he did a yet more noble act by quitting his throne and kingdom, and going to Rome, where he was shorn and ordained a monk by Pope Constantine, and abode to his death (five years later) near the relics of the Apostles.

He made over the crown before his departure to his cousin, Ceolred (709-16), a prince of very different character, warlike, licentious and boisterous, who seduced nuns, plundered churches, and opened a long war with Wessex, of which we shall have much to tell hereafter. (Our chief notice of him is from an unexpected source, a letter of Boniface, the great English apostle of Germany, who lived in the next generation, so is a good authority.)

Meanwhile Aldfrid of Northumbria survived the abdication, of his old enemy Aethelred by a year, dying peaceably at Driffield on December 15, 705. The later part of his reign had been, disturbed by a new quarrel with Wilfred of York, who, does not seem to have been able to agree even with a prince, whom all writers agree in praising for his learning, meekness, and piety. We are told that the trouble arose from Aldfrid's wishing to take from Wilfred his abbey of Ripon, which he held along with the See of York, in order that he might found a new bishopric there. The king seems to have held that Deira, like Bernicia, ought to be divided into two dioceses, according to the scheme of Archbishop Theodore, which Wilfred could not bring himself to accept.

He departed, or was expelled, from his See of York, and removed to Mercia, where King Aethelred gave him the bishopric of Leicester, which chanced at that moment to be vacant. He administered it for no less than eleven years, before he was permitted to return to Northumbria. Naturally he made an appeal to Rome, as he had done before in 678; but though Pope John VI. decided that he had been wrongly expelled, and sent Bulls in his favour to Aldfrid, he was not restored. In 702 the king called a council at Estrefeld (Austerfield) to which came Archbishop Bertwald of Canterbury, and many other prelates.

It seems to have ended by an offer made to Wilfred that he should return to Northumbria, if he would resign the See of York and keep his old abbey of Ripon alone. This meagre compensation was of course refused with scorn, and Wilfred went once more to Rome, to plead his cause in person, though he was now so far advanced in years that the long journey was almost fatal to him (703-4).

The reigning pope, Sergius I. reaffirmed the judgment that had been given in his favour, and wrote to Archbishop Bertwald bidding him assemble a Synod and do justice to the exile. The primate declared himself disposed to carry through the matter; but King Aldfrid, though pious, was obstinate, and nothing had been accomplished when he died in 705. There was a short time of trouble after his decease; his son, Osred was only eight years old, and the reign of a child was a thing unknown in Northumbria. Eardwulf, a distant relative whose lineage is unknown, seized the throne, but held it for only two months, when he was expelled by the ealdorman Bertfrid and other magnates, who had resolved to make the experiment of crowning the child, Osred. Immediately afterwards Bertfrid, who was now practically in charge of the realm, assembled a council on the Nidd, to which came Bertwald the primate, and all the bishops of the North.

The ealdorman and the archbishop being both friendly to Wilfred, a compromise was finally negotiated, by which he received back not his old bishopric of York, but Hexham, a See of much inferior dignity; however, his famous abbey of Ripon and his other possessions were restored to him. With this arrangement Wilfred was fain to be content, though he regarded himself as having been very harshly treated. He held his new See for four years, and died at Oundle in October, 709, while on a visit to Mercia to confer with King Ceolred. His misfortunes, his undaunted spirit, his lavish patronage of monks and monasteries, and his excellent missionary work in Sussex secured him the title of saint. But there can be no doubt that his troubles were largely of his own making, and that his haughty bearing and unconciliatory disposition were the real cause of his long strife with men of such excellent character as Archbishop Theodore and King Aldfrid. The origin of the whole matter lay in his resistance to Theodore's very necessary and profitable scheme for cutting up the unwieldy tribal bishoprics, to which no plea of "vested interests" was a sufficient objection.

Even at that early date his repeated appeals to Rome were resented by the rulers both of Church and of State. But there is no reason to impute blame to him for them, for he had indubitably received hard treatment, and there was no other tribunal to which he could apply for justice. His best title to kindly remembrance, over and above his conversion of the South Saxons, is his zeal for church building, to which he applied all his energy and wealth in the day of his greatness. The foundations of his great minster at Hexham survive, to show the comparative magnificence of his designs, in an age when architecture was in its infancy.

CHAPTER 6

The Eighth Century, 709-802—The Mercian Domination

It has often been remarked that while on the Continent the seventh century was the most miserable period of the Dark Ages, in England the eighth century has that unenviable distinction. While abroad the Merovingian royal house was sinking into senility under a long succession of short-lived and impotent kings, while the Visigoths of Spain were preparing themselves for servitude to the Moor by incessant murder and civil war, while the Lombards were losing their chance of building up a national kingdom of Italy, the English were still a strong and vigorous race.

The impulse of conquest was not yet lost, while the introduction of Christianity had brought with it a higher moral standard and broader aims. Kings like Edwin and Oswald, Oswy and Aldfrid, contrast very favourably with their continental contemporaries. The chronicle of this island, though full enough of battle, murder and sudden death, is not a mere list of horrors, like the history of the Merovingians, as detailed by Gregory of Tours and the meagre analysts who followed him.

Most of all is it to be noted that the English Church, for the first hundred years of its existence, was the most creditable branch of seventh-century Christendom, as much above its Frankish, Visigothic or Lombard sisters in learning and godliness as in energy and missionary zeal. With the commencement of the eighth century we begin to find a change for the worse; it looked as if the experiment of putting the new wine of Christianity into the old bottles of English tribal life had led first to effervescence, and then to a settling down into turbid decay. It took some generations for the process to become complete; for the first third of the eighth century the English Church might still be called learned, disinterested, and zealous, and the English kingly houses still produced on occasion men of vigour and piety.

This was, indeed, in one sense, the Golden Age of Anglo-Saxon England, when scholar-kings like Aldfrid and Ceolwulf of Northumbria reigned, when the school of Greek learning started at Canterbury by Theodore and Hadrian was still flourishing, when Aldhelm and Bede were writing, when Abbot Ceolfrid was causing the *Codex Amiatinus* to be engrossed, and Caedmon the poet was but recently dead. Bede's work, if it were the only thing surviving from the period, would give us a very high idea of contemporary English culture. He was an author of a degree of merit to which no other historian of the Dark Ages attained. Procopius, writing in Constantinople—the centre of all learning—is the only wielder of the pen who can be compared to him in the space of live centuries.

It is only necessary to name the other chief annalists of the West—Gregory of Tours, Isidore of Seville, Paulus Diaconus—in order to realise how far Bede excelled in breadth of view, power of arranging sources, and critical faculty. He is a model to later ages for his admirable habit of citing his personal authority for each statement, and his anxiety to get his chronology correct. Here indeed was a real historian; and the wonder glows when we find that his *Ecclesiastical History of the English People* was only one among very many works of theology and scholarship which engrossed his busy life. And he was no isolated phenomenon, but only the best example of a race of literary men which flourished for at least two generations, and left heirs in Alcuin and other scholars of the next epoch.

But a Golden Age is too often the result of the good work of a previous generation, rather than the start of a continuous period of activity destined to endure. While Bede was still writing, the signs of deterioration were already visible; he himself saw and noted them, and the last paragraph of his continuous narrative ends in a note of doubt and foreboding concerning times "so filled with commotions that it cannot yet be known what is to be said concerning them, or what end they will have." (*E. H., v.* 23)

Evil days were at hand, and it may be said that save for the single great figure of Offa of Mercia among laymen, and save for the great missionary Winfrith (Boniface), the apostle of Germany, among clerks, the rest of the eighth century is a period of dullness and gloom.

★★★★★★

Bishop Aldhelm and the scholar Alcuin, the friend of Charlemagne, can hardly be mentioned along with the other two, though the latter is worthy of remembrance as the last flower of English learning.

★★★★★★

Boniface, writing about 746 to censure a contemporary monarch, remarks that the evil began with the two young kings Osred of Northumbria and Ceolred of Mercia, of whom the former reached man's estate in 714 and the latter ascended the throne in 709. Both were dissolute youths, tyrants, murderers of their noblest subjects, ravishers of nuns, plunderers of monasteries. Both died violent and terrible deaths.

But it is not single sinners, even in the highest places, who break down a well-established system of morality, or ruin a State or a Church. A general decay of energy and a general lapse into ill-living comes from general causes, though particular instances may point the moral. If we have to search for the reasons of the decline of the English kingdoms in the eighth century, we find them to be many and various.

The first was one which worked not only in England, but in all the Teutonic kingdoms of Western Christendom—the want of an established rule of succession in the kingship. This was quite as deadly to the Visigoths of Spain and the Lombards of Italy as to the English. When a kingdom is still in the making, living by the sword, and always in danger from external foes, the rule of the "survival of the fittest" among its rulers may do comparatively little harm.

It is absolutely necessary that the sceptre should be in the hands of the most competent fighting man, or the State may be extinguished. But, in a kingdom which has won its way to a condition of permanent solidity, nothing can be more dangerous than that any descendant of Woden, more or less remotely connected with the reigning royal line, should think it possible to make a grasp at the crown.

In all the English kingdoms the number of princely houses which claimed an ancestry going back to the original founder of the state was enormous. A glance at the genealogical trees of the houses of Cerdic or Ida, of Penda or Aesc, is absolutely bewildering. The succession often moved about in the most unexpected way from one branch to another. Any adventurer of the royal blood who had won fame in war might upset a reigning king who was weak or unpopular. No ancestor of Ceadwalla of Wessex had won the crown for a century, yet he apparently dethroned Centwine with ease. The worthless Osred of Northumbria was murdered and followed on the throne by Coenred, who descended from Ida in the sixth generation, but had no nearer kinship to his victim; and Coenred was followed by Osric, his equally remote relation, to the exclusion of his brother Ceolwulf.

The same was the case in Mercia, where the kings of the later eighth century descended from three separate nephews of Penda in succession. When the crown might be grasped by any successful leader of a warband, civil war tended to become endemic; nearly every king "slew the slayer and must himself be slain," or at least be deposed, tonsured and relegated to a monastery. For, as at Constantinople during the same age, the milder type of usurper contented himself with making his predecessor a monk, while the more ruthless type slaughtered him.

The second cause of trouble was nearly connected with the first: the weakness of the monarchy arose, to a great extent, from the fact that when the age of conquest was over, and no more soil was won from Briton or Pict, the king ceased to have an illimitable power to endow his personal retainers, who were the core of his army, with the land which they required to maintain them. The royal demesne was no longer increasing, and it had actually begun to diminish in a notable way. Not only had much been given to the members of the *comitatus* of each successive king, which did not come back to the crown, but remained with the grantee's family, but much more had been spent in lavish endowment of the Church. (For the way in which this came about and estates got alienated to lay as well as clerical occupants see the notes on *bocland* in chapter 8.)

Bede, though a monk himself, makes in his *Epistle* to Archbishop Ecgbert (734) a strong protest against the way in which monasteries were swallowing up all the available land, with the result that there was not enough to provide for the fighting men needed for the defence of the realm against the "barbarians". It is true that he is mainly thinking of ill-regulated monasteries, which kings and ealdormen were too wont to endow rather as a comfortable refuge for the old age of themselves and their relatives, than as houses for the service of God. But even the better sort of monastic establishments were in that age multiplied beyond all rational necessity. In this comparatively peaceful time, as Bede remarks:

> Multitudes of the Northumbrians, both noble and simple, laying aside their weapons, incline to devote both themselves and their children to the tonsure and monastic vows, rather than to exercise themselves in the studies of war. What will be the end of it the next generation will see. (*E. H., v.* 23)

The kings in all the states without exception set the example. Sigebert of East Anglia, Centwine of Wessex, Aethelred of Mercia, have already been mentioned: Ceolwulf of Northumbria, just when Bede was writing his history, was the first, and by no means the last, example in the Northern Kingdom. Where the retirement was voluntary, and not forced, the king who took the cowl naturally made ample provision from his royal property for the house which he destined as the retreat of his declining yearn. The private monasteries are said to have become an intolerable abuse; when a great man founded such a place of retirement he not only lived there as a law unto himself, but filled it with relatives, some of whom were quite young men, who (save that they were not married) behaved in every way like laymen of a low type, spending their time in idleness, drinking and gluttony, listening to minstrels and buffoons, and not unfrequently lapsing into carnal lusts.

This was all the more easy when, as in some cases, the founder built a double monastery for men and women, taking charge of the first himself, while his wife presided over the others. St. Aldhelm tells us that he had met gay young nuns, who insisted on wearing garments of purple or scarlet trimmed with fur, and paid so much attention to their *toilette* that they habitually used curling tongs for their hair. These young people, male and female, frequently got into trouble—as might have been expected. But when pious fathers devoted sons or daughters to the cloister at their birth, or while they were still in the nursery, without any reference to their vocation, what else could have been expected? The only wonder is that so many of these royal and noble recluses, who had not chosen their own lot, developed into saints: the number of royal abbesses in the English Calendar is surprising, and the cases of scandal much fewer than might have been expected.

The number of members of the great houses diverted into a monastic life for which they had no aptitude, was not the sole bad effect of the multiplication of religious houses. We are told that the scions of the military class, sons of ealdormen and thegns, who would in an earlier age have done fighting-service for their own king, found that they could get no endowment from him at home, and wandered abroad to seek service as adventurers, as members of the *comitatus* of a foreign prince, or as pirates. Those who stopped landless at home were the obvious tools of every aetheling who was meditating a snatch at the crown.

The curse of the land, in short, was that there were too many "aethelings," *subreguli* and ealdormen of royal blood, and too few landholders of moderate status. The king was not strong enough to hold down the nobility, unless he was a man of exceptional ability and energy. It was exactly the same phenomenon which was seen at the same time both among the Visigoths of Spain and the Franks of Gaul. But the fate of the English was to be different from that of either Goths or Franks. They were not destined to be completely overwhelmed by the *infidel*, like the one, nor to find salvation in setting a race of "mayors of the palace" to supersede a decadent royal line, like the others.

The Visigoths perished because they were too few to leaven an alien subject-population; in England such a population hardly existed, save to a small extent in the lands most recently conquered from the

Welsh. The Franks fell under the dominion of the great mayors because the Merovingian kings had become utterly effete. The English royal houses never sank so low; they continued to produce capable men from time to time, till at last one dynasty, that of Wessex, prevailed over the rest because it chanced, in the ninth and tenth centuries, to give birth to a succession of monarchs of more than average ability for several generations, who fought down barbarian invasions as dangerous as those which overwhelmed the Visigoths and bid fair at one moment to overwhelm the Franks also.

The one aspect of the eighth century which gave some promise of better things for the future was a marked tendency towards a closer union between the various tribal units. It seems clear that local particularism was growing less militant, partly because some of the kingdoms and sub-kingdoms lost their royal lines in the civil wars, and gradually learnt to endure rulers of alien origin, but much more because, under the influence of the Church, all the races of England were commencing to regard each other as brethren and countrymen, rather than as neighbours only less to be hated than the Welsh or the Picts. The much-ramified royal houses had intermarried with each other to such an extent that members of one had generally a female descent from one or more of the others, which would make them less intolerable as rulers, if they chanced to conquer or even to inherit another crown.

This was the way in which Kent ultimately got united to Wessex— the father of Ecgbert of Wessex had actually reigned as a *subregulus* in Kent, probably by a female descent. The union of Deira and Bernicia had certainly been facilitated by the fact that Oswy, the heir of Ida, married the daughter of Edwin, so that all his descendants had Deiran as well as Bernician royal blood in their veins.

It seems certain also that the lesser kingdoms by the end of the eighth century were so far losing their particularism that they acquiesced more easily in accepting as sub-kings relatives of one of the greater royal houses, who were from time to time placed over them by some conqueror who had achieved a general "*imperium*" (as Bede would have called it) over his neighbours. Local patriotism died hard, but it was distinctly on the decrease in this age, though the union of all the kingdoms would undoubtedly have taken a much longer time to achieve but for the Danish invasions, which taught Angle and Saxon that servitude to the heathen Viking could only be avoided by combination.

But of all the unifying influences there can be no doubt that the Church was the most powerful. At her frequent Synods, kings and ealdormen no less than bishops from all the realms habitually met, to debate on equal terms for the common benefit of all England. The advantages of the presidency of a single archbishop must have been a perpetual object lesson, to teach that there would be equal profit in the *suzerainty* of a single secular ruler.

Indeed, during the second half of the eighth century, while Offa of Mercia was reigning (757-96), there was a distinct approach to national unity, and if only he had been succeeded by heirs of equal ability a kingdom of All-England might have come into existence under the Mercian royal house. But his male line died out with his only son, who survived him only four months, and when distant collaterals succeeded to his throne the other kingdoms broke loose, and England reverted to disunion and anarchy for a generation, only to be reunited by Ecgbert of Wessex.

Proceeding with our early eighth century annals, we note that although the long peace between Northumbria and Mercia was still to endure for another generation, so that no question of a claim of either to dominate the whole island arose, yet each of the two greater kingdoms had foreign wars to vary its domestic troubles.

In Northumbria, Osred, who succeeded in 705 as a mere boy of eight, seems to have been for many years under the tutelage of the ealdorman, Bertfrid (son of the Beortred who had served as general to both Ecgfrid and Aldfrid). This nobleman is described in 710 as defeating the Picts "between Haefe and Caere," apparently the rivers Avon and Canon, just south of the Firth of Forth; Finguine, the leader of the Picts, was slain, and no doubt the frontier of Northumbria in Lothian was made secure for some years.

A few years later we find Osred governing for himself, though no more than seventeen or eighteen years old. He is said by Archbishop Boniface to have been a youth of precocious wickedness, godless, cruel and debauched, who provoked his subjects until they rose upon him and slew him, "so that he lost his glorious kingdom, his young life, and his lustful soul by a contemptible and vile death" (716). He is said in the *Anglo-Saxon Chronicle* to have been slain "South of the Border," but whether this means the bolder against the Picts, by Forth, or the border against the Mercians, by Humber is not made clear.

The chief of the conspirators who slew him was one Coenred, a very distant relative, since he descended, not from the line of Aethelfrith, which had occupied the Bernician throne ever since 593, but from another branch of the house of Ida, which had never before risen to royal power. He was apparently merely an ambitious aetheling, who saw his opportunity in the unpopularity of his master; at any rate he was saluted as king and reigned for two years, to the exclusion of Os-red's brother Offa and his first cousin, Oslac (the son of that Aelfwin who fell at the battle on the Trent in 679) to one of whom the crown should have fallen if any regular rule of succession had existed.

This was the commencement of that series of murders and *coups d'état* which make the history of Northumbria for the next hundred years a miserable record of blood and treason. Coenred died, apparently by a natural death, in 718: he left a brother, Ceolwulf, but this prince was thrust aside for a time by one Osric, who was as remote a kinsman to Coenred as the latter had been to Osred, since he descended from a third branch of the house of Ida, of which we only know that it had never before been counted royal.

★★★★★★

So at least the genealogy in Florence of Worcester, through Al-ric, Bofa, etc. In Simeon of Durham, however, Osric is called "*filius regis Alfridi*," but is this Aldfrith who died in 705? See notes in Plummer's *Bede, ii*. Bishop Stubbs wished to identify him with the Hwiccian sub-king, Osric, son of Alchfrid.

★★★★★★

He reigned eleven years (718-29), but hardly a single fact has been preserved concerning him, save that he bequeathed his crown to Ceolwulf, the brother of his predecessor. (Bede, *E. H. v.* 23. The *Chronicle of Ethelweard*, ii. 13, says that Osric was slain or murdered—*occiditur*, but this seems incredible when compared with Bede's way of naming his death.) But the transaction was ill received by many of the magnates, so that Ceolwulf's reign began—as it was to end—with dire commotions. A rival king was raised up against him: but whether it was someone of the house of Ecgfrid, the old reigning line, or whether it was his own cousin, Eadbert, who ultimately became his successor, we are not told. Several of the chroniclers inform us that he was taken prisoner, forcibly shorn, and immured as a monk in the monastery of Lindisfarne in 731. Yet some inexplicable revolution drew him from his retirement in less than a year, and he had a second reign from 731 to 737.

Apparently, he was a pious king and a lover of scholars; probably he was, as often happens with princes of such a type, too feeble for the times in which his lot was cast. Bede informs us that Ceolwulf was not only a diligent student of the Scriptures, but an industrious student of the actions and sayings of all ancient men of renown, and that he had often desired that a chronicle of England should be written "to excite the attentive hearer to imitate that which was good, and to shun that which is harmful and perverse" through following the tale of the past. (Bede, *E. H.*, book i., preface.)

Hence it was to him that the *Ecclesiastical History of the English People* was dedicated. He had ample time to study it in his old age, for his later reign ended even as his earlier; in 737 he retired to Lindisfarne for a second time—abandoning in despair the care of a troublous realm which was too much for him. He survived there till 760, in what, it would seem, was a not too comfortless seclusion, for we are told that:

> When this king became a monk, licence was given to the brethren to drink wine and beer; for down to that time water and milk alone had been permitted to them, according to the rule of St. Aidan. (Simeon of Durham, ii.)

Of his reign two events only are recorded, besides a general notice of commotion and civil war. The first is that he procured the pall of an archbishop for his cousin, Ecgbert, who was then holding the See of York—Wilfred and all the other successor of Paulinus had been no more than bishops. The second is that he established a new diocese, seated at Candida Casa (Whiterne in Galloway) for the Niduarian Picts, who were still subjects of Northumbria, though their northern neighbours the Strathclyde Welsh had been independent ever since the Battle of Nechtansmere.

Meanwhile the history of Mercia had remained for a whole generation entirely disassociated from that of Northumbria, but inextricably mixed with that of Wessex. Ceolred (709-16), the contemporary of Osred and his rival in turbulence, lawless cruelty and evil living, was apparently drawn into war with Ine of Wessex, because the latter had made his kingdom so strong that it had now become—what it had never been before—a serious rival of Mercia, and a competitor for the supremacy in England, south of the Humber. Ine (688-726) had succeeded to the throne when his distant relative Ceadwalla went on his famous pilgrimage to Rome.

Our first notice of him is that he continued or resumed the war with Kent which his predecessor had begun, and brought it to a successful conclusion, since he received from King Wihtraed and his subjects the enormous war indemnity of 30,000 gold *solidi*, each of 16 *nummi*, which is equivalent to 3,750 pounds, as compensation or *weregeld* for the death of the West Saxon prince, Mul, the brother of Ceadwalla, whom the Kentishmen had burnt seven years before.

★★★★★★

So Ethelweard: the best texts of the *Anglo-Saxon Chronicle* say simply "30,000," with no name of coin added. But probably Ethelweard and Florence of Worcester are right in making it *solidi*, or *mancuses* as these gold pieces were afterwards called. They weighed 65.6 grains, and eight equalled a pound.

★★★★★★

Nor was this all; Sussex, which had been in the hands of Wihtraed's brother, Eadric, fell under the power of Ine, who there established his kinsman, Nunna (or Nothelm) as *subregulus*. This least of the Saxon kingdoms seems to have been for the future habitually dependent on Wessex, and its rulers are as often styled *duces* (*i.e.*, ealdormen) as kings. It is probable that in consequence of Ine's victories not only Sussex but also Kent and Essex yielded him some sort of homage. But the only proof of this is that in his famous code of laws of 693 he styles Earcon-wald of London "my bishop," along with Haedde of Winchester. The phrase seems to imply definite *suzerainty* over London and its district.

Having established his borders in a satisfactory fashion in the East, Ine would appear to have turned his attention towards the Damnon-ian Welsh. His wars with them must have begun early in his reign, for Exeter was English before 700. But the only entry concerning them in the *Chronicle* is that in 710 Ine and his vassal Nunna fought against Gerontius (Geraint) of Damnonia, beat him and won from him much land. Taunton was occupied and fortified as a royal *burgh* to guard the newly acquired district, which extended even to the Exe.

★★★★★★

Ine is mentioned as having built it some time back in 722, so there can be little doubt that it arose after the campaign of 710, or even earlier.

The main evidence for believing that Exeter now came un-der Ine's hand is that the great missionary Bishop Winfrith is recorded by Willibrord to have been educated at Exeter by an abbot named Wulfhard. Unless the city was English it is hard to see how this could have happened. And as Winfrith was born before 690, Ine must surely have been fighting with the Welsh much earlier than 710.

★★★★★★

The growth of the West Saxon kingdom had already been marked by the division of its territories by Ine into two bishoprics, instead of the one at Winchester which had hitherto served for the whole realm. On the principle introduced by Theodore a new See was created for the parts west of Selwood, in Dorsetshire and Somerset, with its seat at Sherborne. St. Aldhelm, the learned Abbot of Malmesbury, was its first bishop (705-9).

Our most precious information as to the early part of Ine's reign is given not by the meagre entries in the *Chronicles*, but by the text of his code of laws of 693, already alluded to above. (So, to be dated by the mention of St. Earconwald, Bishop of London, who died in that year. For details about this Code see Chapter 7.) Its interest lies in the proof which it gives that, just about the time when Ine's conquests were beginning, the western parts of the realm of Wessex contained a large subject population of Welsh, who had settled down as landed proprietors, small and great, and were so far amalgamated with their conquerors that they sometimes became royal officials, and served in the king's *comitatus*, though they retained a separate name and status. Evidently the old days when conquest implied extermination were long over, and a favourable *modus vivendi* for the Celt had been devised. That the system was successful is shown by the fact that in a few generations, West Somerset and East Devon had become entirely English. Of this Code we shall have more to say in its due place.

In 715, five years after Ine's campaign against King Gerontius, we find him engaged in war with Ceolred of Mercia. We cannot be far wrong in concluding that while the pious and peaceful Coenred had endured the rise of Wessex without offering opposition, the fierce and violent prince who succeeded him had resolved to check it, and to win back for Mercia the supremacy over the whole South which Penda and Wulfhere had held in an earlier age. The Mercian king entered Wessex, evidently through the land of the Hwiccas, and engaged in a great pitched battle at "Wodnesbeorg," apparently the same spot, somewhere in North Wilts, where Ceawlin had fought and failed 130 years before.

The result was perhaps indecisive—certainly not in favour of the Mercian. But the war would probably have continued if in the next year Ceolred had not perished. His end was sudden and awful—St. Boniface, writing only thirty years later, tells us that while he was feasting in state among his nobles, he suddenly became possessed by an evil spirit, burst out into boisterous madness, and died raving, without being able to receive the last sacraments of the Church. Presumably an attack of *delirium tremens*, consequent on a long course of evil living and hard drinking, is implied (716).

Ceolred's sudden death was followed by the accession of one Aethelbald to the Mercian throne. He was a young aetheling, whom Ceolred had exiled and persecuted, probably not without good cause, for the record of his career shows that he was violent and ambitious. His kinship to his predecessor was very remote, since he descended not from Penda, but from that king's brother Eowa, who had fallen at the Battle of Maserfeld nearly a century before. In all probability his rise was accompanied by civil war and commotion, which prevented him from continuing the struggle with Wessex which was on hand. It seems also likely that he may have had trouble with the Welsh, as two battles in Glamorgan, at Garthmaelog and Pencoed near Bridgend, are recorded in the Cambrian Annals early in his reign. In both, as it is said, the Britons were victorious, and their enemies can only have been the Mercians.

★★★★★★

This note is under the year 721 both in *Annales Cambriae* and the *Brut y Tywysogion*. They are noted along with a battle in Cornwall in which Rodri Malwynog, a King of Wales, took part. Was this against Ine?

★★★★★★

It seems, at any rate, certain that Ine of Wessex found no hindrance from Aethelbald in the last years of his reign. The *Anglo-Saxon Chronicle*, always interested in the acts of the house of Cerdic, gives a number of notes concerning him, but they are all occupied with civil wars in the South, not with any struggle with Mercia. In 721, as we read, Ine slew the aetheling Cynewulf, apparently a domestic rebel. In the following year another aetheling, one Ealdbert "the exile," raised Sussex and Surrey against him, but was beaten and expelled. In connection with this incident we are told that Aethelburh, Ine's consort razed Taunton, which her husband had previously built. This puzzling entry has been interpreted as meaning that, while the king was busy elsewhere, some of his enemies seized Taunton, which Aethelburh took and destroyed, fighting in her husband's behalf.

★★★★★★

So, Henry of Huntingdon interpreted the story, and he seems for once to be right, though there is no sign that he had anything to go upon save the mysterious words of the *Anglo-Saxon Chronicle*.

★★★★★★

Three years later, we are told that Ealdbert returned to the charge, once more found harbourage and assistance among the South Saxons, and was for a second time defeated by Ine: on this occasion, however, he failed to escape, and was slain in battle.

Three years later Ine, now an elderly man, for he had reigned thirty-seven years, copied the example of his predecessor Ceadwalla by laying down his crown, and going on a journey to Rome "desirous to spend some time of his pilgrimage upon earth in the neighbourhood of the holy place" (728). He was accompanied by his wife, who (according to a late version of the story) had spared no pains to persuade him to the step. Apparently, they survived for some time, in pious seclusion, near the tombs of the Apostles. (William of Malmesbury, we know not on what authority, says that Ine "*plebeio amictu tectus clam consenuit cum uxore*" i. 39).

Before starting on his voyage Ine had made over his crown to his distant kinsman Aethelheard, who was also the brother of his wife Aethelburh. But the succession was not undisputed; an aetheling named Oswald, a descendant of another branch of the house of Ceawlin, also aspired to the throne; probably he was some relative of the Ealdbert and Cynewulf whom Ine had slain, and was supported by their faction. He kept up civil war for two years, till Aethelheard slew him in 730. By this strife all the work of the last thirty years was undone, and Wessex lost its predominance in the South and sank very low.

It was, no doubt, Aethelheard's misfortunes which tempted Aethelbald of Mercia to fall upon him. This prince was now firmly seated upon his throne, and had his hands free for conquest. He was the greatest fighting man of his day, vigorous, unscrupulous and untiring: apparently, he was not without his virtues, since St. Boniface, who sent him a letter of bitter rebuke for his misdoings, grudgingly concedes that he had a liberal hand and was a lover of justice. But he was an enemy of the Church and a notorious evil liver. The Mercian successfully invaded Wessex, defeated Aethelheard, and besieged and took the royal town of Somerton (733)—probably the place of that name in Somerset, not the one in Oxfordshire. (A victory in Somerset seems better to account for the complete collapse of Wessex than one in Oxfordshire.

Yet it is likely enough that the region around the latter, the land of the Chilternsaetas, now lapsed once more into Mercian hands, Wessex, it would appear, became tributary to Aethelbald, and remained so during the rest of the life of Aethelheard and part of that of his successor Cuthred. Indeed, the victor now became *suzerain* of all England south of Humber, and was, as Bede shows, as powerful as any of the great holders of the "*imperium*" who had preceded him. (*E. H., v.* 23.) Of all the English states only Northumbria was wholly free from his overlordship, and this exception he was determined to make an end of. The King of Northumbria was now Eadbert, the cousin of Ceolwulf, to whom that feeble monarch had resigned his crown, when he retired for the second time to the cloisters of Lindisfarne (737).

★★★★★★

The *Anglo-Saxon Chronicle* wrongly ascribes Eadbert's accession to 738, and so makes Aethelbald attack Northumbria in the last year of Ceolwulf. But there is no doubt that the war began after the latter king's abdication.

★★★★★★

We have now arrived at a period when the invaluable history of Bede at last fails us. His last chapter ends in 731, and he died on May 26th, 735. For the future we get no aid from his innumerable character-sketches, his illustrative anecdotes, and his careful record of dates and sources of information. We are now following the *Anglo-Saxon Chronicle* as our main source of information, and this work was drafted more than a century later, and was primarily concerned with the history of the house of Wessex. It can be supplemented to some slight extent from the short annalistic *Chronicle* appended at the conclusion of Bede's fifth book, from the two Welsh chronicles, the *Annales Cambriae* and the *Brut y Tywysogion*—both too late to be completely trustworthy—and with equal caution from Ethelweard, a tenth century chronicler full of errors, and from Simeon of Durham, whose twelfth century book preserves the remnants of a lost Northumbrian history.

Nor are the biographies and letters of certain saints—notably Boniface the English apostle of Germany and Alcuin without their value. Yet the whole period 730-810 is very dark and difficult of comprehension. For many of the English kingdoms we have hardly a note—the succession of kings in East Anglia from 793 onward is lost, and that in Kent and Essex very imperfectly known. Even where we have some sort of a continuous narrative, as in the cases of Mercia, Northumbria and Wessex, the bare facts only are before us. The local colour of the times, the causes and meaning of events, is hard to determine, and deductions are hard to draw.

It is curious to note that while on the Continent the blackest darkness of historical knowledge lies between 600 and 750, in England it is from 730 to 850 that the obscurity is thickest To put things shortly, the age of Charlemagne fell ninety years before the age of Alfred, and in each case the bright period casts a certain light on all sides of itself. But outside that radius things are dim and often inexplicable.

But to resume—Eadbert of Northumbria was the strongest monarch who had sat on the throne of Oswy and Ecgfrid for many years, so that Aethelbald's attack on him, which broke up the sixty years' peace that had reigned on Trent and Humber since 679, might be reckoned unwise and hazardous. But the Mercian had chosen his moment with care, when Eadbert, but newly invested with the crown, was occupied in a war with the Picts. This stab in the back, "an impious fraud" as the continuator of Bede calls it, in his Northumbrian patriotism, enabled Aethelbald to lay waste a considerable part of Deira, before his adversaries' forces could be disentangled from the northern war and brought to bear against him (740).

But when the full force of Northumbria stood at bay under a capable king it was still too strong for the Mercian invader. We hear of no conquests made by Aethelbald, and since, two years later, we find him occupied by a Welsh war, while Eadbert has returned to his northern campaigning, it is clear that a peace had been patched up, after one or at the most two summers of war. The power of the two kings was too nicely balanced to encourage either in further strife; the union of England was to come neither by Mercia conquering Northumbria, nor by Northumbria conquering Mercia.

The northern wars of Eadbert were apparently brought about by new combinations among the Celts of Scotland. In this region there was at the time a great warrior, Aengus, king of the Picts, who had put down many competitors, and then turned upon his neighbour, the Dalriad Scots and the Strathclyde Britons. The former he harried to extremity, slaying their king Alpin and driving his family to take refuge in Ireland, and it would seem that the latter also were suffering from his sword. Whether Eadbert in 740 was defending the borders of Lothian against Aengus, or suppressing a rising of his own subjects, the Galloway Picts, is not clear. But it is probable that the latter was the case, for Aengus and Eadbert are soon after found in close alliance for many years, endeavouring to make an end of the Strathclyde Britons, old enemies of both. In 744 we get a note that the Picts were attacking Strathclyde, apparently with indecisive results.

******

For all this see Skene's *Celtic Scotland*, i. But it is impossible to follow that author in all his deductions. Of the details, the continuator of Bede only mentions the war in 744 and the conquest of Kyle by Eadbert. Simeon of Durham gives the alliance of 756 and the capture of Alclyde. The rest comes from the *Annales Cambriae* and the Irish chronicles.

★★★★★★

But in 750 an attack upon that realm was made by the Picts and the Northumbrians at the same moment, no doubt by friendly arrangement. The northern inroad was beaten off; in a battle at Mugdoch (Mocetauc, Maesydog) in Dumbartonshire the Britons routed the invaders and slew Talargain, the brother of Aengus. But Eadbert at the same time ravaged all their southern borders, and added the region of Kyle to his kingdom, with other lands—perhaps the adjacent Carrick and Cunningham. In 756, however, the cooperation was better managed—Eadbert and Aengus joined their armies, overran Strathclyde together, and besieged and captured Alclyde its capital, which made formal surrender to the allies (August 1st, 756).

Apparently, Aengus stripped off the northern border of the Britons, beyond Clyde, while Durmagual, son of Tudor, the King of the Welsh, did homage to Eadbert for the rest of his dominions. We are told that the Northumbrian Army suffered heavy losses while returning from Alclyde to Newburgh in the valley of the Tweed, (Simeon of Durham, *sub anno* 756), but this did not prevent Eadbert from keeping the overlordship of Strathclyde, which seems to have continued in vassalage for some years to Northumbria, till the domestic troubles of that kingdom caused it to lose all its outlying dependencies in the latter part of the eighth century.

After a reign that seems to have been in every way successful, and which forms the last bright spot in the Northumbrian annals, Eadbert, in 758, followed the example of Aethelred and Ine and the numerous other princes who retired to a cloister to finish their days. Unless he was in extreme old age, which does not seem to have been the case, for he survived nine years as a monk at York, his abdication can only be styled criminal, for the domestic commotions and strife for the crown, which he had put off for twenty-one years, broke out with redoubled vigour on his disappearance from the scene. (There is a curious tale that his abdication was so much dreaded that his vassals offered him untold lands if he would only consent to postpone it.)

The time of absolute chaos began with the murder of his son and successor Oswulf, "slain by those of his own household," apparently in a palace conspiracy, after he had held the throne for less than a year (July 25th, 759).

Meanwhile we must turn back to Aethelbald of Mercia, of whom nothing has been said since he turned back from his ineffectual attempt to overrun Deira in the year 740. The energy which he could not employ to good effect upon Northumbria seems to have been turned aside upon the Welsh. In 743 we find him accompanied by his vassal, the King of Wessex—Cuthred had now succeeded to his kinsman Aethelheard's crown, and also to his obedience to Mercia—to harry the Celts. The details of the campaign are unrecorded, but it was presumably successful, since Aethelbald is found continuing in full power, and maintaining his supremacy over all England, south of Humber, for nine years more. His long reign, however, was destined to end in defeat and gloom.

In 750 we are informed (by Simeon of Durham only, while the *A. S. Chronicle* gives the note about Aethelhun), that Cuthred rebelled against him; the same year bears the note that the Wessex king fought against "Aethelhun the proud ealdorman," possibly one of his own nobles set up against him by Aethelbald; we are told, though on late authority, that they contended *pro aliqua invidia reipublicas*. (Ethelweard, i.) But it was not till 752 that the war came to a head, at a great battle fought by Burford in Oxfordshire; presumably Cuthred was advancing to win back the old West Saxon district of the Chilternsaetas. The King of the Mercians was completely defeated, and lost not only the territory in dispute but his supremacy over Southern England.

He survived for five years longer, but with diminished power, and probably among civil dissensions, for his end was that he was "miserably murdered at night by his own bodyguard" (*a suis tutoribus*) at Seckington in 757. Treason on the part of the thegns of the royal *comitatus* was such a rare thing—this case and that of Oswulf in 758 just narrated are almost unique—that it is probable that Aethelbald, soured by defeat, had goaded his followers to desperation by a course of tyrannical acts. The throne fell to Beornred, a distant relative, who may either have been already in arms against the old king, or have been the contriver of the assassination plot. But "he held the kingdom for a little while and unhappily." Before the year was out, he was defeated and expelled by Offa, the son of Thingferth, Aethelbald's cousin (grandson of his first cousin, to be exact), and natural heir.

This prince was destined within a few years to raise the Mercian realm to an even higher level of imperial power than Aethelbald had achieved, but at the beginning of his reign he had much to set right and restore. It appears that his opportunities of greatness originally came from the temporary collapse of the West Saxon kingdom, under the successors of Cuthred, the victor of Burford.

After that successful campaign Cuthred, as it seems, had made peace with Mercia on favourable terms, and turned his energy against the Damnonians, who may have taken the opportunity to assail him in the rear while he was engaged with Aethelbald. We are assured that he was victorious, and it is quite possible that he may have won some territory on the side of Devonshire. But in the following year (756) he died, to the great detriment of Wessex, which at once fell into times of trouble. His successor was his near kinsman, Sigebert, who, unhappily for his subjects, was a reckless and cruel tyrant

★★★★★★

He was *propinquus* (or *maeg* in *Anglo-Saxon Chronicle*). Here begins an error of two years in the *Chronicle*, which goes on for a century and causes vast confusion in dates till the middle of the ninth century, when right figures recommence after. See Plummer's *Bede*, ii., ciii.

★★★★★★

The West Saxons endured him for a year, when sedition broke out and the witan declared him deposed, and gave the kingdom to Cynewulf the aetheling, who represented another branch of the royal house, though his descent from Cerdic and Ceawlin is not preserved. But Sigebert maintained himself in Hampshire "until he murdered the ealdorman who longest remained faithful to him," one Cumbra by name. After this Cynewulf drove him out of his small remaining dominion, and chased him into the forest of Andred. There he lurked, until he was slain by a certain swineherd, who slew him to avenge ealdorman Cumbra, his late master, at Privetsflood (Privet, Hants).

It would seem that these domestic troubles broke the power of Wessex, which under Cynewulf does not appear as an aggressive state, and for many years made no attempt to check the restoration of the Mercian *imperium* under Offa. Indeed till Cynewulf came into collision with that great king in 777, we have no information about his reign, save that he fought incessantly with the Damnonian Welsh, probably rather to defend lands already won, as we should gather, than in order to extend his borders westward, for his realm was clearly in a weak condition. It is possible that the aetheling Cyneheard, the brother of the deposed Sigebert, was giving trouble all through Cynewulf's time, though it was only at the end of a rather long reign of thirty-one years that the king fell a victim to the aetheling's hatred (786).

While this obscure monarch was reigning in Wessex, Offa was restoring the glories of Mercia. His first recorded campaigns were against the Welsh; in 760 he defeated them in front of Hereford; since this was the capital of the Magesaetas, and lay well within the border of their territory, we must conclude that the Celts had been the aggressors. It does not appear that the King of Mercia made any attempt to avenge himself for some years, though when the chastisement did come it was heavy and unsparing. In the early section of his reign it was rather in Southern England that he was active.

Between 760 and 777 he apparently conquered one after another all the minor States. We know that by 771-72 he was so far master of the South that he was able to dispose of land in Sussex, by charters to which Ecgbert of Kent and Cynewulf of Wessex set their hands in consent, evidently as vassals. Probably their submission was at first uneasy, for Offa is found beating the Kentishmen at Otford, near Sevenoaks, in 774, and then three years later in collision with Cynewulf, who fought him at Bensington near Dorchester-on-Thames in 777, but was utterly defeated. (The dates 774 and 777 in the *Anglo-Saxon Chronicle* are apparently, as usual in this period, two years out.) The town was taken, and with it all the land of the Chilternsaetas was annexed to Mercia, for the last time; it never went back to Wessex until, in common with other Mercian lands, it became subject first to Ecgbert, the great unifier, and then to his grandson, Alfred the Great

With the Battle of Bensington, active opposition to Offa in South England seems to have come to an end, and for the remainder of his reign—nearly twenty years—he ruled with undisputed sway over vassals who had been taught obedience. The state of the smaller kingdoms seems to have been in some cases peculiar—several kings reigning in them at once under Offa's supremacy.

This would be well suited to the *suzerain's* ends, as it would keep his subjects weak. In Kent, from 760, with or after Eardwulf and Alric the last certain descendants of Hengist, there were reigning at different times, as charter's show, Sigered who called himself "*rex dimidiae partis provinciae Cantuariorum*" (about 760-62); Ecgbert II., whose dates run between 765 and 779; Heahbert whose *floruit* is about 775; and Ealhmund, a prince of West Saxon blood who signs as *subregulus*, about 784-86. (Concerning whom, see Chapter 9.)

Apparently as many as three of them must have coexisted simultaneously in the one small kingdom. There are some signs of a divided kingship in East Anglia also, but here, in the very end of his reign (793), Offa took the high-handed step of slaying the ruling prince and annexing his realm to Mercia. There was evidently something particularly atrocious about this business, as the young king Aethelbert was reckoned a saint, and became one of the more popular names in the English Calendar. Later legends told how he was lured to Offa's court by the promise of the hand of his daughter, Aelfthryth, and then murdered by the contrivance of Queen Cynethryth. Cynewulf of Wessex (767-86), who was contemporary with the greater part of Offa's long reign, came to an evil end in circumstances which throw a lurid light on the troubled condition of his realm during the Mercian supremacy.

The entry concerning his death in the *Anglo-Saxon Chronicle* is too characteristic to be omitted. It is written at such unwonted length, and with such picturesque detail, that we must suspect it to be some fragment of a heroic poem which the chronicler thought too good to be lost. Cynewulf "purposed to expel from his realm the aetheling Cyneheard, brother of his predecessor Sigebert" apparently a pretender to his throne, rather than an overgrown subject. The aetheling was in arms with a small body of his followers, when he heard that the king was near him almost unattended. For Cynewulf was intending to visit a lady dwelling at Merantun (Merton in Surrey) who was his mistress.

Therefore, he had left the greater part of his retinue behind him, and took to Merton only a few of his most confidential attendants. While he was sitting alone with the lady in her bower, Cyneheard and his men rode suddenly up to the homestead, poured into the courtyard, and rushed in straight to the king, who snatched up his sword and fought for his life at the door, till noticing the rebel prince in the rear, he charged out upon him, and wounded him, but was immediately encompassed and slain. The thegns of Cynewulf, alarmed by the screams of the lady, came rushing out of the hall just in time to see their master fall. The aetheling cried to them that the king was dead, and that all of them should have not only their lives but rich endowment, if they would take service with him.

But the outraged retainers laughed him to scorn, attacked him, and were slain every man, save one, "and he a hostage, a Welshman, and sore wounded". Next morning the house where the slaughter had taken place was beset by the main body of Cynewulf's retinue, under Osric the ealdorman, who had heard of the king's death during the night. Through the barricaded doors the aetheling offered them "their own choice of lands and money if they would take him as king, and showed them that he had with him many of their own kinsmen, who would be true to him". But the besiegers cried out that no one was dearer to them than their lord, and that they would never follow his murderer, and they bade their kinsmen who were within to quit the aetheling and depart. Then Cyneheard's men answered "that they were no more minded to quit their lord than your companions yesterday, who fell with the king". Whereupon the ealdorman and his band assaulted the gate, and after hard fighting won their way in, and slew the aetheling and all who were with him, save one man who was Osric's godson, "and he was wounded in several places".

The tale illustrates well enough the old English ideal of chivalry, the boundless fidelity due from the sworn member of the war-band to his lord. But it also bears eloquent witness to the uncertainty of a kingship under which any ambitious prince could hope to buy over the chief officers of his master by lavish offers. Doubtless many another such adventurer as Cyneheard thus won the crown; similar scenes had another end in the cases of Osred and Aethelbald. The uncertain law of succession was a curse to the land, and was to remain so for many a year more.

Cynewulf was succeeded by one Beorhtric, of whom we know nothing more than that "his right paternal kin went back to Cerdic": he was apparently no close relation either to the dead king or the aetheling who had slain him. He reigned sixteen years (786-802), and was evidently a quiet vassal to Offa, whose daughter, Eadburh, he married. Wessex legend related that this lady was the instrument of her husband's death; she much hated a young thegn whom Beorhtric favoured, and prepared poison for him in a cup, which the king, coming in by chance, took up and drank. She fled to France, and was sheltered for a time by the Emperor Charlemagne, who gave her a nunnery as endowment. But she there lived such a scandalous life that she was expelled, and died an outcast in the streets of Pavia. So, Asser tells the tale, having learnt it (as he says) from the mouth of the unlying Alfred himself, two generations after the tragedy.

★★★★★★

Asser says (§18) that the story of Eadburh's evil doings and end was told him by Alfred, and corroborated by the witness of several English travellers, who had seen her begging her bread in the capital of Lombardy when they were young. He adds what seems to be a mere folk tale, concerning a humorous offer which Charlemagne made to marry the lady when first she arrived in his dominions. It is told of other persons in other ages.

Offa's later and more serious invasions of Wales all belong to the second period of his reign, when South England was already subdued. The first was in 778, when we are told that he devastated all South Wales. In 784? comes his second spoiling of South Wales, which befell at Midsummer, and is said to have been provoked by previous incursions of the Celts into his own land. It was apparently after this that he drew from sea to sea the great earthwork that still preserves his name.

> He caused a dyke to be made as a boundary between him and Wales, to enable him to withstand more easily the raids of his enemies, and that is called *Clawd Offa* from that time till this. And it extends from the southern to the northern sea, from opposite Bristol at one end, to above Flint on the other, between the monastery of Basingwerk and Coleshill. (*Brut y Tywysogion.*)

To describe its course more exactly, we may say that it follows the east bank of the Wye from its estuary as far as a point seven miles west of Hereford, and then turns north-west past Kington, Knighton and Montgomery to the Severn near Welshpool. From thence it strikes across Denbighshire, by Chirk and Ruabon, till it reaches the mouth of the Dee five miles north of Mold. In this part of its course much that is now reckoned Welsh, in the counties of Montgomery, Denbigh and Flint, is marked as Mercian; farther south, on the other hand, it leaves as Welsh much in Herefordshire that is now reckoned English— all the region of Ercyng (Irchenfield) and the Golden Valley. Since Hereford had been an English town for more than a century, (see chapter 5), it seems that the boundary had not been moved forward in this direction.

But in the north the advance was considerable, and placed all the lowlands north of the great bend of the Severn in Mercian hands. Offa's last Welsh invasion, which included a devastation of Rhuveniog (West Denbighshire) in 795, (*Annales Cambriae, sub anno* 795), was probably caused by an attempt of the princes of Gwynedd to rebel, and win back some portion of the lost lands, when they thought that their conqueror had grown old and feeble. The Dyke, as has often been pointed out, is not a work defensible along its whole length, but rather a boundary line, in the style of the first Roman *limes* in Northumberland, intended to mark clearly the border between Mercia and the vassal Welsh, which the latter could not overstep without definitely trespassing on their *suzerain's* land and challenging him to war.

From 777, the date of the Battle of Bensington, down to his death in 796, Offa ruled England south of Humber with a completeness of authority which none of his predecessors had enjoyed for such a long period of years. On the continent he seems to have been regarded as monarch of the whole English nation—Pope Hadrian I. formally addressed him as *Rex Anglorum,* Charlemagne dealt with him almost as an equal. Normally their relations were friendly, and at one time there were long negotiations for the marriage of one of Offa's daughter to Charles the Younger, the eldest son of the great Frankish king. We are told that they failed because Offa wished to secure in return the hand of one of Charlemagne's daughters for his son Ecgferth, which was refused him—for the Frank would never allow his daughters to marry, a thing that caused much wonder and scandal then and thereafter.

The coolness that ensued soon passed over, and in 786 Charlemagne, when returning in triumph from his great victory over the Aval's on the Danube, sent to Offa some of his trophies, gold, swords, and embroidered garments, as testimonies of his regard and friendship. We have a good deal of incidental information regarding the relations of the great king of the Franks and the overlord of Southern England from the letters of the English scholar Alcuin, who, though he had settled down on the continent and become a member of Charlemagne's court, never ceased to remain in close touch with his native country.

Not the least important side of Offa's life was his ecclesiastical policy, in which he evidently took a deep interest. He was a very zealous builder and benefactor of monasteries—like all the better kings of his age: St. Alban's was undoubtedly one of his foundations, and perhaps the house on Thorney Island near London, which Edward the Confessor developed into the Abbey of Westminster, was another. But in one respect he was a poor friend both to the Church and to the unity of England. He seems to have resented the fact that the primate to whom all his bishops owed obedience was placed at Canterbury, outside the limits of his own realm, and designed to break up the ecclesiastical union of Southern England by creating a new archbishopric within his own borders, which should be independent of the successors of St. Augustine.

This was a retrograde step, and unnecessary also, considering that Kent had been politically subject to him for many years, and had made no attempt to get free since the Battle of Otford in 774. But Bregwine and Jaenbert, the archbishops of Offa's central years (76193) were not Mercians by birth, and probably were not so subservient as the great king desired. At any rate he determined to have a primate of his own, dwelling under his own eye at Lichfield, who should rule over all that lay between Thames and Humber.

This plan was carried out, with the consent of Pope Hadrian, in 786: perhaps the papacy acquiesced in the scheme merely to please the king, perhaps, however, because archbishops ruling over smaller areas were less likely to give trouble and assume an independent attitude than those whose sphere of influence was conterminous with a whole national or imperial unit. At any rate the papal legates, George and Theophylact, visited England, and after being hospitably entertained by Offa, executed a sort of visitation of the whole country. George went north to York, and in company with Archbishop Eanbald held a provincial council for Northumbria, at which Alcuin (then in England) chanced to be present. Theophylact visited Mercia and its subject kingdoms.

Then in the following year (787) both the *legates* were present together at the Council of Chelsea. Its first business was to discuss and assent to twenty decrees concerning details of church-governance, which were proposed under papal authority. One provided for the holding of two provincial Synods every year; another ordered the bishops to carry out annual visitations of their dioceses; a third and most excellent clause gave the bishops the duty of inspecting monasteries, to see that their rule was duly kept. One of the greatest ecclesiastical troubles of the Middle Ages, the independence of religious houses, who so often defied the diocesan, would have been prevented if only this arrangement had continued. But undoubtedly the most important part of the proceedings was the carrying out of Offa's scheme for the cutting up of the Archbishopric of Canterbury: the plan was vehemently opposed, so that the meeting is called in the *Anglo-Saxon Chronicle* "the contentious Synod." (Under the erroneous date 785. But all the years in this part of the *Chronicle* are two years out, as has been previously noted.)

But Offa, backed by the legates, was far too strong for Archbishop Jaenbert and his friends, and the matter was carried through. Higbert of Lichfield was designated as primate of all the lands of Mercia and East Anglia, seven dioceses in all, while Canterbury was for the future to have authority only over the Bishops of Rochester, Selsey, Winchester, London and Sherborne. Pope Hadrian sent the archbishop his pall, and Offa in gratitude promised to send every year 365 gold *"mancuses"* to Rome, to be used for alms and supplying the lights in St. Peter's. This donation was probably the origin of the well-known "Peter's pence" of which so much is heard in later history.

Chance has preserved a single specimen of Offa's *"mancus,"* which we find to our surprise was copied not from any late Roman coin, but from the *dirhems* of the Saracen *Caliphs*. It bears on both sides a blundered Arabic inscription, across which the words *Offa Rex* are engraved in large characters. This was a most exceptional piece of money; there had been a little gold coined in England at an earlier date, very small pieces copied from the Frankish *tremissis*, but it had long gone out of currency, and the striking of this larger coin was abnormal; there is nothing to compare it with in the Heptarchic age except a *solidus* of Archbishop Wigmund of York (837-64)—an equally rare issue, and equally notable in its type, which presents a full-face bust of that prelate, in a style far better than that of other contemporary coins English or continental. Offa is much better remembered for his silver than for his gold coins; he was the first king who discontinued the old *sceatta* and adopted the Carlovingian *denarius* or silver penny.

The humiliation of the See of Canterbury was only destined to last for sixteen years, as after Offa's death and that of his son Ecgferth, Coenwulf, the next King of Mercia, forced Higbert to resign, and restored his lights to Archbishop Aethelheard. His political reasons for doing so will be explained in their due place, and he had to do with a primate who was a Mercian by birth and a loyal supporter, and not with a more or less open enemy, such as Jaenbert had been in the time of his predecessor.

Offa died in the summer of 796, still undisputedly supreme over all Southern England, in great amity with Charlemagne, and full of years and prosperity. (July 26th, according to Simeon of Durham or 28th according to the *Anglo-Saxon Chronicle*.) His dynasty might have become permanent rulers of all the smaller States if it had but continued. But Fate intervened; his only son Ecgferth died in the flower of his youth only 141 days after his father, and with him the line was extinct. An heir was sought by the Mercian witan in one Coenwulf, a very remote relative, since he descended from a brother of Penda different from that Eowa from whom came the line of Aethelbald and Offa. His reign will be dealt with elsewhere, for just ere he came to the throne the great central dividing line of old English history was reached—in Offa's thirty-sixth year (793) the first Danish raid on this island had taken place, and the new age of the Viking invasion had begun.

Before turning over this new leaf, it is necessary to dispose of the history of the unfortunate kingdom of Northumbria dining the years that correspond to Offa's long reign. We had followed it no farther than the death of Oswulf, the son of that Eadbert who had laid down the crown against his subjects' desire in 758. This short-lived prince was slain after a reign of less than a year by conspirators among his own thegns (July 25, 759). The place of the murder was "Mickle-Wongton," apparently Great Whittington near Corbridge. Eleven days later one Aethelwald, nicknamed "Moll," was elected *"a sua plebe,"* as the continuator of Bede puts it—a phrase which seems to hint that it was rather the popular voice than the will of the *sapientes*, greater councillors, which placed him on the throne. He was supposed to have been the instigator of the murder of Oswulf: his descent is uncertain; the statement that he was an illegitimate brother of Eadbert, and so the uncle of Oswulf, whose death he was accused of contriving, is certainly wrong.

******

It has been suggested that he was a descendant of his namesake, Aethelwald the son of Oswald, who was Sub-King of Deira during Penda's ascendency. But see Haddan and Stubbs, iii., and Cadwallader Bates, *Northumberland*.

******

His, election, however, was not undisputed. The son of the late king was still a mere child, but the aetheling Oswine, apparently a younger brother or cousin of Oswulf, took up arms against Aethelwald, and found much support in Bernicia. However, "King Moll" went northward against him, brought him to action at Eildon Hill, near Melrose, on the Tweed, and there scattered his army. (The *Anglo-Saxon Chronicle* calls the battle-spot "Eadwin's Cliff.") The aetheling was left on the field mortally wounded (Aug. 6th, 761). This victory, however, only gave Aethelwald four years of troubled and uncertain kingship, in which the chroniclers find time to note the "mickle winter" of 763-64, which lasted from December to March, two years of "a great tribulation of mortality, several grievous dysentery, raging, but more especially the dysentery," and disastrous fires which destroyed York, Doncaster and other places.

Aethelwald was apparently regarded as an unlucky sovereign, and "fires seen in the air lasting almost the whole night" (*aurora borealis* or a shower of meteors?) on January 1st, 765, were considered ominous

158

of more trouble to come. It took the shape of a turbulent meeting of the Northumbrian witan at Finchale (Winchanheal), near Durham, in the following autumn, at which the king was deposed and, much against his will, tonsured and sent into a monastery. The chaotic rule of succession in the North is sufficiently shown by the fact that although Aethelwald himself had a son, and Aelfwald, the heir of his predecessor Oswulf, still lived, the *sapientes* went out of their way to elect and crown one Alchred, the head of a line which claimed to descend from Ealric, one of the younger sons of Ida, though none of his ancestors had ever worn the crown, and their royal descent seems not to have been unquestioned (Nov. 3rd, 565). Thus, at this time there were no less than three separate races contending for the Northumbrian throne, and their representatives succeeded each other in chaotic alternation.

To strengthen his elective title to the throne Alchred took as his wife Osgeofu, daughter of the murdered Oswulf, but it availed him little when her brother was alive to claim the throne. A curious letter of the royal pair to Lull, Bishop of Mainz, the successor of St. Boniface, has been preserved, in which they set forth that the state of affairs both in Church and in State is troubled and unsatisfactory, but that they accept it as a divine dispensation. Rebellion was apparently rife; at any rate, in 769 the royal town of Catterick "was burned by Earnred the tyrant, and the wretch himself, by God's just judgment, perished by fire within the same year". We have no knowledge which of the contending lines claimed him as a member, but he was clearly an unsuccessful pretender to the throne. Yet Alchred was not destined to close his eyes in peace; his rule evidently gave little satisfaction, and at Eastertide, 774, "by the counsel and consent of all his subjects, deposed by a combination of the royal house and the princes, he changed his majesty for exile".

Aethelred, the son of Aethelwald Moll, was elected in his place, but got no secure footing. The banished monarch first seized Bamborough at the head of a few faithful adherents, and, when evicted, then fled to Cynoht, King of the Picts, the successor of Aengus, who seems to have kept up his predecessor's friendship with Northumbria. There he died in exile, but his son Osred remained as a pretender to the throne, which he was one day to enjoy for a short space.

Aethelred, the son of Moll, was apparently one of those princes who in a time of trouble think murder the sole remedy for all evils; the recipe has been known to succeed, but only when its employer was a man of genius—like Chlodovech the Frank or Ivan the Terrible—and this was evidently not the case with Aethelred. His whole record is one of blood, culminating in 778 in the simultaneous slaying by treachery (*fraude*) of three ealdormen (or high-reeves, as the *Anglo-Saxon Chronicle* calls them)—Eardwulf of Bamborough, Cynewulf and Ecga. This apparently was too much for his subjects, and he was expelled a few months later, "and compelled to turn to the tone of sorrow and to utter pitiful complaints". For eleven years he remained in exile, waiting for a second chance for a snatch at power, which was ultimately to be granted him, much to the detriment of Northumbria, for he was in every way evil, an adulterer and a profaner of sanctuary, as well as a murderer.

The witan, on the expulsion of this wicked prince, gave the crown to Aelfwald, son of Oswulf, attracted perhaps not only by his descent from Eadbert, the last successful king in the land, but by his personal virtues. He was a pious and just monarch, "men called him God's friend," and miracles attested his sanctity. He ruled for nine years (779-88), a long period as Northumbrian reigns went, in this period of chaos; his four predecessors had only filled twenty-one years among them. It was also, as it seems, a period of comparative quiet: we have no mention of civil war, and the best remembered incident of the time was the visit to Northumbria of the papal legate George Bishop of Ostia, who held (as has been already mentioned) a provincial council at Finchale (786), when with the consent of the king.

Archbishop Eanbald, and the other prelates of the North, those same twenty decrees were promulgated which were afterwards laid before the Council of Chelsea. But not even blameless life and general popularity could save a Northumbrian king in this age from the common fate of his race. Aelfwald was "miserably murdered by his ealdorman Sicgan at Scythlecester near the wall, (apparently Chesters, near Chollerford), on September 23, 788, as the result of a conspiracy He was buried with much wailing in Hexham Abbey, and a light was seen to shine for many nights, so the tale went, over the spot where he had been slain; a chapel was afterwards built upon it.

Aelfwald left two infant sons, Aelf and Aelfwine; they were too young to reign, and the witan chose the exile Osred, son of Alchred, to take the crown. But the evil days had begun again; after a reign of somewhat over a year (788-90), the new king was "circumvented by the wiles of his princes, arrested, deposed, and forcibly tonsured in his city of York." More fortunate than his predecessor, he got off for the moment with his life, and succeeded soon afterwards in escaping to the Isle of Man. The crown fell to Aethelred, the cruel son of King Moll, in whose interest the conspiracy had been managed. He returned to the throne, which he had lost in 779, in no wise improved by the bitterness of prison and exile. (We know of the imprisonment from Alcuin, who was visiting England at the time.)

He took the young sons of the saintly King Aelfwald out of their sanctuary in York Minster with false promises of safety, and sent them away to be secretly drowned in Windermere. Another of his crimes had a curious end: he ordered that the aetheling Eardwulf should be put to death; his assassins led out their prisoner before the gate of the monastery of Ripon, and there slew him, as they supposed. His body was taken up by the monks, and placed under a tent outside the church, for burial on the next day. But after midnight the supposed dead man was found alive, and seeking sanctuary at the altar; he had been only wounded and had come to himself after a swoon of many hours, and crawled into the church. He was apparently assisted to escape by the brethren—certainly he fled into exile and survived to become King of Northumbria sixteen years after.

In 792 the exiled king, Osred II., made an attempt to recover his kingdom, being invited to return from his refuge in Man by a faction of nobles, who told him that the rule of Aethelred had become un-bearable. He landed secretly in Northumbria and raised his standard, but his followers flinched from him, and he was captured by the king, who immediately ordered him to be beheaded. This seemed to make Aethelred's throne secure, despite of all his cruelties, and he was hon-oured with the hand of the great Offa's daughter, Aelflaed, a sign that the ruler of the South regarded him as a neighbour whose friendship was worth securing.

But a disaster was impending over him of a different kind from any that had gone before. It was no wonder that the spring of the fourth year after his restoration (793) was filled with dire prodigies—showers of meteors, perpetual thunderstorms, fiery dragons seen in the mid-night sky, and such-like—for in the summer occurred the first great Viking raid that penetrated to England. It was wholly unexpected, since the struggle between Charlemagne and the Danes, which pre-cipitated the outbreak of this pest, had apparently roused little interest on this side of the North Sea. An attack from the side of the sea by a foreign enemy was a thing which never had been seen, since the first of the Angles settled in Bernicia and Deira.

Hence the terror aroused was dreadful, when it was reported that a squadron of pirate vessels from the Pagan North had descended upon the island sanctuary of Lindisfarne, sacked its church, plundered its treasures of gold and silver, slain some of the brethren with the sword, drowned other's, and carried off a remnant as slaves. It was at first hoped that this was an isolated and abnormal phenomenon; but in the next spring the heathen appeared again, and plundered Jarrow, the monastery where Bede had lived and died.

It was some consolation that on this occasion they did not escape unscathed: their leader—traditionally said to have been the famous Ragnar Lodbrog—was captured and put to a cruel death; later generations said that the Northumbrian king cast him into a pit filled with adders. (An error: Ragnar's sons were harrying England eighty years later.) Many of the Danish ships were cast on shore by a violent north-east wind, and of their crews some were drowned and others taken and slaughtered. King Aethelred was not the man to spare an enemy of any sort.

But his bloodstained reign was just at an end. In the seventh year of his reign, on April 18th, 796, he was slain at Corbridge by conspirators, who proclaimed as his successor one Osbald, an aetheling who was also an ealdorman. We know nothing of his ancestry. But his party had miscalculated their strength. After reigning only twenty-seven days he was driven out by a faction headed by Eardwulf, the ealdorman of whose miraculous escape from death at Ripon we heard a little while back. Three kings reigned in a year, and Charlemagne, who had been an ally of the cruel King Aethelred, expressed his high disgust, and declared that the Northumbrians were worse than their pagan enemies the Danes.

The kingdom had indeed sunk to the very depths of degradation. It would seem to have been at this time that it lost its long-preserved *suzerainty* over the Galloway Picts, whose last recorded English bishop was consecrated in 791, and apparently died or withdrew from his See about 803. There are some signs that the border against the Strathclyde Welsh was also receding. The only wonder is that Offa of Mercia never seems to have thought it worthwhile to assert his supremacy over the decadent realm. Perhaps he considered that the turbulent and faction-ridden kingdom was safer as an impotent neighbour than as a troublesome vassal-state.

It is clear that he might have had it as his own, by assisting one faction against another, at any time that he chose during the last twenty years of his reign. But he preferred to keep on terms of friendship with the *de facto* king of the moment: the only case in which he seems to have committed himself to anything more, was when he gave his daughters hand to the cruel king Aethelred. When his son-in-law was murdered, he made no attempt to avenge him; but this may have been because he was already sickening for his final illness; the Northumbrian tyrant died on April 18th. Offa expired on July 26th, 796.

Having once reached the commencement of the Viking raids, we must consign the remainder of the miserable annals of the Northern kingdom to the chapter which deals with the struggle between Dane and Englishman. The troubles of Northumbria were to be protracted for another seventy years, under a succession of seven kings, whose record is quite as miserable as that of the last age, though one of them, Eanred (808-40), succeeded in prolonging his reign for the unprecedented term of thirty-two years, through no great merit of his own. Nothing short of the extermination of all the branches of the house of Ida by the sword of the Danes could teach these misguided Northumbrians wisdom.

They finally found themselves the servants of the stranger, and only achieved a kind of freedom when, in company with their conquerors, they were absorbed into the new kingdom of All-England, through the annexation of the whole North by the great kings of the house of Wessex—the descendants of Alfred—in the middle of the tenth century. Melancholy as is the whole later history of the Heptarchic kingdoms, that of Northumbria certainly constitutes its most depressing page.

CHAPTER 7

The Social Organisation of the Early English Kingdoms

Any attempt to give an account of the social and political organisation of the Teutonic kingdoms in Britain during the first two centuries of their existence must necessarily proceed by the method of working backward. Contemporary records there are none: but starting from the very moment of the conversion of the Jutes of Kent to Christianity, we find a long series of codes of laws, charters, and other instruments, which cast a light on the previous condition of the English peoples. And information no less precious is to be elicited from the literary documents of the early Christian period, and most especially from the long and detailed *Ecclesiastical History* of Bede, who is almost as valuable for the social facts which he records incidentally, in the course of his countless anecdotes and divagations, as for his political narrative. The process of working backward has its dangers, particularly when the nation and the state have just passed through a period of rapid development and transformation, caused by the introduction of Christianity.

But these dangers of this method are no whit greater than those which lie in the way of those who have taken the opposite course, and have endeavoured to reconstruct the social organisation of the Early English kingdoms by working forward from the picture of the second-century Teutonic tribes contained in the *Germania* of Tacitus. The Roman author gives a sketch mainly derived from his knowledge of the races just beyond the Rhine, on the frontier of the empire. He sometimes errs from misconception, and sometimes seems to be more set on pointing a moral than on supplying an accurate analysis of facts. More than three hundred years passed between the time when he wrote and the settlement of the English on the coast of Eastern Britain, and in that long period all the Teutonic tribes had gone through many new experiences.

We do not even know how far his picture of the German states, if correct in the main for the frontier peoples whom he had seen, would have served, at the moment when he published his book, for a description of the remoter races, dwelling by the Elbe or the Eider. Caution, in short, is necessary on either hand: it is even more dangerous to argue that a second-century institution was still unchanged in the sixth century, than to deduce that a social fact observable in the early eighth century was already existent in the days of Ida or Ceawlin. Still, within certain limits, argument and deduction are possible, and it is only by their use that we can make any statement with regard to the dark space between Hengist and Aethelbert.

The first problem that confronts us, when we face this most problematic age, is one on which most of the constitutional difficulties of Anglo-Saxon history ultimately depend. Was the conquest of Britain carried out purely and solely by the personal warbands of individual chiefs—*duces, heretogas, ealdormen*—or was it to any extent a settlement of tribes and families, as opposed to a settlement of individuals dependent on their chosen war-lords? Looking at the mere probabilities of the case, we should be inclined to accept the former alternative, and to think it probable that the first Teutonic communities in this island must have been started by the gift of land, with or without servile dependants dwelling upon it, by a conquering king to the members of his comitatus, the sworn followers whom he was bound to maintain in return for their loyal service in battle.

The nucleus of the invading hosts was undoubtedly composed of such retainers, and in most cases, it is clear that the English settlements were not made by races migrating *en masse*, and carrying the whole tribal community and its customs with them, but by parties, larger or smaller, conducted by adventurous leaders. The main body of the Saxons and the Jutes certainly remained behind in their old continental sites, whatever may have been the case with the Angles, (see chapter 2), of whom we have seen reason to believe that the majority emigrated, and left that gap behind them, in the *"Angulus"* in Schleswig, which Bede describes. Fragments of a race, who had left the ancestral home at various dates and under many leaders—as did the Saxons at least—and who formed many settlements, not under the old tribal king, but under princes representing younger branches of the royal house, might be expected to organise themselves as new military states, dependent on their chiefs, rather than as tribal groups.

In short, we should expect to find reproduced in Britain the state of things which certainly prevailed among the Frankish conquerors of Gaul, where the royal power was all-important, and the settlers regarded themselves as the sworn liegemen of the conqueror who had parcelled out among them the lands of the Roman provincials, not as a mere tribal community owing a traditional allegiance to its ancestral monarch.

We have seen reason to believe that the war-bands which invaded Britain were decidedly more heterogeneous in blood than the Franks, and have noted that the first names of the English states are not drawn from old designations of sub-tribes in Germany or the Cimbric peninsula. When they are not purely local (like East-Saxons, Mercians, or Mid-Angles) they are either borrowed from the Celtic lands recently conquered (like Bernicians, Deirans, Lindiswaras, Kentings) or obviously designate a new and artificial unit like Gewissae "the confederates". (See chapter 3.)

It is impossible to point out a single name for the peoples of any Anglo-Saxon kingdom or sub-kingdom which was clearly in use on the continent for an already existing community before the invasion began.

Notwithstanding all this, we are confronted with the stubborn fact that the social organisation of the English states, when first we can

165

visualise them with some approach to detailed accuracy, in the seventh century, does not seem to have been the simple military monarchy that we should have expected. We should have looked to find an all-powerful king, surrounded by subjects who derived their endowment from him, and who only differed in importance, one from another, in proportion as they had received a greater or less share of his bounty. Among such a community "nobility by service," *i.e.*, the differentiation of rank according to the scale on which the settlers had commended themselves to the king's liberality, and approached more or less nearly to his person, might have been expected to prevail.

And as a matter of fact, nobility service—as we shall see—did ultimately become the main feature of the Anglo-Saxon social system. But just where we should have looked for it in its most marked shape, in the earliest document available, the Kentish laws of the seventh century, we find in fact something different.

The first document in which the ranks and classes of one of the Teutonic kingdoms of Britain is set forth is the short Kentish code known as the "Laws of Aethelbert". This compilation, which dates from a few years after the king's conversion to Christianity, is followed at a distance of two and three generations by later Kentish laws issued by his descendants—Eadric, Lothere, and Wihtraed. Like other early codes, the Kentish laws deal mainly with fines to be imposed for the various degrees of breach of the peace, from homicide downward, and are largely devoted to the setting forth of the exact compensation due for injury to members of each class in the state. The notable point about them is that they divide the population of Kent into three classes, *eorls, ceorls*, and *laets* (besides slaves who stand apart in the reckoning) *i.e.*, nobles, freemen, and tributary dependants, a partition apparently corresponding very nearly to the threefold classification found in the continental codes of several North-German tribes.

For example, the Frisian laws give the division into *nobiles*, freemen, and *liti*. So, do those of the Old Saxons by the Elbe. The code of the Thuringians (*i.e.*, the Netherland Thoringi, we have seen reason to believe; chapter 2) has a similar division, but calls the noble *adalingus*. While agreeing with these, the Kentish laws show a sharp contrast with the Frankish codes, where the only legal distinction between persons (outside that between Frank and Roman) is that the king's ministers and henchmen, the *comites, antrustions*, etc., are estimated at a value far greater than that of the ordinary Frankish freeman. There is little trace of birth nobility in the Merovingian realm, where the king alone is the source of all power and honour.

In Kent, on the other hand, as in Frisia or Saxony, birth-nobility certainly existed. And it seems probable that the same may have originally been the case in other English kingdoms. The *eorls* of the Kentish codes find their parallel in the *nobiles* of Bede's *Ecclesiastical History*. In the account of the great baptisms in Northumbria in 627 (ii 14) the *nobiles* among the converts are as carefully distinguished from the *regii viri* (the king's thegns and other ministers), as in another passage they sure from the "*privati*" or ordinary freemen (*v.* 23). Similarly, when Bede in another chapter (*iii.* 30) contrasts the "*optimates*" with the "*plebs*" of the East Saxons, the only natural way to understand his phrase is to think of the nobly-born as distinguished from the merely free-born, not to imagine that we are confronted with royal retainers as opposed to the *ceorls*.

So too when in the *Historia Abbatum,* he tells us that Benedict Biscop was *nobili stirpe gentis Anglorum progenitus,* (*E. H. iii.*) he is most evidently referring to ancestral blood; Benedict has been a member of King Oswy's following, but it was not this but his *stirps* that made him noble in Bede's eyes. Similarly, the unfortunate King Oswin, whom Oswy slew unrighteously, is said to have been so kind *nobililus suis atque ignobilibus* that even from other states *viri nobilissimi* would frequently come, with the request that they might be allowed to join his household. They were not ennobled by adhering to him, but were already "*nobilissimi,*" obviously by blood.

The Kentish codes would have called all such people *eorlcund*. Indeed the term *eorl* was so well known as the title of the well-born, as opposed to *ceorl* the ordinary man, that the jingle "*eorl* and *ceorl,*" as expressing the whole body of the king's free subjects, continued to be used for long generations after the cross-division into persons belonging, or not belonging, to the nobility of service had become the dominant fact in social life. It was employed even by Alfred in the ninth century in general phrases, though long before his time the other form of classification had become the really important one for all practical dealings, both between man and man, and between the state and the individual.

It seems then that a clear distinction between the nobles by birth and the mere freemen existed in the English kingdoms so far as we can trace them back, and that the former had marked and manifest superiority by reason of their status, quite without reference to their relations to the king. A Kentish *eorl* in Lothere's time had a *weregeld* of

300 gold *solidi*, while the death of a mere *ceorl* could be atoned for by a fine of 100 *solidi* only—and so in all the scale of valuations.

Nor is this the only sign that the king's favour was not the sole factor in differentiating social privilege in Early England. The family group appears as an important feature in all legislation. The individual, *eorl* or *ceorl*, is not merely a unit whose welfare concerns himself and the state alone: he is a member of a *maegth*, or kindred, organised in a joint association for mutual protection, and liable also to take up the responsibility for all the misdoings of its component personages. This family group is not an artificial invention, but a band of actual relatives, whose pedigree is carefully traced out to the fifth and sixth generation. It is by no means a mere gathering together of individuals for police purposes, like the frank-pledge groups of a later age, nor even a body which any stranger can easily enter by the fiction of adoption, like the old Roman gens. It is very jealously guarded by those who, in virtue of their birth, have a right to belong to it.

These two phenomena which we have just noted, the existence in the earliest organisation of the old English states of a hereditary nobility, anid of a powerful and important system of family groups allied for purposes of self-defence and mutual responsibility, are by no means what we should have expected to find in kingdoms newly established by military adventurers. A war-band following a chief to a settlement overseas would, we should have supposed, be composed of individuals drawn from many families, and only connected by their common allegiance to the heretoga or ealdorman to whom they had bound themselves. And within the war-band birth would have been of little importance, compared with the favour of the chief, the source of all honour and endowment. But since these two phenomena are observed, we are forced to make certain deductions.

The first is that the original settlers must have been to a much greater extent than might have been supposed, drawn from particular kindreds and families, who retained their mutual ties, despite of their having individually made themselves over to the king or ealdorman as members of his *comitatus*. The second is that a considerable number of noble families must have taken part in the original settlement— enough to be able to assert their old privilege of status, both against the king and against the other members of the war-band, who were but "*ceorlish*" in descent. In short, the population of a newly-founded English kingdom—Kent, Bernicia, Sussex, or what not—must have been much more of a section sliced off from the whole of the continental tribe which had sent it forth, and much less of a mere *comitatus*, than might have been expected.

This we could understand well enough in the case of the Angles, where (as has been already stated) the bulk of the race seems to have migrated, so that *eorl, ceorl* and tributary dependant would naturally come over together, with their old status and rights. It is more surprising in the case of the Jutes and Saxons, where only a moderate part of the old tribe abandoned its Continental home. But our evidence is very strong for the Jutes of Kent, since it is their code which is the oldest, and in it the position of the noble-by-birth is particularly well marked. A suggestion has sometimes been made that all the nobles of an early English kingdom may have derived their rights by inheritance from the original royal stock, of which they would represent younger branches.

But though it may be granted that some of the royal houses, especially that of Wessex, had countless ramifications, and though individuals descended from *subreguli* or *aethelings* may have been an appreciable element in the nobility, it seems difficult to believe that they were its sole members. It seems indeed that while connection with the royal line was carefully remembered and highly esteemed, it was not the ordinary qualification for nobility. Bede speaks of *viri de regio genere*; the *Anglo-Saxon Chronicle* was careful to speak of persons "whose right paternal kin went back to Cerdic," though their ancestors had not reigned for many generations (*e.g.*, King Beorhtric; *A. S. C.* year 784). In Northumbria we have a special note of surprise in the same authority when Aella was chosen as ruler, because he was "ungecyndne cyning" a king not of royal blood. (*A. S. C.* year 867.) Such facts are just what we should not find if all *nobiles* had originally been aethelings.

We must take it then that in the early English kingdom the two phenomena of birth-nobility and family-groups were clearly displayed. It has been suggested that the easiest way of accounting for the existence of something like tribal kingdoms with a well-marked social stratification by birth, where centralised military monarchies might have seemed the natural form of settlement, can best be discovered by supposing that when some adventurous king and his *comitatus* had made the first lodgement, free tribesmen were invited in to strengthen the new community.

The chief, finding his warband too few to settle up what he and they had won, may have offered liberal terms to powerful *eorls* of his own tribe, and to whole family-groups of *ceorls*, if they would come over the water to his aid. They would stipulate for the perpetuation of their old privileges in their new homes, so that the state, when formed, would be much less autocratic in constitution than might have been expected. This is pure hypothesis, but we have to account somehow for the phenomena before us. And thus, does it seem easiest to explain the preponderance in most parts of Eastern England of the family settlements which are its characteristic development. For it is impossible to regard the typical village names of those regions, all the Effinghams and Walsinghams, the Tootings and Wokings, the Whittingtons and Bridlingtons, as anything but the original homes of powerful *maegths*.

★★★★★★

Kemble's view on this point still stands, despite of much criticism. See also Vinogradoff, *Growth of the Manor*, 140, who finds Kemble's theory "conclusive," the constant recurrence of these forms is sufficient to convince us … that the occupation must have been effected largely by connecting the territorial division with a kindred For a statement of the contrary view see Mr. Stevenson in *Engl. Hist. Rev., xiv.*, 1894.

★★★★★★

The normal holding of the *ceorl* who formed part of one of the large kindred-settlements was the *hiwisc*, or in later phrase the *hide*, the amount of land which was considered competent to support a free household. Hence Bede and other early authorities use *terra unius familiae* as the equivalent for a hide, and a large estate may be called equally the land of five hides or of five families. The hide must not be conceived as consisting of a precise number of acres: soils are of unequal fertility, and the amount necessary to maintain a household would differ in area. Nor does it consist solely of arable land in the stripes dear to the early Teuton. To supplement them grazing ground in the common meadow is required, moreover there are rights over the wood of the common waste of the settlement.

For the typical free settlement of an English *maegth* consisted first of the large arable fields divided up into narrow strips, of which each household possessed several, next of the almost equally prized meadow, which was hedged off into appropriated lots in summer, but thrown back into common in winter, and lastly of the undistributed waste, from which the whole community would draw its wood supply, and on which it would pasture its swine, or even turn out its cattle for rough grazing at some seasons.

The normal method of agriculture was the "three-field system," with a rotation of wheat, barley or oats, and in the third year fallow— to allow of the exhausted soil regaining some measure of its fertility. In the last year the field was left unfenced, and the cattle of the community picked up what they could from it, when they were neither on the waste, nor being fed with the hay that had been mowed from the meadow. There seem to have been exceptional cases in which the strips of the arable were not permanently allotted to different households, but were distributed, by lot or otherwise, to different holders in different years. But this was an abnormal arrangement: usually the proprietorship of the strips in each field was fixed. (See Vinogradoff, *Origin of the Manor.*) And the usual arrangement would be that the fully endowed *ceorl's* household had just so much arable in its various strips as a full team of oxen could plough.

The king's comitatus appears clearly enough in the Kentish Laws, but in a less prominent way than we should have expected. Apparently, there are already two classes of persons comprised in it. These are the *gesith* (later called *comes*) who is the superior of the two, a regular member of the king's war-band, already endowed with landed estates, and the thegn (*minister* as he was afterwards called) who was still the household servant of the king, and in many cases not yet a landholder by his master's bounty. There are only two allusions to the class, both in the latest additions to the code, those made by Wihtraed in 695. In one place the member of the royal following is called a "*gesithcund-man*," a term that we shall meet more frequently when dealing with the Wessex code of Ine.

In the other place he is styled a "king's thegn" (*cyninges theng*). The superior status of both is shown by the fact that the *gesithcundman* is fined twice as much as the *ceorl* who commits the same offence, while the thegn is given the privilege of clearing himself from an accusation by his own oath at the altar, while the *ceorl* similarly accused has to bring forward four men of his own class to make oath for him.

There is one more element to take into consideration when dealing with the social organisation of the earliest English kingdoms. Besides "*eorl* and *ceorl*" and besides the mere domestic slave (*theow, esne*) who existed in this island as in every other home of the Teutons, we find already existing in the code of Aethelbert, a third class not enjoying complete freedom, yet certainly not merely servile, the *laeta*. Their name at once suggests the *litus* and *lazzus* of the Continent, and we cannot fail to see in them tributary dependants of alien blood. But a difficult problem at once crops up: are these persons the descendants of the old Romano-British peasantry, taken over along with the lands which they cultivated, by the Teutonic conqueror? At the first glance this would seem to be their most probable origin, and the analogy of the similar class in Gaul would serve us well

But a second thought reminds us that the *lazzus*, a similar tribute-paying person of inferior status, crops up also among the Saxons and Frisians, in lands where there is no question of a survival of Roman provincials. In Saxony or Frisia he must have been the descendant of conquered tribes or of emancipated slaves. What are we to assign as his origin in Kent? We know from the moans of Gildas that a certain proportion of the old British population had survived the Conquest—the people whom (in a passage already quoted) he describes as:

> Going, worn out by famine, to the enemy, and surrendering to them on the condition that they would serve them for ever, if only they were not slain at once, for this was the best privilege that they could obtain.

This passage alone would almost by itself suffice to prove the perpetuation of a certain amount of British population in Eastern Britain. And when we find a considerable class of tributary peasants, existent in Kent in the year 600, it is tempting to recognise in the *laets* of Aethelbert's code the descendants of the broken provincials of whom Gildas wrote. Yet on the other hand it is only fair to plead that *laets* may also have come over from Germany, along with the *eorls* and *ceorls*, in whose company they must already have existed on the Continent. And if the surviving British population in Eastern Britain had been numerous, it is hard to explain why the English tongue won such a complete victory over the speech that preceded it, in direct contrast to what happened in Gaul, where the debased Romance dialect of the conquered overcame the old Frankish speech.

Moreover, as has been already pointed out in an earlier chapter, it seems hard to believe that if the Romano-British peasantry had survived as the base of the agricultural population in Kent and elsewhere, we should have no trace whatever of Christianity surviving also. Yet the narrative of the conversion in Bede most distinctly implies that Augustine found no pre-existing Christian population within the English states, and that Queen Bertha and those of her household were the only baptised persons whom he met on his arrival in Britain.

It is true that the missionaries received permission from Aethelbert not only to build places of worship where they pleased, but to repair old Roman churches where they found them. (See chapter 5.)

But the whole tenor of the story implies that these last were ruins, not live churches with congregations composed of British *laets* and served by a surviving British clergy. Are we then to conclude that Christianity had become extinct among the tributary subjects of the old English kings? Or must we be driven still further, and doubt whether the *laets* were Britons at all, accounting for them as immigrants from Germany along with the *eorls* and *ceorls* among whom they lived? In either case the problem presents great difficulties.

One thing, however, is certain. About ninety years later, when the West Saxon King Ine drew up his code about the year 693, not only was there a considerable tributary population in his realm—as there seems to have been in Kent in the days of Aethelbert—but this population was British in blood, so much so that a member of it is invariably called a *Wealh*; no such non-national term as *laet* appears in this king's laws. It has sometimes been suggested that this fact is only the reflection of the recent conquest of mid-Somersetshire, in which the West Welsh had just become Ine's subjects, and that the whole code is the settlement-charter of a newly subdued region.

But if the *Anglo-Saxon Chronicle* can be trusted Ine's Damnonian campaigns belonged to his middle years (710), while the date of his code is fixed at some period before 693 by the appearance in its preface of Bishop Earconwald, who died in that year. On the other hand, there are reasons for thinking that Ine had already won land as far as the Exe by 690, (see chapter 6), so the problem is left still unsettled.

As to the proportion in which the old provincial population endured, the only deduction that can be made is that, as has been already said, the English tongue prevailed everywhere in Eastern and Southern Britain. This shows that the surviving stratum of Romanised Celts cannot have been nearly so thick as in Gaul—not to speak of Spain or Italy. Even in the vocabulary of husbandry and servile industry the number of loan-words to be discovered in the old English tongue is by no means large. Indeed, the language seems to have been far more affected by borrowings from Latin in the sphere of Church life, after the conversion, than by those from either Celtic or Latin in the sphere of domestic life made in the earlier centuries.

In short, the base of the state in seventh-century England must have been the *ceorl*, the small freeman, rather than the *laet* or *Wealh* of tributary status. And long before the Norman conquest the surviving alien population seems to have been absorbed in the conquering race in all districts save the extreme West.

Ine's Laws are interesting as showing the full development of the "nobility by service," which is so slightly touched upon in the Kentish codes. To the West-Saxon king the primary distinction among his subjects (putting the *Wealhs* aside) was not that between "*eorl* and *ceorl*," but that between those who belonged to his personal following and those who did not The former, as in the Kentish laws of Wihtraed, are called *gesithcund*, whatever their rank or status, and this term is used in normal contradistinction to the *ceorl*. The *sithcundus homo* and the *cyrlisus homo* balance each other in many paragraphs of the Latin translation of the code. A *gesithcund* man might be holding land by the king's grant, or not; in the latter case he is evidently one of the domestic retinue, who has not attained sufficient importance to be endowed with an estate.

The code says:

If a *gesithcund* man with land neglects the summons to war, let him pay 120 shillings; if he owns no land, 60 shillings; but let the *ceorlish* man pay 30 shillings for his *fyrdwite*" (fine for evasion of military service). Apparently the *gesithcund* men were not in full permanent and hereditary possession of the land which the king has given them: it was held purely on condition of service. One law lays down that:
If a *gesithcund* man wishes to depart, he may take with him only his reeve, his smith, and the fosterer of his children.

The rest of the dwellers on his land must be left behind. It seems also that by accepting the land from the king he binds himself to bring it under cultivation, and to people it, for another law says that:

He who has twenty hides of land must leave twelve hides of settled land (*gesettes londes, terrae vestitae*) if he wishes to depart; he who has ten hides, six; he who has three, one and a half hides of settled land.

A very curious paragraph gives the rate of rent at which estates were let out to the king's men.

Whoever has ten hides shall pay yearly ten jars of honey, 300 loaves, twelve *ambers* of Welsh beer (mead) and thirty of clear

174

beer, two fully grown oxen or ten wethers, ten geese, twenty fowls, ten cheeses, a full *amber* of butter, five salmon, twenty measures of fodder, and one hundred eels.

These provisions presumably fed the king's domestic retinue in his constant journeyings around his realm.

It is important to note that the royal following included men of Celtic blood, as well as the English *gesithcund* men. Among the statements of the *weregeld* of each rank—the sum due as compensation for manslaughter—we find the valuation of "the king's horse-*Wealh* who can do him service as messenger": he is reckoned at 200 shillings, which should be compared with the counting of the ordinary Welsh landholder at 120 shillings, and of three classes of Englishmen at 1,200, 600 and 200 shillings respectively.

★★★★★★

We find, however, from law 24 that there were exceptional Welsh subjects of the king who had as much as five hides of land, and these attained to a *weregeld* of 600 shillings, that of the second class of English.

★★★★★★

The fact that the "horse-*Wealh*" is in the king's service has raised his value by 60 *per cent.,* and equated him with one of the third and lowest category of the superior race.

Another point of obvious significance in Ine's law is that the *gesith-cund* man of the superior class with his 1,200 shilling *weregeld* is worth six times the *ceorl* with his 200 shilling valuation. In the Kent of Lothere and Wihtraed, one generation before, the *eorl* had been worth no more than three times the *ceorl*. The relative estimation of the ordinary freeman to the great landowner has evidently fallen in the interval.

The piece of information which we should have been most glad to discover in the laws of Ine is, most unfortunately, withheld from us, *viz.*, the proportion in which the population of Wessex about the year 693 was divided between free *ceorls* living on their hides of land in the old fashion, dependent peasants living on the land of the king's *gesith-cund* men, and tributary *Wealhs*. From the amount attention devoted to the rights and liabilities of the second-named class we should suppose that it must have been very large. But whether it, as yet, formed a majority of the whole race of the West Saxons we are not in a position to say. At any rate we may be sure that what may be called the elements of feudalism were already well established in the land.

Wessex was full of great landowners holding ten or twenty hides from the king, and working those hides by the labour of peasant families, English or Welsh, who paid them rent and service, just as they paid these same dues to the king. The lord was already entitled to share, along with the king, in the *weregeld* of his dependants if they were slain. He was already responsible in some degree for their good conduct: in the case of theft, for example, if the dependant (*geneat*) escaped with his plunder and had no kin pledged for him, the lord would have to pay up the fine and compensation for his crime. We seem to detect two classes amongst the peasantry on the estates of the *gesithcund* men: the one get their dwellings and probably their outfit of cattle, etc., from him: the other have taken up land under him, but apparently have dwellings and stock of their own.

Both might, as it seems, migrate with their lord's permission; but if they passed into another shire clandestinely, they were liable to be reclaimed, and sent back charged with a fine of sixty shillings. Among the paragraphs, however, of Ine's code which deal with dependents settled on the land of a lord, there are a considerable number of others concerning the other sort of community "where *ceorls* dwell having meadow land in common, and other land (*i.e.*, tilled land) in shares": here we recognise the old free village that had started with the settlement of a *maegth*.

There are many rules laid down about the duties of hedging in fields so as to prevent trespass of cattle, and of making no more than moderate use of the common wood. The man who in greed felled too many trees might be fined as much as sixty shillings: the same penalty fell on him who by carelessness set the wood ablaze, "for fire is a thief". In these sections there is, of course, no question of payment or compensation to anyone but the injured persons, there being no lord to claim a share. If, for example, cattle have done damage because some of the community have well fenced their fields and others have not, the owners of the unfenced shares have to compensate those who have taken proper precautions, and have suffered because their neighbours had not done the same.

Notwithstanding all this, we are undoubtedly driven to the conclusion that Ine's Wessex was a state in which the free *ceorl* was not nearly so important, when compared to the landholder belonging to the kingly comitatus, as he was in Kent. His only evidence forthcoming for the other two kingdoms which grew great at the expense of the Welsh, Northumbria and Mercia, would seem to point to the conclusion that their social organisation was more similar to that of Wessex than to that of Kent.

It may very likely have been the case, on the other hand, that East Anglia, Essex, and Sussex, where the conditions of settlement were more similar to those of Kent, and where extension at the expense of the Britons became impossible at an early date, showed the opposite phenomenon. But here we have no evidence at all: not a single law has survived from these kingdoms, nor have we even a series of charters to replace them. Once more we have come upon one of the numerous gaps in Anglo-Saxon history—gaps which are as frequent in social as in political annals.

CHAPTER 8

The Political Organisation of the Early English Kingdoms

Having dealt, so far as is possible, with the social organisation of the early English kingdoms, we must turn to their political organisation. The governmental machinery by which the people of Kent, *eorls*, *ceorls* and *laets*, were ruled in the time of Aethelbert and his descendants is passed over in the most surprising fashion in the Kentish codes. (Ine.) There is a clear indication of the existence of a council of wise men in the prologue to Wihtraed's *Dooms*. The king has gathered "an advisory assembly of his great men" at Bersted and, as we then read:

> Every rank of churchman spoke, in unison with the loyal folk: and the great men resolved, with the assent of all, to add to the rightful customs of the men of Kent these following laws.

Beyond Bertwald, Archbishop of Canterbury, and Gebmund, Bishop of Rochester, no one of the "great men" is named. That there were present a great many of the ordinary *ceorls* must be inferred from the allusion to the "loyal folk". But how far their approval to the new legislation was asked or given is not clear from the phrase that the great men enacted it *mid ealra gemedum* "with the assent of all". This may or may not imply that the laws were formally submitted to the whole crowd of men of Kent. The gathering itself is called a *gemot*.

The only other allusions to any public assembly in the Kentish laws occur, one in the Code of Aethelbert, where in the first clause it is stated that there is a double fine for breaking the peace of the "*Maethel*," the other in Lothere's law, where it is called "*Medle*". This is apparently the local assembly akin to the Frankish *Malus*.

The preamble to Ine's code is in a quite different form. He states that he has published it:

> With the advice and counsel of his father Coenred (a *subregulus* who never attained to the royal crown), of his two bishops Hedde of Winchester and Earconwald of London, of all his ealdormen, of the senior wise men of his kingdom (*thaem ieldstan witum minre theode*), and of a great assembly of clergy.

There is no allusion whatever to the presence of any general body of the firemen of the West Saxon kingdom, or of their assent to the legislation, though the code is stated to be "for the profit and better governance of our folk The impression given to the reader by this, as by so much more, of Ine's terminology, is that Wessex was a state in which the royal power was in a much more advanced condition than in Kent, and in which the smaller freemen counted for far less. But what of the greater? What was the relation of a Saxon king to the assembly of notables who gave him advice—the *sapientes* or *consiliarii*, who composed his witan?

The constitutional position of the witan and its relations with the king on the one side, and the general assembly of the freemen of the tribe on the other, have long been debated upon. In the days when "primitive Teutonic freedom" was the watchword of historians, it was usual to write as if there existed a regular system by which the power of the king was limited, by his being obliged to act by the counsel and consent of his "wise men," while the ultimate legislative power lay in the hands of the whole body of freemen, who had to confirm any laws or ordinance laid before them. In this view there is something of misconception and much of exaggeration.

The witan, so far back as we can trace it, is an assembly of royal nominees, not a body of hereditary peers with a right to advise the king. And we look equally in vain for any sign that it was a representative body, which could speak in behalf of the people. In the seventh century, when we get our first view of it, as in the later times when documents grow numerous, it appears to have consisted of the ealdormen, who governed under the king the various units of his realm, of the archbishops and bishops, and of a limited number of other councillors.

It would seem that these last constituted a definite and recognisable class. There is a law of Ine which lays down a precise fine for breaches of the peace, in the houses of such persons. If any man brawls in the house of an ealdorman or of any other "exalted wiseman" (*oth-*

res getkungenes witan) he has to pay a certain fixed and heavy fine. Clearly then it was known who was and who was not of this status. Presumably they were gesiths or thegns of the greater sort, with ample landed endowment. But whether in Kent at the same time independent "*eorls*" of great landed wealth might not have sat among Wihtraed's "great men" "it would be dangerous to speculate.

At any rate this was not the custom in later centuries, when among the signatures of members of the witan, annexed to some deed or charter, we can distribute all among four classes—(1) members of the royal family; (2) archbishops, bishops, abbots and other clergy; (3) ealdoraien; (4) king's thegns (*ministri*) and other officials. There is no category of wise men of lay status who do not belong to the "nobility of service". Ine's code does not give us the smallest indication that this was not already the case in his day: there is no allusion whatever to great men who enjoy inherited eminence, and are not members of the body of *gesithcundmen*.

Since, then, the council was a council of nominees, its function was to advise rather than to guide or restrain the king, and a headstrong ruler might ignore its advice at his own peril, without committing a constitutional solecism. At the same time the witan was not without its importance. If a king grew unpopular, deservedly or not, there were always members of the royal house in existence, who would naturally be members of the witan, and who in unison with the other councillors would apply to him the most stringent check—resistance and rebellion. A tyrannical ruler could not rely, beyond a certain limit, on the loyalty of his dependants. We need only recall the cases of Aethelbald of Mercia, and Oswulf and half a dozen more Northumbrian kings "slain by those of their own household". This might be called mere "despotism tempered by assassination". But there are distinct cases where the unpopular ruler seems to have been formally deposed, and where the witan are spoken of as carrying out or at least assenting to the deposition.

Such was that of Sigebert of Wessex (A.D. 755) of whom it is said that his kinsman Cynewulf and the West Saxon witan deprived him of his kingdom for his unjust doings. (*A. S. Chronicle, sub anno* 755.) Equally clear is the instance of the Northumbrians, Alchred who in 774 was dethroned by the counsel and consent of all his subjects (Simeon of Durham), and Osbald who in similar terms is recorded to have been deposed in 796. The same no doubt was the case in 765 with that king Aethelwald, "*qui regnum Northanhymbrorum amisit*

179

in Winchanheal III Kal. Novembris," Finchale being one of the regular meeting-places of the Northumbrian witan. For if the fall of Aethelwald had been the effect of mere rebellion and tumultuary violence, it could not be said to have happened on a particular day and at a particular place.

Clearly some sort of definite form of deposition must have been carried out. It would be mere playing with words to say that the proceedings of the witan in such a case were not constitutional. For the word constitutional in all times, early and late, save when a fixed framework of laws exists to define the polity of a state, means little more than "habitual, and generally accepted by the nation If witans on many occasions declared kings deposed, and deposition actually ensued, it is surely quibbling to say that the action had no legal validity, and was only a form of rebellion. (For a lucid statement of the opposite view, denying any such power to the witan, see Chadwick's *Anglo-Saxon Institutions*.)

The witan had also its part to play in another sort of case, where the question was not one of the deposition of a tyrannical or unpopular king, but simply one of the regulation of the succession to the crown. In many, probably in most, cases, a king who had reached middle age, and had sons of his own, would get his natural heir recognised as his successor-designate during his lifetime. Often, he gave him a sub-kingdom to rule, by way of starting him in the necessary training, as did Penda or Oswy. Sometimes a king who was setting his house in order, either because of age and infirmity, or because he wished to enter the religious life, would commend a relation who was not his son to the witan and his subjects at large.

This happened in the case of Aethelred of Mercia, who resigned in favour of his nephew Coenred (704); while Coenred in his turn went on pilgrimage to Rome in 709, after handing over his sceptre to his cousin the worthless Ceolred. So, too, we read in Bede how Osric of Northumbria, "*successorem fore Ceolwulfum decrevisset, fratrem illius qui ante se regnaverat, Coenredi.*" Clearly the will of the reigning king was in such instances the main factor in the determining of the order of succession, and he took measures, before his death or abdication, to get his subjects to recognise the heir whom he preferred. Probably the witan went through some ceremony of taking the successor as lord and doing homage to him.

But in other cases, the order of succession was determined in a less smooth fashion. If a king who had no designated heir fell in battle, or if an unpopular king was deposed, someone had to be set in his place. In many cases a pretender might make a mere snatch at the crown with the aid of his relatives and dependants, like that Osbald who "*a quibus principibus ipsius gentis in regnum est constitutus*," (Simeon of Durham), only to be deposed immediately after by the witan of Northumbria. But in others there seems to have been something like a definite election. Aethelwald Moll of Northumbria (759) is said, by the contemporary annalist who continued Bede's history, to be "*a sua plebe electus*," and the same is implied of his son Aethelred, when the *Anglo-Saxon Chronicle* says that "the Northumbrians drove out Alchred from York at Easter-Tide and took Aethelred to be their lord." (Florence of Worcester paraphrases this by "*in regem levaverunt*," a clear allusion to the old Teutonic elevation of a newly elected sovereign.)

For the taking of a prince to lord must surely have been something more formal than the recognition of a *de facto* king who has won the crown already by arms. When Ine of Wessex is "*functus in regem*," and Ecgbert, a century later, "*in regnum ordinatur*," some sort of an election seems equally implied. In each of the two latter cases the throne was vacant, and the late king had left no heir. Later cases, where the phrase "elected as king" is used, sometimes with the addition that the witan is definitely stated to do the electing, may be found in the *Anglo-Saxon Chronicle* under the years 924, 1016 and 1043. But in all cases, we cannot doubt that the wise men, and not any tumultuary meeting of the folk, must have been the body which made the choice.

Passing on from the witan to the other governmental machinery of the early English realms, we are surprised to find in our earliest documents, the Kentish codes, no allusion to ealdormen (though they certainly existed in Kent in the eighth century and later, and are repeatedly mentioned in the *Chronicle*) or to any royal officials save the king's *wicgerefa* or ton-reeve, before whom, as is casually mentioned in a law of Lothere, the vouching for the honesty of a bargain may be made.

******

Lothere, §16. This often-quoted passage does not seem to presuppose a Kentish wic-reeve in London, as some suppose, but only provides that a bargain made in London should be vouched for before the nearest wic-reeve.

******

He appears again (but called *gerefa* only) in Wihtraed's laws, as the person to whom anyone who has a charge to bring against one of the king's slaves ought to make his complaint. We have mention of the king's retainers, as has already been stated in the preceding chapter, both as his *gesithoundmen* and as thegns. We hear also of his smiths and other servants, but there is a sad want of detail as to actual officials.

Ine's code gives us much more information in this respect. It clearly mentions the ealdorman as governor of a "shire" under the king—the thirty-sixth law is to the effect that an ealdorman who lets go a captured thief or hushes up a robbery, shall "lose his shire" unless the king grant him pardon. As early as 755 we have a definite mention of a Wessex ealdorman by name and title, *viz.*, of that Cumbra who ruled "Hamtunscire" for King Sigebert, and was so ungratefully treated by him. (See chapter 6.) In that century and the next we are able to account for all the later shires of Wessex as already in existence, and there is no reason to doubt that all save Devon were created before Ine's time. But as to their origin speculation only is possible.

Some have supposed that they represent the successive local units created by each advance of the Wessex border against the Welsh—that Wiltshire, Dorsetshire, Somersetshire were formed by bodies of settlers called Wilsaetas, Dornsaetas, Somersaetas, from the regions in which they took up their abode, and the names lend themselves to this hypothesis. A later view is the shires represent, more or less, the realms of the numerous *subreguli* who parted the West Saxon realm among themselves on several occasions in the seventh century.

A plausible explanation for Berkshire, at least, is that it represents the principality of 3,000 hides which King Coenwalch granted to his nephew Cuthred "in Ashdown". (See Chadwick's *Anglo-Saxon Institutions*.) The ealdorman, under this hypothesis, would be a royal official administering what had been once the realm of a *subregulus* from its most important centre.

But again, it is suggested that the shire names may be traced back to districts administered from important royal "*vills*," Hamton and Wilton, Dorchester and Somerton, which last obscure place was perhaps of some note in the seventh and eighth centuries. (Outside Wessex, Winchcombshire and the later Liberty of Bury Saint Edmunds are examples of which documentary evidence survives. See the Charters in Thorpe.)

Be this as it may, we find in Ine's laws besides the ealdormen a person called the shireman, who has generally been identified with the shire-reeve or sheriff of the tenth century. He appears as a legal official before whom accusations have to be enrolled. It seems hard to believe that he is not an early form of the sheriff, and in the later days of the

Anglo-Saxon monarchy the two terms shireman and sheriff were certainly used indifferently for the same official.

✶✶✶✶✶✶

Mr. Chadwick, in the work cited above, (chapter 2), disputes this. He apparently thinks that Ine's shireman is the ealdorman, and that the later sheriff only came into existence in the tenth century.

✶✶✶✶✶✶

He is apparently in Ine's time the most important of the king's reeves, or local stewards and bailiffs, having not a single estate, nor a single town, under him, but a large district, wherein he would be responsible for all the royal finances derived from litigation and taxation, no less than from the king's landed property. Every royal estate had certainly a minor reeve (*gerefa*), and probably every town also: we have seen already that Kent had "*wicgerefas*" or town bailiffs when Wihtraed, Ine's contemporary, was publishing his "dooms"; and in later centuries we have definite mention of Wessex "*Wicgerefas*," *e.g.*, at Winchester and at Bath, who seem to have been persons of some importance. (Sufficiently so have their deaths mentioned in the *Chronicle*, as in 906 and 897.) It is noteworthy that in the other English kingdoms which were large enough to require administrative ealdormen, Mercia and Northumbria, we seem to have no trace of an early shire system.

In Mercia there were ealdormen who governed districts for the king, but these all seem to be much larger than the Wessex shires. Indeed, the ealdormen whose local habitat is ascertainable seem to have ruled the old sub-kingdoms, in succession to the *subreguli* who died out in the eighth century.

We have definite mention of ealdormen of the Hwiccas, and of Lindsey; presumably Mercia proper, the Magesaetas beyond Severn, and the Middle Angles were ruled by others. Possibly the Gyrwas and the Chilternsaetas formed separate units also. The charters of the great Mercian kings, like Offa and Coenwulf, are signed by a good many *duces*, but many of them were clearly not the rulers of Mercian districts, but came from Kent, Essex, and other regions which were vassal to the greater kingdom but not incorporated in it.

If the statement in the *Anglo-Saxon Chronicle* under the year 827 (825) could be taken as strictly meaning what it says, when it states that King Ludecan was slain by the East Angles "and his five ealdormen with him," we should be obliged to conclude that there were precisely five administrative districts in Mercia when its vassal king-

183

doms had shaken off the yoke—presumably Lindsey, Mercia Proper, Hwiccia, the Middle Angles, and the Magesaetas. But it is not certain that the possessive pronoun "his" can be pressed to this extent; for Ethelweard's *Chronicle* translates what is evidently the same original into "*et quinque duces cum eo*," not into "*cum suis quinque ducibus*". (He makes the strange error of putting Beortwulf instead of Ludecan.)

Moreover, in late ninth century Mercian charters, issued after the Danes had occupied all the eastern part of the kingdom, we sometimes seem to find three or even four ealdormen signing. It is hard to find territories for them all, unless we suppose that there was an ealdorman for the Chilternsaetas, or whatever name we apply to the Mercian district lying north of the Middle Thames.

★★★★★★

But possibly Aethelred, then ruling with *quasi*-regal power, had kept no region immediately under himself, and the other three ealdormen were those of Hwiccia, the Magesaetas, and Old Mercia (or such part of it as obeyed Aethelred).

★★★★★★

As to Northumbria, there were certainly ealdormen therein, but we get no visible trace of a shire system. (See *A. S. C.*, 684 and 778.) If there were permanent local divisions, it seems that they were under *praefecti* (as Bede calls them) or high-reeves as the *Anglo-Saxon Chronicle* prefers to name them. One family of such high-reeves can be traced at Bamborough for several generations, and its last members seem to have exercised as much power as a *subregulus* after the breakup of the Northumbrian kingdom before the Danish invaders. (For this race of Eardwulfs and Ealdreds, sec Cadwallader Bates' *History of Northumberland*.) It is notable that Simeon of Durham calls *duces* three notables whom the *Chronicle* styles high-reeves, all murdered by King Aethelred I. in 778. The *Chronicle* distinctly gives them local titles "Eardwulf high-reeve at Kingscliff," etc. If there existed a regular system of administrative division in the seventh and eighth centuries, it was certainly swept away by the Danes in the ninth.

Another class mentioned by Ine, of whom we would gladly know more, are certain judges (*derman* in the Saxon original, *judices* in the Latin version) who are named along with the shireman. They seem to be royal officials, but what was their status or the extent of their sphere we are unable to say. When so much of justice consisted in the administering and accepting of oaths of compurgation, and while "the suitors were the judges," the position of the presiding official at a court is a perplexing one to realise. Conceivably this *judex* was the "dooms-man" of a hundred, though of the existence of that territorial unit we have no mention in Ine's Law, nor indeed till the time of Eadgar, more than two centuries and a half later.

Yet it would be dangerous to deny that hundreds existed in all the early English kingdoms. The idea of the unit of a hundred households supplying a hundred warriors was very early, and current in most or all Teutonic lands. If it is alluded to in Tacitus and found current as far as Scandinavia when historical times begin, it is no very perilous hypothesis to believe that it existed in seventh- or eighth-century England.

★★★★★★

Among the Franks there was no shire-court, but only what was practically a hundred-court. If the English had shire-courts always, and only introduced the hundred-court in the tenth century, their line of development was abnormal.

★★★★★★

It has indeed been suggested, with great plausibility, that the reason why all early calculations of the area of districts were made in round numbers of hundreds, both in narratives such as Bede's history and in statistics such as the "Tribal Hidage," already alluded to, (see chapter 7), is that the notion of the hundred in households or hides as the national primitive unit was well established.

★★★★★★

Mr. Chadwick, though conceding that "the distribution of the nation according to hundreds of hides goes back in principle to early times" (*Origins*), will not allow that there were actual administrative divisions, in the sense of the Doomsday Book hundreds, before the tenth century.

★★★★★★

It is of course unfortunate that Ine and his councillors, when setting forth their code, were not intent on furnishing posterity with constitutional information, but on formulating in detail the precise penalties of various crimes. Their dooms mainly consist of clauses dealing, on a scale which the modern student finds minute and irritating, with the valuation of offences against life, person, and property, and the machinery by which those offences shall be dealt with. But this is equally the case not only with the Kentish laws, but with all the continental codes—Frankish, Lombard, Saxon, etc., of the Dark Ages. The most striking feature in Ine's legislation is the employment of the system of compurgation for the decision of all manner of cases. Instead of dilating on the fashion in which witnesses should be called and examined, Ine takes it for granted that the normal decision in the shire court will be made according to the scale on which the defendant will bring oath-helpers to vouch for him. The man who is known to be a bad character will be unable to collect compurgators, and will presently fall into the most unpleasant position.

> The *ceorlish* man who has been several times accused of theft, and is then again taken in cattle-stealing, clearly guilty, shall have his hand or his foot cut off.

When the accused is not a notorious offender, and when his guilt in the particular' charge laid against him is not clear, he will be able to get his lord, if he is a dependant, or his kindred and neighbours, if he be a free villager, to swear for him. Their swearing power is elaborately defined according to their rank, and is stated in terms of hides, as if credibility increased in exact proportion with the extent of landed property which a man enjoyed—a strange hypothesis to the modern mind.

> A man accused of gang-robbery shall clear himself by the oath of 120 hides, or pay up.
>
> A royal tenant, if his *weregeld* valuation is 1,200 shillings (*i.e.*, if he is a freeman of the highest class among the *gesithoundmen*) may swear for 60 hides, if he is a regular communicant.
>
> If any man is accused of having stolen cattle, or harboured stolen cattle, then he may swear himself off the charge by the oath of 60 hides (*i.e.*, by the oath of one or more persons whose valuation comes to 60 hides) if he be oath-worthy.
>
> If the accuser is an Englishman the charge must be rebutted with twice as strong swearing: if only a Welshman, the sixty-hide oath is enough.
>
> If a man be accused of homicide, and wishes to rebut the accusation by oaths, then, in every body of oath-helpers that he produces, out of 100 hides of swearing there must be an oath by a man of the royal following with 30 hides, whether the slain be *gesithound* or *ceorl*. (If this is the meaning of the curious phrase stating that 30 hides of the oath must be provided by a person with a "king's oath"; Ine, §54).

Such are the curious provisions which continually meet the student who runs through the laws of Ine. If the practical working of the system be considered, it is clear that a first offender who had devoted relatives, or a lord who valued his service, must have found it easy to swear off a charge. But it would grow progressively more difficult to collect oath-helpers to the required amount when accusations began to be repeated, so that the habitual offender would ultimately reach the stage of finding no one to swear for him.

At the best, the system was equivalent to letting off the man who had a good local reputation: at the worst it must have amounted to giving an opportunity for all unscrupulous families or lords, on whom an oath sat lightly, to cover the misdoings of their connections. One may guess what must often have taken place in Wessex by picturing to oneself the results that would follow today, if compurgation prevailed in the West of Ireland for the crime of cattle-driving!

The offences on which Ine dilates at greatest length are homicide, theft—especially of livestock—gang-robbery, and brawling, a list which gives the impression that his realm cannot have been a happy residence for persons of peaceful disposition. Brawling was clearly liable to break out anywhere, even in the vicinity of the royal person.

> If any man fights in the king's house, he is liable to lose all his goods, and his life is at the king's disposal: if any man fights in church, he shall pay 120 shillings, if in an ealdorman's house, 60 shillings to the ealdorman and 60 more to the king. But if he fight in the house of a tax-paying man (*i.e.*, an ordinary freeman) or a smaller peasant, the 120 shillings go to the king and six only to the householder. (Ine, §54)

Gang-robbery evidently prevailed on a very large scale: for, says Ine:

> We call men thieves if the party did not exceed seven persons; if it was between seven and thirty-five it is a band (*hloth*), but if over thirty-five then we call the gathering an army (*here*).

Owing to the public danger caused by such felonious assemblies, the amount of penalty (or of compurgation) was heavily increased above that of mere theft when the larger numbers were reached.

The influence of the Church is to be traced throughout all the early laws, in those of Kent no less than in the later code of Ine. It expresses itself in the high valuation given to ecclesiastical persons, and the severity with which injuries due to them are punished. He who stole goods from the king paid nine-fold value of what he had taken, but he who stole "God's and the Church's goods," twelve-fold. (Aethelbert, §1 and §4.) Theft from a priest cost nine-fold, from an ordinary *ceorl* only threefold. The bishop's word, like that of the king, is indisputable, even without an oath. (Wihtraed, §16.) A priest can clear himself from an accusation by standing before the altar of his church and asseverating "*veritatem dico in Christo, non mentior,*" when ordinary laymen would be obliged to bring oath-helpers.

But the most notable feature of all is that the state intervenes from a very early date to punish purely ecclesiastical offences. Wihtraed lavishes the heaviest penalties on every man, free or unfree, who is caught secretly worshipping the pagan gods: he even enforces Sabbath rest with the enormous fine of 80 shillings. Ine goes so far as to punish with a penalty of 30 shillings the man who has not had his child baptised within thirty days of its birth, and to inflict a crushing fine on the negligent person who has omitted to pay his church-scot. The privilege of sanctuary, destined to lead to so many abuses in later ages, was already known.

> If a man who has incurred the death penalty flee to a church, let him keep his life and make (pecuniary) compensation according to the law: if he has incumd corporal punishment and so flee, let the chastisement be forgiven him. Ine, §5.)

Ine's law shows the Church possessed of much land, and mentions abbots and abbesses with servile dependants. This is only what we should expect from our reading in Bede, where the kings are found, from the very foundation of Christianity, lavishing large estates upon the missionary clergy, and later founding monasteries on the most splendid scale. Two or three generations of liberality such as that of Aethelbert and Edwin caused Church-land to become an appreciable part of every realm in England.

The habit spread from the kings downwards, till already Bede, in 730, was growing frightened at the enormous growth of the number of religious houses—many of them ill-managed, and unworthy of their name. But this tendency and its consequences have been dealt with elsewhere, (see chapter 6): it never ceased till the Danish invasions swept over the land and destroyed monasteries by the score, so that a new monastic revival was required in the tenth century, when the land had once more settled down to peace.

From another point of view the growth of Church property is of high importance in English constitutional history, as being the main instrument in the breaking up of the old land-holding system of the original settlers, and its conversion into a more modern and individualistic type. It seems to be proved that the land divided up on the first conquest of a British region, and held according to the tribal rules of family inheritance, was called *folkland*, whether it went to king, to *eorl* or to *ceorl*, as being held by *folkright*, national custom. (For Folkland and its meaning, see Vinogradoff in *English Historical Review for 1893*, with additional explanation in the *Growth of the Manor*, and in *Mélanges Fitting;* 1908.)

The later Latin term for it seems to have been *terra publicae juris*, or (more clumsily) *reipublicae jure conditionis*.

★★★★★★

The very important term folkland only occurs, oddly enough, three times in documents; the odd Latin translations of it quoted above only once each, in two charters of Coenwulf of Mercia. Thorpe, *Dipl.* See Vinogradoff's views in the places mentioned in the last note.

★★★★★★

Such land, whether owned by king or *ceorl*, could not be alienated from the family or devised by will, the proprietor being nothing more than a life-owner. It passed on his death to his heirs automatically, according to the rules of the tribal custom. It was subject to all the usual obligations to the state, military and *fiscal*—the *trinoda necessitas* of sending warriors to the host (*fyrdfare*), repairing of forts (*burhbot*) and work on roads and bridges (*bricgbot*), the obligation to entertain the king and his retinue on his progresses, and to pay his tax (*gafol*), etc. When once a region had been divided up, even the king could not permanently alienate the royal estates held as folkland, though he might distribute them as life-maintenance to members of his following. But the death of either the grantor or the grantee would bring the land back into the royal domain, or the king could terminate the grant at his good pleasure if his *gesith* or thegn had displeased him.

The first serious objection to this ancestral system, as it appears, came when the kings of the seventh century wished to endow churches and found monasteries, a desire in which their ealdormen and thegns soon came to participate. To alienate land during the grantor's life was all that was in has power, so long as folkright prevailed. To render permanent endowments possible, however, a new device was soon found—this was the institution of *bocland*, land held by a "book," *i.e.*, a charter, instead of by folkright. Such estates could only be created by a formal act of the king and his witan, royal land as well as private land having to be freed from the old restrictions by a charter, since the king was (after all) only a life tenant of his own domain. Presumably the consent of the kindred ought to have been obtained in each case, for they had a clear interest in the land alienated by the creation of such a grant.

"The proper course was to obtain the consent of the interested relations of the actual holder" (*Growth of the Manor*)—though it is not clear that this was always done. The immediate result of the invention of *bocland* was the rapid diminution of the royal domain, not only when the king transferred lands in his own actual possession to a bishopric or a monastery, but also when he gave leave for royal folkland, in the temporary occupation of one of his ministers or officials, to be treated in the same way. This last form of liberality was very tempting both to the thegn and to the king, since the former was alienating to the Church land which was not permanently his own, while the latter was not making any new grant out of land in actual possession, but only consenting to part for good with an estate which was already in the hands of someone else—though it would ultimately have returned to the crown, and have been available for the rewarding of another generation of thegns.

The pernicious effect on the royal revenue became even more marked when the king, on giving away a piece of royal domain or permitting other persons to make similar grants, added to the charier a clause exempting the newly-made *bocland* from a greater or lesser part of the services and taxation which it owed the state—occasionally it was let off even the *trinoda necessitas,* the common obligation incumbent on all land under normal conditions.

These facts make it easy to understand the dismay with which farsighted and statesmanlike minds, such as that of the Venerable Bede, regarded the wholesale alienation of "*bocland*" to the Church, which had been going on for a century in Northumbria when he wrote. How was the king to maintain an adequate revenue, or provide for endowment of his military retainers in the future, if all the royal domain was being gradually given away, and much of the private land once held under folkright being freed from more or less of its dues to the state?

It was not long before it was discovered that if "*bocland*" could be made for the Church, it could also be made for private individuals. No boon could be greater to landowners than to give them leave to turn folkland into *bocland*, since they thereby became its actual owners, instead of merely the life tenants of what was bound to pass to their kin on their decease. For one of the main characteristics of the new tenure was that land held by it was alienable by gift or by will. Hence many favoured subjects of the king were anxious to get their estates chartered into *bocland* by the king and witan, in order that they might be free to deal with them according to their desires. In the course of a century or two the larger part of the land of England had passed from family ownership into real private ownership in this fashion.

It is interesting to note that, in most of the great eighth and ninth century wills which have been preserved, the *bocland* in the possession of the testator enormously exceeds the land of which he is possessed on other tenure. (*Growth of the Manor.*) King Alfred, at the end of the ninth century, seems to have been displeased by the way in which the kindred was suffering from this tendency, and in the forty-first clause of his code expresses his opinion that *bocland* which had been received from kinsmen ought not to be left outside the family. Probably he had lay public opinion at his back, as gifts to the Church were still the most frequent incident by which such land was being alienated. But it is clear from many instances that it was also being sold, or left in inheritance to those who were not the actual nearest kinsmen.

It has been suggested that another undesirable result of the whole-sale creation of *bocland* was that it contributed to that depression of the *ceorl* which characterises the later centuries of Anglo-Saxon period. As long as he was seated on royal folkland as a rent-payer (*gafolgelder*) he would be better off than when that folkland had been turned into *bocland*, and passed to a monastery or a great thegn. For thus he ceased to be in direct connection with the king, and became subject to a territorial lord, lay or spiritual.

LEONAUR

ALSO FROM LEONAUR
AVAILABLE IN SOFTCOVER OR HARDCOVER WITH DUST JACKET

A DIARY FROM DIXIE by *Mary Boykin Chesnut*—A Lady's Account of the Confederacy During the American Civil War

FOLLOWING THE DRUM by *Teresa Griffin Vielé*—A U. S. Infantry Officer's Wife on the Texas frontier in the Early 1850's

FOLLOWING THE GUIDON by *Elizabeth B. Custer*—The Experiences of General Custer's Wife with the U. S. 7th Cavalry.

LADIES OF LUCKNOW by *G. Harris & Adelaide Case*—The Experiences of Two British Women During the Indian Mutiny 1857. A Lady's Diary of the Siege of Lucknow by G. Harris, Day by Day at Lucknow by Adelaide Case

MARIE-LOUISE AND THE INVASION OF 1814 by *Imbert de Saint-Amand*—The Empress and the Fall of the First Empire

SAPPER DOROTHY by *Dorothy Lawrence*—The only English Woman Soldier in the Royal Engineers 51st Division, 79th Tunnelling Co. during the First World War

ARMY LETTERS FROM AN OFFICER'S WIFE 1871-1888 by *Frances M. A. Roe*—Experiences On the Western Frontier With the United States Army

NAPOLEON'S LETTERS TO JOSEPHINE by *Henry Foljambe Hall*—Correspondence of War, Politics, Family and Love 1796-1814

MEMOIRS OF SARAH DUCHESS OF MARLBOROUGH, AND OF THE COURT OF QUEEN ANNE VOLUME 1 by A. T. Thomson

MEMOIRS OF SARAH DUCHESS OF MARLBOROUGH, AND OF THE COURT OF QUEEN ANNE VOLUME 2 by A. T. Thomson

MARY PORTER GAMEWELL AND THE SIEGE OF PEKING by *A. H. Tuttle*—An American Lady's Experiences of the Boxer Uprising, China 1900

VANISHING ARIZONA by *Martha Summerhayes*—A young wife of an officer of the U.S. 8th Infantry in Apacheria during the 1870's

THE RIFLEMAN'S WIFE by *Mrs. Fitz Maurice*—*The Experiences of an Officer's Wife and Chronicles of the Old 95th During the Napoleonic Wars*

THE OATMAN GIRLS by *Royal B. Stratton*—The Capture & Captivity of Two Young American Women in the 1850's by the Apache Indians

LEONAUR

ALSO FROM LEONAUR
AVAILABLE IN SOFTCOVER OR HARDCOVER WITH DUST JACKET

ESCAPE FROM THE FRENCH *by Edward Boys*—A Young Royal Navy Midshipman's Adventures During the Napoleonic War.

THE VOYAGE OF H.M.S. PANDORA *by Edward Edwards R. N. & George Hamilton, edited by Basil Thomson*—In Pursuit of the Mutineers of the Bounty in the South Seas—1790-1791.

MEDUSA *by J. B. Henry Savigny and Alexander Correard and Charlotte-Adélaïde Dard* —Narrative of a Voyage to Senegal in 1816 & The Sufferings of the Picard Family After the Shipwreck of the Medusa.

THE SEA WAR OF 1812 VOLUME 1 *by A. T. Mahan*—A History of the Maritime Conflict.

THE SEA WAR OF 1812 VOLUME 2 *by A. T. Mahan*—A History of the Maritime Conflict.

WETHERELL OF H. M. S. HUSSAR *by John Wetherell*—The Recollections of an Ordinary Seaman of the Royal Navy During the Napoleonic Wars.

THE NAVAL BRIGADE IN NATAL *by C. R. N. Burne*—With the Guns of H. M. S. Terrible & H. M. S. Tartar during the Boer War 1899-1900.

THE VOYAGE OF H. M. S. BOUNTY *by William Bligh*—The True Story of an 18th Century Voyage of Exploration and Mutiny.

SHIPWRECK! *by William Gilly*—The Royal Navy's Disasters at Sea 1793-1849.

KING'S CUTTERS AND SMUGGLERS: 1700-1855 *by E. Keble Chatterton*—A unique period of maritime history-from the beginning of the eighteenth to the middle of the nineteenth century when British seamen risked all to smuggle valuable goods from wool to tea and spirits from and to the Continent.

CONFEDERATE BLOCKADE RUNNER *by John Wilkinson*—The Personal Recollections of an Officer of the Confederate Navy.

NAVAL BATTLES OF THE NAPOLEONIC WARS *by W. H. Fitchett*—Cape St. Vincent, the Nile, Cadiz, Copenhagen, Trafalgar & Others.

PRISONERS OF THE RED DESERT *by R. S. Gwatkin-Williams*—The Adventures of the Crew of the Tara During the First World War.

U-BOAT WAR 1914-1918 *by James B. Connolly/Karl von Schenk*—Two Contrasting Accounts from Both Sides of the Conflict at Sea During the Great War.